Words as Weapons

V

Words as Weapons
Selected Writing 1980–1990

—————◆—————

PAUL FOOT

VERSO

London · New York

First published by Verso 1990
Selection © Verso 1990
Individual articles © Paul Foot

Verso
UK: 6 Meard Street, London W1V 3HR
USA: 29 West 35th Street, New York, NY 10001-2291

Verso is the imprint of New Left Books

ISBN 0 86091 310 4
    0 86091 527 1 (Pbk)

British Library Cataloguing in Publication Data available

US Library of Congress Cataloging-in-Publication Data available

Designed by David Williams
Typeset in Ehrhardt by Leaper & Gard Ltd, Bristol
Printed and bound in Great Britain by Biddles Ltd, Guildford and Kings Lynn

Contents

PROFESSIONS AND CONFESSIONS

Introduction

For many years I have castigated friends and relations (including my revered uncle Michael) who have published volumes of journalistic excerpts. Journalism, my argument ran, is by its nature ephemeral. It cannot stand the test of time – and if it does, it was probably useless when it was written. Then Robin Blackburn of Verso wrote to me asking if I would be willing to publish a volume of excerpts from my own journalism. At once, I began to see the argument in an entirely different light. Now Verso are on again demanding an introduction! I shall try to resist the temptation to write another few thousand words about myself – there is far too much of that in the articles already. But since most of the articles were written after 1980, here is the briefest account of how I got there.

I come from a West Country family of enormous repute, which was presided over in my childhood by my grandfather, Isaac Foot. He had been a Liberal MP and a Methodist lay preacher, though I never saw him in either role. He lived in a rambling house in Cornwall, whose every nook and crevice was filled with books. He paid well. For committing to memory (and reciting) the whole of Macaulay's 'Horatius' (a very long poem) he paid me, aged eight, half a crown. For Tennyson's 'Revenge', a florin. For innumerable gobbets of Shakespeare, one shilling each. As I grew up he told me I ought to read novels; not just Dickens, Thackeray and Scott, but the novels of his own contemporaries – Joseph Conrad, Thomas Hardy, Arnold Bennett, D.H. Lawrence. I didn't take his advice until much later in life, though I did steal a copy of *Lady Chatterley's Lover* long before it was legally published and ran away to read it, very suitably, in the woods. I didn't read enough all those years, but owe to my grandfather a lifelong bibliomania.

I was sent to a ludicrously snobbish preparatory school (Ludgrove) and an only slightly less absurd public school, Shrewsbury, about which there are one or two excerpts here. By the time I went to Oxford to complete the last round of my privileged education, I knew next to nothing. I read Law, which enormously increased my ignorance and inexperience. And I was a Liberal for the excellent reason that my grandfather was. During the term I was President of the Oxford University Liberal Club, I went along for the first time to meetings of the Labour Club and heard some arguments for socialism. To my horror and embarrassment, they seemed unassailable. I managed to cover up the confusion by committing myself to the Campaign for Nuclear Disarmament, which included Liberals as well as socialists. But by the time I left Oxford I was a keen supporter of the left-wing weekly *Tribune* (proprietor: my Uncle Michael) and the *New Left Review*.

In 1961, I went to Glasgow to join the *Daily Record* as a reporter. Stuart Hall, one of my heroes on *New Left Review*, warned me that one of my first jobs in Glasgow would be to 'sort out the Trots'. The Trots turned out to be young workers from shipyards and engineering who had joined the Young Socialists. Their politics were entirely different to anything I had come across in formal education. I was encouraged, for the first time, to read Marx, Engels, Lenin, Rosa Luxemburg, Trotsky (especially the wonderful biography of Trotsky by Isaac Deutscher which was just being published). What I read there (and heard in the debates among the Young Socialists) seemed to fit the reality of the city of Glasgow far more closely than anything I had read before. It seemed suddenly clear from what I read and saw that society was cut into classes, and that the classes were forever at war with one another. The result, in Glasgow at any rate, was a city of monstrosities, and an impoverishment of mind and body which was at once incredible and intolerable.

Could capitalism be reformed? Could these stinking slums be cleared and the threat of unemployment lifted by acts of Parliament? My experience in the Labour Party (and my reading of Ralph Miliband's *Parliamentary Socialism*) suggested otherwise. To the contrary, what seemed to happen was that intelligent, competent and eloquent people who came to politics out of the working class quickly became converts to 'the gradual road to socialism'. They started by wanting to do things by degrees, and ended by not wanting to do them at all. When, rarely, there were revolts against the system, chiefly in the form of strikes, the Labour people rushed to quench the flames.

We argued a lot about Russia. Most of the Trots (who had by now succeeded completely in sorting *me* out) thought Russia should be defended against the West because of its planned economy and its legacy of socialist revolution. One of the groups which was forming among these Trots was the 'Socialist Review' group, whose acknowledged leader was an ebullient Palestinian Jew called Tony Cliff. Cliff came to Glasgow to argue about Russia in a tiny, packed shop in Weir Street, the meeting-place of the Gorbals Young Socialists. His case was that Russia was state capitalist: that its central economic drive was competition with the capitalist world and that Russian workers were as much, if not more, cut off from economic and political power as they were in the West. His slogan was: Neither Washington nor Moscow but International Socialism. The argument swayed back and forth, intense and serious throughout, but I thought Cliff won hands-down. He had the extraordinary gift of articulating in simple language and in effervescent style what seemed to be entrenched in his listeners' minds. Unlike all the others, Cliff and his group seemed to be casting their net and organizing outside the laager within which Trotskyist grouplets savaged one another in search of the 'right line'. The right line, Cliff argued, was far more likely to emerge through activity around a strike or a tenants' protest.

In 1963, I joined the newly formed International Socialists, whose national membership could meet in one room. I became editor of the *Labour Worker*, an important four-page broadsheet published monthly, most of whose 1,500 printed copies ended up under the beds of the faithful. I have been an active member of the IS and its successor, the Socialist Workers Party, ever since.

Of all the many lessons I learnt in those three years in Glasgow, the one which most affected my life was a passing remark by Rosa Luxemburg that socialists cannot take office under capitalism. She predicted that, however strong people's socialist commitment, as soon as they are involved even to the slightest degree in managing the system on behalf of capitalists, they will be lost to the socialist cause.

In 1964, I came to London to work on the new *Sun*, the replacement for the old *Daily Herald*. I was put into a department called Probe. The idea was to investigate and publish stories behind the news. The excitement of the project soon vanished when the man in charge turned out to be a former *Daily Express* City editor whose response to our idea for a background feature on capital punishment was to clap his hands in approval and ask: 'How much would we save by that? How much does an execution cost?'

The whole Probe team resigned after six months. I went to work on the Mandrake column on the *Sunday Telegraph* chiefly because I was allowed to work only three days a week while I wrote a book about the Tories' racist election campaign in Smethwick. In 1967, to the consternation of my family, I left Fleet Street to join *Private Eye*, which promised me at least two pages a fortnight for what has since been described as investigative journalism. Writing for *Private Eye* is the only journalism I have ever been engaged in which is pure enjoyment. It is free publishing of the most exhilarating kind. There is nothing in this book of what I wrote for *Private Eye*, and that is an obvious gap. But I left the full-time staff of the *Eye* a long time ago and much of what I have written since, like most of the information published in the *Eye*, depends for its strength (and its sources) on anonymity.

The awful failures of the Harold Wilson Labour Government of 1964 to 1970, the uprisings in Europe in 1968, and the successful miners' strike of 1972 (which threw a Tory government into reverse gear) seemed to vindicate everything the IS had predicted in those tiny meetings in the 1960s. Capitalism couldn't be reformed from above but it could be shifted by action from below. Soon after the miners' triumph, I got an irresistible offer from *Socialist Worker*, which had replaced *Labour Worker* in 1968 and was now publishing weekly with a circulation of some 20,000. The International Socialists now had more than 1,000 members and were growing all the time. The proposition was that at the age of thirty-four I should give up a promising journalistic career, a high salary and plenty of spare time, to join *Socialist Worker* at half the salary and with not the slightest prospect of any spare time. I accepted at once, and worked for *Socialist Worker* for six years.

It was invigorating to write not only what I saw, heard and discovered but also what I thought. But the revolution we had all expected did not happen. It was easy to predict that the Labour Government would hammer the people who had voted Labour, but less easy to believe that the organized working-class movement, so strong and confident in 1974, would roll over onto its back and ask for more. I left *Socialist Worker* in 1978, and was out on a limb. I was half-rescued by *Private Eye*, though I couldn't rekindle the old enthusiasm for it, and by Bruce Page, editor of the *New Statesman*, for whom I wrote a fortnightly diary.

One evening in June 1979 I had an urgent invitation to dinner from Mike Molloy, editor of the *Daily Mirror*. He asked me if I would like to join the *Mirror* to work on investigations. My immediate reply was No. I knew how unrewarding it is to fight for space in papers like the *Mirror*, and I reckoned I would be lucky to get more than a handful of investigations (most of them, probably, sententious and unreadable) printed. Of course, I added, partly as a joke, if I had my own space every week, that would be a quite different matter. He said he thought that might be possible. I thought not. 'After all, Mike,' I explained, 'I am a Trot.' He was sure, he replied, that he and his mates could soon cure me of that delinquency.

Our unspoken and unwritten agreement was that I would not make political propaganda for the SWP in the *Mirror*, but that my page (it very soon became a page) should take the side of the poor against the rich, public enterprise against private enterprise, Labour against Tories, wrongly convicted prisoners against the judiciary, and so on. The idea was not so much to express my views as to publish information of assistance and interest to the people at the wrong end of society. For this I needed the help of *Mirror* readers, and solicited information from them at the bottom of every column. The result has been an enormous and rich correspondence which tells the real story of what has happened in the forgotten part of society during the Thatcher years. I became fascinated in particular by people who were brought up to believe in God, Queen and Country, but who were treated shamelessly by all three. Such a man was the former Leeds policeman, Ron Smith, whose daughter Helen, a nurse, died in mysterious circumstances in Jedda in 1979, and who led a long and powerful campaign to discover the truth; or Rob Green, a former naval intelligence officer, who still wants to know who killed his aunt, the 82-year-old anti-nuclear campaigner Hilda Murrell; or Colin Wallace, who was victimized by the Ministry of Defence for refusing to smear elected politicians.

People are always asking me: 'How can you work for the *Daily Mirror*?', 'How can a SWP member work for Robert Maxwell?' The short answer is that most people in capitalist society work for capitalists of one kind or another. But there is a more serious answer.

I don't share the view widely expressed on the left that the media are chiefly responsible for the fact that most people accept the horrors of capitalist society. I think the media reflect those horrors – but do not create them. Marx wrote that the 'prevailing ideas' in any class society are certain to be the ideas of the ruling class; as long as class society remains, so the media will, by and large, support the rulers. The more confident the rulers, the more sycophantic will be its media. Thus Rupert Murdoch's *Sun* supported the miners' strike of 1972, but opposed the miners' strike of 1984.

Nor do I share the snobbish and contemptuous view that people think exactly what they read in the newspapers. Often, when the enormous majority of the media have supported the Conservative Party, the majority of people have not voted that way. On the other hand, I certainly don't accept that the media can be changed by enlightened editors or executives fighting their way into the corridors of power. On the whole, they go the same way as Labour MPs who go to Parliament to change the world. They get changed themselves. Many a first-rate reporter and columnist has been ruined by his or her ambition.

I do not, however, conclude that there is nothing socialists and revolutionaries can do inside newspapers or television. There is a curious contradiction about journalism. While the proprietor, and perhaps even the editor, wants to keep everything 'even-handed' and 'normal' (that is, without disturbing the rich), there is always a demand for a news item that does not come off the wires; that is fresh, new and the result of an individual journalist either noticing something or investigating something. Mike Molloy, in my first meeting with him about the *Mirror*, used a phrase I had not heard before. 'We need more self-starters', he said. He was fed up with the passivity of reporters who wait to be told what to do, and even how to do it. The whole of society is a teeming mass of stories, many of them interesting and invigorating, the enormous majority of which, since they don't immediately involve important people or their bank accounts, never get told. A society founded on exploitation spawns countless injustices every day, all of which can and should be exposed.

I was especially lucky to be a young reporter when British post-war society was at its most tolerant and liberal. Quite contrary to what was promised by the union-busters at Wapping in 1986, the increasing uniformity of news in newspapers is one of the scandals of the 'free eighties'. My good fortune at having had for so long such a lot of influential space to fill in my own way is, I recognize, formidable. But there are still tiny crevices, in which doubtful journalists and revolutionary journalists whose inquisitiveness stems from a general contempt for the way society is run should get to work.

If all my work in the 1980s had been for the *Mirror*, I might perhaps have got stuck. In 1984, Chris Harman, editor of *Socialist Worker*, persuaded me to write a weekly column. 'We'll like it,' he said, 'but that's not the point. It will do you good.' He was right, and I have continued to write the column ever since. A hefty sample has found its way into this volume. I am especially grateful to Pete Alexander of the SWP for taking time to slog through all the *SW*s of the eighties to make his own selection; and to Mike Marqusee (the final editor and selector) who is not in the SWP (though he ought to be), and who has included here many items which a more sectarian editor would have held out.

In the same year, I was approached by Mary-Kay Wilmers, then deputy editor (now joint editor, with Karl Miller) of the *London Review of Books*. 'We never take less than two thousand words' was her seductive formula. The *LRB* is, in my view, much the best literary journal in the country, and just about the only place where decent writing mixes with genuinely challenging ideas. A lot of my pieces for the *LRB* have been included here. They mingle with others from the *New Statesman*, for whom I write less since it dropped its socialist guard; the *Spectator*, which never pretended to be other than a right-wing journal but sent me books to review and for some reason published every word I wrote; and the *UK Press Gazette*, for whom I wrote a monthly column for about two years.

Almost everything here was written in the 1980s. The main reason for that, obviously, is that the more recent the journalism, the less dead it is when it is repeated. There's another reason, though. Of all the wretchednesses and tragedies of the Thatcher years, none has been more disastrous than the retreat of the socialist Left. The two great props of socialist thought and ideas over the century – social democracy and Stalinism – have been exposed for the shams they were. Neither aimed at anything which could properly be described as socialist, but the collapse of both has dragged the name of socialism in the mud. People who only a decade or two ago were lambasting capitalism as an evil and ugly system are now sighing that it is the best system we have got. Some modern socialists even pretend that capitalism works.

This judgement comes at a time when the universal and catastrophic failure of the market system has never for fifty years been more apparent. Mrs Thatcher's wonderful 'cure' for the economy when she came to office was an old-fashioned recession and mass unemployment (by far the worst since the war). Just as she starts telling us we are out of the woods, we are faced with a new and yet more drastic dose of the same medicine. The only answer to inflation, we discover, is ... an old-fashioned recession and mass unemployment. This follows years and years of 'free enterprise' policies whose chief effect has been to enrich the already disgustingly rich, chiefly at the expense of the desperately poor. Checks and balances, introduced in the past by governments obliged by full employment to develop some kind of social conscience, have been shovelled away. Little bits of sticking plaster which held people's lives together at the bottom of the social scale have been torn off. There is poverty, homelessness, sheer unadulterated misery of a kind which would not have been thought of, let alone tolerated, twenty or thirty years ago. Into the gaps left by the half-regulators and the half-correctors have stepped a new generation of Thatcherite guttersnipes; bullies to their underlings and cowards to their bosses.

The whole mess stinks of corruption, and the British and American governments are up to their armpits in it. Ronald Reagan, fêted everywhere as a master politician, had more officials and advisers who went to jail than any other president before him (yes, more even than Nixon). Thatcher and her advisers were hands in pockets with the wealthy swindlers who went to prison after the great Guinness scandal.

Every single one of the contradictions and nastinesses of capitalism which Marx predicted has come true. The system cannot begin to provide even growth or even development. It can flourish only by lurching from boom to slump; by dishing out more and more to the rich, and squeezing more and more from the workers and the poor. For all its rhetoric about free enterprise and competition, it is creating larger and larger corporate monopolies, hugely powerful and out of all democratic control.

In the month I write this, the World Bank comes out with a report which ought to terrify the wits out of the complacent bankers who commissioned it. It shows that in 1985 – for the first time since the Second World War – the poor countries of the 'underdeveloped world' paid more to the rich countries than they received from them. In the 1950s and 1960s we used to amuse ourselves by arguing how much aid should go to the poor countries of the world. Was one per cent of the economy enough to stop the Apocalypse? Maybe it was; maybe it wasn't. Then, in the middle of the decade of the Market, wealth began to flow the other way. Each year since, the figures have got worse. Last year the 'deficit' (from poor to rich) was an astonishing 42 million billion dollars. The World Bank's desperate conclusion – published just before the Iraqi invasion of Kuwait and the mobilization of the most fantastic weaponry for a war in the Middle East to prop up a feudal dictator and to keep down the price of oil – was that the governments of the world, to save themselves, must cut down on military spending.

Never in my lifetime has the disaster which is capitalism been more exposed for all to see. Yet at this time, socialists of every persuasion can be heard prevaricating, apologizing, pretending that they never were socialists anyway. The *New Statesman* joins in a witch-hunt against the President of the National Union of Mineworkers and *Marxism Today* carries on its cover a glamorous picture of the Prince of Wales.

The very most I can hope about this selection is that it will help to reassure socialists that the rot can and must be stopped. The case for socialism has never been stronger, and is not at all weakened by the fact that something which was called socialism (but was in fact its opposite) has at last been exposed as a sham. Even if we are nervous to call it socialism, the only alternative to the market capitalism which is dragging us all to the rim of hell is a society whose means of producing wealth are owned, controlled and planned by the people who produce it. William Morris, a socialist writer who never for a moment trimmed his opinions to catch the prevailing wind, made the point in his *Dream of John Ball*:

> I pondered all these things, and how men fight and lose the battle, and the thing that they fought for comes about in spite of their defeat, and when it comes turns out not to be what they meant, and other men have to fight for what they meant under another name....

Paul Foot
September 1990

THEM

1. The Tories

Thatcher: class warrior

Thatcher-worship, which goes on all the time in a continuous Mass in T, will rise to a crescendo in the next few weeks. A new excuse to sing the praises of the Prime Minister in otherwise difficult times comes with the tenth anniversary of her becoming leader of the Conservative Party.

A suitable prelude is an article in the *Mail on Sunday*'s colour magazine by the reactionary critic, Anthony Burgess. His piece, gloriously entitled 'The Sexuality of Power', ends by comparing Margaret Thatcher to Venus de Milo. He makes the subtle point that whereas Venus had no arms, Mrs Thatcher has plenty.

Grateful and sycophantic press barons will be eager to impress on their readers that Mrs Thatcher is a wonder woman, her political intelligence and grasp far greater than anything else seen in Britain (or any other country) in the postwar period. Above all, she will be heralded for her *convictions* and her *passions*, which, it will be argued, contrast magnificently with the dull pragmatism of her two predecessors, Heath and Macmillan.

When I try to read all this, I remember an evening in Plymouth some sixteen years ago when I first appeared on the BBC radio programme *Any Questions*. A Labour government was in office with a majority of 100. A Labour MP and I were 'balanced' on the right by Malcolm Muggeridge and Margaret Thatcher MP.

When, after the programme, I said that I thought the Labour government was behaving rather like a Tory one, she blithely agreed. *But,* she insisted, in a very maternal way, there *was* a crucial difference between the two parties: in the people they represent.

When I next came across her, she was speaking as minister for education at the Tory Party conference in 1970, declaring with tremendous passion that the school-leaving age would be raised to sixteen, and that much more money would be spent on the state sector.

She is not someone who fights when she thinks she may be beaten. The miners' strike of the winter 1980–81 is a very good example of that. She withdrew a pit closure programme *at once*.

Mrs Thatcher's real skill comes from her deep sensitivity to the ebbs and flows in the fortunes of her class. She is a class general, who knows no sentiment in the struggle.

The old aristocratic leaders of the Tory Party believed they were superior to the lower orders chiefly through divine intervention or God's will. They were therefore inclined to dilute their class passions with occasional bouts of compassion, doubt or hesitation.

Margaret Thatcher and her *arrivistes*, people whose parents had to hang on by their fingertips to stay in the ruling class at all, believe that they are superior *because they are superior*. There is, therefore, in their class war strategy not a hint of doubt or guilt. They have a better sense of the state of the battle, and a stronger will to win it.

Unlike Macmillan, Thatcher was deeply suspicious of the Keynesian economics and full employment of the postwar years. She sensed that although these things could not be reversed at the height of the boom, they were fundamentally corrosive of her class. Long before most Tory leaders she sensed an ebb in that confidence, and she seized the time.

She knew that mass unemployment breeds despair in workers, and that that despair would breed its own confidence among her people. She knew that trade union leaders were only powerful as long as they were allowed to seem so. She sensed the union leaders' special weakness, their suspension between the two classes, and their unwillingness to side with either. She reckoned that if the union leaders were expelled from the corridors of power, they would be reduced to pleading to be allowed in again.

Mrs Thatcher is not an intellectual giant, nor has she risen to such heights through her beauty or her oratorical skills. She is a new-fashioned two-nation Tory who understands the simple truth, which evades far too many of us: that class confidence comes out of class strength, and that her class can win only if the other class loses.

The wets

A great song and dance has been made in the newspapers about a country gentleman called Pym, who, not for the first time, has made a speech in the House of Commons. Francis Pym says he is descended from a more famous man of the same surname who once struggled for human rights, a struggle which no one could possibly accuse the present Mr Pym of even contemplating.

Mr Pym comes from Bedfordshire where he has a very nice 500 acres and a country mansion, valued rather meanly at half a million pounds. He has been a career Tory politician all his life, was elected in a safe seat when he was thirty-nine and almost at once spent eleven years in the Tory Whips' office. He is not reported to have said a single word against the policy of his party in all his twenty-two years as an MP. Though a friend of Edward Heath, he gaily took office under Margaret Thatcher, and never lost an opportunity to praise her policies and recommend them to the nation.

During the recent election campaign he was pathetically rebuked over the Falklands by Thatcher at an election press conference featuring all the cabinet. The rebuke stung him into more and more abject support for Thatcher's policies, especially over the Falklands. He rushed to her aid on the one issue over which she was rattled: the *General Belgrano.*

He explained to anyone who would listen that it was 'perfectly right' that the *Belgrano* should have been sunk while he was negotiating for peace in America. It mattered not one whit that he was not consulted about the sinking, he emphasized. After all, he was just the foreign secretary.

After all these years on his face in front of his party leaders, Mr Pym has now suddenly turned over on his back – and become a rebel. Newspapers are looking to him to lead Tory revolts against Mrs Thatcher!

What has happened? Has anything changed?

Well, yes, something has, actually. Poor old Francis has been sacked, and his salary has come down by about 50 per cent. Everybody knows that people of the calibre of Francis Pym, the decent old Tories of yesteryear, can take just about anything except being sacked. The suggestion that somehow Pym (or anyone else) will organize any-thing substantial by way of a 'revolt of the wets' is almost as ridiculous as Pym himself.

Newspapers prattle about a brand of Tory who *cares* about unemployment, and believes that Britain is 'one nation' and that all sectors of the nation must be 'looked after'. The fact that there have been such Tories in the past, however, has nothing to do with their personalities or independent political ideas.

The heyday of the Tory 'wets' was the time when there was full employment, when the working-class movement was strong and confident and when capitalism could afford to be relatively generous to the dispossessed. Capitalists, and their Tory spokesmen, were no less determined to maintain two nations then than they are now. They simply bent with the wind, and managed to keep the two nations apart by pretending that they were together.

Times have changed. We now have mass unemployment, a weak and despondent working-class movement, with a spineless leadership, and a rampant Tory government more and more openly committed to the class war. In such times, a new type of Tory fits the bill: an aggressive, mean-mouthed and belligerent Tory, who makes no secret of his or her contempt for the organized working class and the 'drop-outs' from that class, such as the unemployed or the sick.

The 'wets' are irrelevant. In all the last four years, who has heard a peep of protest against any of the awful priorities of the Thatcher government from Prior, Walker, Whitelaw – or any of the rest of them? The only time they speak out is when they lose their jobs, thus making themselves even more contemptible in the process.

Socialist Worker, July 1983

The Tories and the junta

Every time I hear Margaret Thatcher going on about the cruel military dictatorship in Argentina, I am bound to repeat that no government in Europe has snuggled closer to the junta than hers has. From the moment it came to office, Mrs Thatcher's government set out to make friends with South American tyrannies, especially in Chile and Argentina. The first victims of this policy were the political prisoners in both countries.

In 1974, the Labour government had set up a special programme for refugees from the right-wing terror in Chile. Political prisoners were 'adopted' by union branches and other groups, and granted visas to come to Britain. These prisoners were allowed to choose between staying in prison and going into exile. In 1978, the scheme was extended to Argentina. Altogether, nearly 3,000 people were rescued from Chilean and Argentine concentration camps by the programme.

As soon as the Tories were elected in 1979, the Home Office started refusing applications for visas. Juan Martin Guevara, for instance, had been held for political 'offences' in the horrible Rawson prison, Argentina, since 1976. He had been viciously tortured and was seriously ill.

The Transport and General Workers' Union asked the Home Office if he could be given a visa to Britain. No, replied the compassionate William Whitelaw, Home Secretary. He wrote: 'Mr Guevara has no ties with this country and I believe his presence here would not be conductive to the public good.'

Mr Whitelaw's junior minister, Timothy Raison, took the same view when the college teachers' union NATFHE wrote about Celina de Torres Molina, a political prisoner in Argentina. He replied: 'Mr and Mrs Torres do not appear to have any ties with this country which would make a settlement here appropriate. I note, for example, that neither speaks English.'

In October 1979, the Tories abruptly cancelled the entire special programme, and the following year, cut off all its funds. Nicholas Ridley, then a Foreign Office minister, described the programme as 'a public relations exercise of the last government which is better buried'.

Daily Mirror, May 1982

Torpedoing the peace

Did Mrs Thatcher order the sinking of the aged Argentine cruiser *General Belgrano*, on Sunday 2 May 1982, in order to scupper a peace settlement which had been hammered out between Lima, Peru and Washington over the previous weekend and which was on the point of being signed? For several months, Tam Dalyell, the Labour MP for West Lothian, has been making this astonishing charge against the Prime Minister. His view is that she deliberately gave the order to sink the cruiser at a time when an honourable peace settlement was almost secured – one which could have prevented the subsequent bloodshed of the Falklands campaign.

The charge has been met in the main with faintly amused disdain. Tam Dalyell, it is pointed out, is an eccentric with weird views on many subjects. But whenever a specific reply has been given to any of his questions, the mystery surrounding the sinking of the *Belgrano* has deepened. The 45-year-old cruiser was not 'closing on the Task Force', as Defence Minister John Nott told the House of Commons at the time. It was heading away from the Falklands and was at least 350 miles from the nearest task force surface ship. The range of its guns was thirteen miles. Even its missiles would hardly have reached into the 'exclusion zone' established round the islands. After spending four days in Lima and talking to Dr Javier Arias Stella, Peru's Foreign Minister at the time, the picture I got strongly confirms Dalyell's charge.

Thursday 29 April The Organization of American States, the alliance which binds North and South America, met to consider the Falklands crisis. It passed a motion proposed by Peru which called for a ceasefire and a peace on the basis of recognizing Argentina's sovereignty over the Falklands. Several countries, including the United States, abstained.

Friday 30 April United States Secretary of State Alexander Haig declared that his efforts to get a peace settlement between Britain and Argentina had failed. He had tried to reach an agreement on the basis of United Nations Resolution 502 – which called for Argentine with-drawal followed by negotiations. His stumbling block was that the British would sign nothing which did not include immediate Argentine withdrawal from the Falklands and the Argentines would not withdraw unless their rights to the islands were sanctioned. It seemed a hopeless impasse.

Haig declared, moreover, that the United States supported Britain in the conflict, and would assist economically and militarily. This statement was greeted with fury in Peru, which has close ties with Argentina.

Saturday 1 May The British forces attacked Argentine positions on the Falklands by sea and air. The barrage included a hail of cluster bombs. The Argentines admitted to fifty-six dead. There were probably many more.

In Lima, that evening, the ageing President Belaunde Terry and his foreign minister, Dr Arias Stella, held urgent talks. They decided to intervene to seek a settlement. Belaunde rang Washington and spoke at length to Haig, offering to act as broker in new peace negotiations. Haig leapt at the suggestion. He had not given up hope of a last-minute compromise. Moreover, he was about to welcome the British Foreign Secretary, Francis Pym, who was flying into Washington that evening. In the frenzied negotiations over the next two days, the Peruvians 'acted' for the Argentinians and Alexander Haig for the British.

At once, Haig told Belaunde that any new proposals, if they were to have the slightest chance of succeeding, must move a long way from what had been previously rejected. He suggested (to satisfy the main Argentine objection) that no position on sovereignty should be adopted, but that a treaty should recognize the 'conflicting claims' of both countries; and (to reassure the British) a separate clause to sanction the 'points of view and interests' of the islanders.

If these two clauses could be agreed on both sides, he thought that a peace was possible on the basis of an instant ceasefire, withdrawal of all forces, an interim administration of the Falklands that involved neither Argentines nor British, and a 'contact group' of four countries – then suggested as the USA, Peru, West Germany and Brazil – to supervise the withdrawal and the negotiations. The last point was that agreement would have to be reached by 30 April 1983.

The seven-point plan was not agreed with Haig until nearly midnight. At once Belaunde phoned the Argentine dictator Leopold Galtieri. Galtieri was delighted with the new initiative. The day's attacks on the Falklands had frightened him and his high command. They were now facing a humiliating defeat. He assured the Peruvian President that the new proposals satisfied him. Would they not remove the British from the Falklands without any more shots being fired? And did they not at least accept that Argentina had a claim to sovereignty? He would talk to his high command in the morning, he promised; but he was hopeful.

Sunday 2 May That optimism was increased considerably when Galtieri phoned Belaunde in the early morning. The high command, he said, was almost unanimous in approving the terms, though there were a number of small points to be negotiated.

Throughout that morning, Belaunde negotiated these points in calls to Washington and to Buenos Aires. In Washington, General Haig was in close touch with Francis Pym (he was probably in the same room for most of the time – certainly the two men had lunch together). In Buenos Aires, Galtieri kept open his hotline to the junta's hard man, navy chief Admiral Anaya.

The proposals were amended. 'Points of view and wishes' of the islanders was changed to 'needs and aspirations'. The membership of the contact group was left open, though it was suggested that Canada might come in for the USA and Venezuela for Peru.

By noon, an agreement seemed secure. A final draft of a treaty was prepared by officials who had been at work in the eighteenth-century Torre Tagli mansion (the headquarters of the Peruvian Foreign Office) since the early hours. It was drawn up for signature by the British and Argentine ambassadors in Lima. The ceremony, it was confidently expected, would take place that night.

General Galtieri, who had given the go-ahead for these preparations, made it clear that he must first get the approval of his official junta meeting, scheduled for 5pm that afternoon. But, he insisted, the agreement of the junta was a formality.

This is confirmed by the *Sunday Times* Insight book on the Falklands war, which quotes a 'senior official' of the Argentinian Foreign Ministry as saying, 'I was in the room when Foreign Secretary

Costa Mendes came in and said: "We have an agreement. We can accept this." Everybody was very excited.'

Once the junta meeting started in Buenos Aires, President Belaunde decided to hold his weekly press conference, which had been long delayed. At 4.45pm, he went in front of the cameras with his prime minister and foreign minister to tell the world that a settlement was at hand 'this very night'. All three men made it quite plain that a settlement was imminent.

Very soon after the press conference, these high hopes were dashed. News came in of the sinking of the *Belgrano* some three and a half hours earlier (it was sunk at about 4pm Argentine time, 2pm Lima time). Communications were slow, since the cruiser's signalling systems were destroyed and its escorts and the submarine wanted to protect their positions.

An admiral stormed into the junta meeting in Buenos Aires shouting the news. Many junta members had sons and nephews on the *Belgrano*. The method of its sinking and the huge loss of life completely changed the mood of the meeting. Although they went on formally discussing the proposals, all hope of a settlement was dead. The State Department was the first to convey the bad news to the presidential palace in Lima.

At 6.30pm, Foreign Minister Arias Stella received the ambassadors of Britain (Mr Charles Wallace) and Argentina (Mr Louis Sanchez Mareno). Perhaps they came to sign the treaty. They were told the bad news and left.

Soon after midnight, after a seven-hour meeting, the junta formally rejected the Peruvian peace proposals, specifically mentioning the *Belgrano* sinking as the cause.

During the next few days, the Peruvian president, prime minister and foreign minister all explained to the Peruvian parliament that peace had been in their grasp, only to be sunk with the *Belgrano*. All three endorsed the unequivocal view of the prime minister, Mr Manuel Ulloa Elias: 'Argentine rejection of the Belaunde peace proposals was due to the fact that Argentina had been attacked with the torpedoing of the *Belgrano* at the very moment that Peru was trying to find a dignified way out of the contest.' (Quoted in *El Observador*, Lima, 5 May 1982.)

Ulloa also strongly rejected the widely held view that the Belaunde proposals were just a re-hash of Haig's earlier efforts – 'Haig in a poncho'. On the contrary, he said, the package was very different both from the Haig proposals, which failed because they leant too far to the British, and from the OAS resolution of 29 April, which leant too far to Argentina. In the Belaunde proposals, unlike those of both Haig and the OAS, an immediate Argentine withdrawal was matched by the temporary removal of British administration from Port Stanley; and the matter of sovereignty was left entirely neutral.

The Belaunde proposals, it is safe to conclude, *were* taken seriously by both sides. They *were* drawn up into a treaty which was expected to be signed. And they *were* put to flight by the sinking of the *Belgrano*.

Senor Arias Stella, who is a fellow of the Royal Society of Pathologists in London and has no anti-British feeling, generously ascribes the *Belgrano* sinking to military accident. He told me that he and all his colleagues had assumed that some hothead submarine commander had let fly at the cruiser without any idea of the state of negotiations in Lima, Buenos Aires and Washington.

This has been indignantly denied by the submarine commander himself. He insists he received clear orders to sink the cruiser.

Nor have Tory ministers been slow to claim their part in the action. Margaret Thatcher told the House of Commons on 4 May 1982: 'With regard to that particular event [the sinking of the *Belgrano*] and all events other than the mere tactical ones in the South Atlantic, the task force clearly is and was under political control.'

A few minutes later, Nott, the Defence Secretary, was asked by Willie Hamilton: 'Will the minister confirm ... that the decision to launch the torpedoes was a political decision – in other words, it was made either by the Prime Minister or by the Rt Hon. gentleman, or by both together? Or was it made by an admiral on the spot?' Nott replied, rather evasively: 'The overall political control remains with the government.'

There the matter rested until last October, when a mysterious leak to the newspapers (printed in all of them) 'revealed' that the decision to sink the *Belgrano* had been taken by the 'war cabinet' (minus Pym) in pre-lunch discussions with the service chiefs on 2 May.

This version comes out in *The Battle for the Falklands* by Simon Jenkins and Max Hastings as follows: 'Sir Terence Lewin went to the war cabinet meeting at Chequers on the morning of Sunday 2 May to request permission under the rules of engagement to sink the *General*

Belgrano some forty miles southwest of the total exclusion zone.' After some discussion the book goes on: 'No minister demurred. The order was issued before lunch.'

One difficulty about this is that the cruiser was not actually sunk until about eight hours afterwards (between 3 and 4pm Argentine time – 8 and 9pm GMT). Even given the difficulties of contact with a submerged submarine, this does seem a huge time gap.

Another problem is that the war cabinet meeting with the defence chiefs was not just a discussion about the *Belgrano*. It was, as reported in the newspapers on 4 May, a full-scale assessment of the state of the war, which went on for four hours.

At any rate, the direct responsibility of Thatcher, Whitelaw, Nott and Parkinson for the *Belgrano* sinking has never been denied. The question then arises: how much did they know of the progress of the Peruvian peace talks?

The seven-point plan had been agreed between Haig and Belaunde the previous night (in Britain, the early hours of the morning). Was it conveyed to Chequers that night? Did the war cabinet meeting not have before it 'the latest from Francis in Washington'? Even if they did not, they knew that Pym had gone to Washington in a last bid for peace. However hopeless such a mission seemed in the eyes of the hawks in the war cabinet (and by all accounts they were all hawks, except Pym), they knew that the armed forces could not be seen to cut the ground from under the Foreign Secretary's feet.

On arrival in Washington the previous evening, Mr Pym gave an impromptu press conference. He explained that the attacks on the Falklands that day had been intended to concentrate the Argentines' minds on a peaceful settlement. He went on: 'No further military action is envisaged at the moment, except to keep the exclusion zone secure.' (*Times*, 2 May 1982.) This pledge was kept – right up until the sinking of the *Belgrano*.

At the very least, then, the cabinet that Sunday morning knew that Pym was trying for peace and that a period of calm was vital if he was to be seen to be trying. That is the background, apparently, in which they gave the order to attack a ship on the high seas, with a complement of 1,000 men, when it was outside the war zone they themselves had designated.

As the afternoon and evening went on, however, Mrs Thatcher and those ministers who stayed in contact can have been left in no doubt as to the progress of the Peruvian peace talks. By noon US time, 5pm GMT, after all, the seven-point plan had been agreed between Belaunde, Haig and Galtieri. Even before he sat down to lunch with Haig, Francis Pym must have known about this, and expressed his own agreement. He must, too, have conveyed it back to Chequers. If the order to sink had in fact been given at lunchtime, there was still time to countermand the order, or to try to countermand it. For the *Belgrano* was not sunk until three hours later.

The British government does not deny that it was prepared to accept the Belaunde proposals. The official Foreign Office document, 'The Falklands Islands: Negotiations for a Peaceful Settlement', published on 20 May 1982, says: 'The next stage of the negotiations was on proposals originally advanced by President Belaunde of Peru and modified in consultations between him and the United States Secretary of State. ... Britain was willing to accept the final version of these proposals for an interim agreement, but Argentina rejected it.' The document does not point out that Argentina rejected it under the most savage provocation imaginable; namely, the sinking of the *Belgrano*.

If the interim agreement had come into force, what would have happened? All forces would have withdrawn. A thousand lives (and several thousand million pounds) would have been saved. The British forces would have left the Falklands for the time being. Some sort of settlement respecting the needs and aspirations of the islanders would probably have been reached. Not everyone would have been satisfied, but at least the Falkland Islands would have had a future as a place where people lived and worked, not as a military bunker.

The only organization seriously undermined by the settlement would have been the British Conservative Party. Its press and its right wing had been let off the leash. Only war and conquest would have satisfied them. For the Iron Lady, donning the ill-fitting garments of peace and compromise, the future would have been bleak indeed.

Tam Dalyell's questions stand up well to the facts. They were not even asked by the Franks Report. Franks and his colleagues stopped at the Argentine invasion. If they had asked why the war was allowed to start; in particular, who gave the order to sink the *Belgrano*; when; above all, why – then I doubt whether Margaret Thatcher would have read their conclusions to the House of Commons with such gusto. For the sinking of the *General Belgrano* was, at best, a crass blunder, based on false information, which made a laughing stock of Pym's negotiations. At worst, it was, as Tam Dalyell suggests, a desperate attempt to force the other side back from a peace treaty which could have sunk the Tory leadership.

New Statesman, May 1983

Thatcher and Galtieri

Andrew Wilson's splendid scoop in the *Observer* could supply the missing link in the *General Belgrano* mystery. I've always been puzzled by the official story, that the war lords persuaded the Prime Minister to agree to the sinking of the *Belgrano* at lunchtime on 2 May 1982, just while Foreign Secretary Pym was starting a day of negotiations in Washington. Could she really have been callous enough to give the order to sink the cruiser outside the exclusion zone at such a delicate time? The new leaks tell a different story. They say that the rules of engagement were changed to sink not just the *Belgrano*, but any Argentinian warship anywhere. In other words, the war cabinet had before it not a specific proposition to sink a specific ship at a specific time – but a general proposition to attack any ship which might move into view. This must have seemed quite easy to accept, and much less immediately threatening to negotiations. But the vagueness of it was deceptive. The *Belgrano* had been in *HMS Conqueror*'s sights for some twenty-four hours. Could it be that the Chiefs of Staff, anxious to get on with the war, bounced the war cabinet into an apparently general change in the rules of engagement which would enable them specifically to sink the *Belgrano* as soon as the peace negotiations threatened to succeed?

Which reminds me of a story I picked up in Peru earlier this year. It seems that on General Haig's first visit to London during his 'peace shuffle' over the Falklands last year, he greeted the Prime Minister jovially. 'Come on, Margaret,' he apparently said, 'you mustn't be too hard on Galtieri. He keeps telling me he's always been your biggest fan in South America.' The Prime Minister, I gather, was not amused. Which was rather churlish of her. For, just as the Argentine junta reached its highest pitch of repression, it got a boost from the British government. Someone has sent me a remarkable article from the summer issue of *Resurgam*, the journal of the Federation of British Cremation Authorities. It reveals that in March 1981 the City Authority of Buenos Aires put out to international tender a huge new crematorium. The scheme called for 'three banks of five cremators capable of dealing with 200 bodies a day' and facilities for taking bodies out of coffins and reusing the coffins. The article points out that there is little or no demand for civilian cremations in Argentina and that the new crematorium was obviously needed to 'deal with' the 'disappeared' dissidents. In March 1981, when the specification went out, the British government policy of appeasing South American dictatorships was in full swing. The debonair Cecil Parkinson had flown to Buenos Aires to butter up the junta. At the Buenos Aires Chamber of Commerce, he made the debonair point that the economic policy of the junta was an example to the British government. Peter Walker had also just visited Buenos Aires and Willie Whitelaw had obliged the junta's Minister of the Interior by cutting off the previous Labour government's assistance for political refugees from Argentina.

I was remembering this appeasement on a recent visit to poor old Plymouth which never did anyone any harm, but is represented in Parliament by David Owen and Alan Clark. I am still basking in a glorious attack on me by Mr Clark in the House of Commons last May, during a debate on the sinking of the *General Belgrano*. 'Paul Foot and others like him,' he said, 'hate their country so much that they will even take sides with President Reagan's favourite hit man in that hemisphere – President Galtieri.' Mr Clark forgot to mention that while I and others like me were demonstrating against the Galtieri government, his own government was wooing and arming it.

New Statesman, August 1984/August 1983

Heseltine's principles

The greatest Tarzan of them all – Johnny Weismuller – is dead, but Michael Heseltine is still around to maintain the traditions of the white man in the jungle.

He's just back from a much-publicized trip to the Falklands, where he had a good look at the fifty-four houses which have been built for 'senior business personnel' there, at a cost of £133,000 each. He also surveyed the site for the airport to be built by three construction firms which paid handsome contributions to the Tory Party, and will cost the British taxpayer £800m *without a penny return*.

The reporters who fawned about Heseltine were normally too 'moved' by the graves of dead heroes to do anything but murmur their appreciation. But one of them plucked up courage, as Heseltine was leaving, to ask if it really was worthwhile spending about £500m a year on the Falklands (that is, a quarter of a million pounds for every islander – increasingly fewer as the islanders, terrified and infuriated by the military circus which their own intransigence has brought down on them, pack up their bags and go).

'Oh,' replied Tarzan breezily, 'it's a question of principle.' The government, he explained, had decided to defend the Falklands and the islanders, and the decision had to be upheld *whatever the cost*.

Back in Britain, Heseltine found he had to go down to the House of Commons and vote for the government to cut still further into the housing benefits, whereby the bottom quarter of society manage to save themselves from starvation. *Four million people* are now so poor that they *do* worry how to feed themselves and their families. The cuts in housing benefit will hit mainly the working poor, the labourers and pen-pushers in dead-end jobs who keep the system going, the one-parent families who strain their whole lives to get out and work for small wages. These people will find themselves, thanks to the housing benefit cuts, with another £1 or £2 or up to £7 a week less to hold their lives together. These cuts mean hundreds of thousands more old people staying in bed all day because they can't heat the house enough to keep warm.

None of this, for Mr Heseltine, is a question of principle. It's a simple matter of necessity. 'We just can't afford any more,' he whines with all the others. 'There just isn't the money in the kitty.'

They have got to save £250m by cutting housing benefit for the four million desperately poor. There is no alternative. But when it comes to finding twice that much to defend the dubious right of 1,500 people to 'be British' in a barren island 7,000 miles away, then somehow, the money is there. There is an alternative. By magic, the money *arrives* from somewhere. The kitty is full.

For the Tarzans of this world, a fight with a foreign foe about next to nothing a long way away is much better for prestige and power than the fight against disease and poverty on their doorstep. That's what they mean by 'principle'.

Social Worker, February 1984

Westland Ho!

It was the end of a cabinet meeting and Mrs Thatcher was cross. It was all so silly, so unnecessary. She was half-way through her second term as prime minister – a bad time for most governments, but hers was doing surprisingly well. Earlier in the year, the most dangerous of all the 'enemies within', the miners' union, had been thoroughly beaten in a tough fight. The trade unions everywhere else were humbled and split. The Opposition was fighting itself, and was unconvincing. For a brief moment, almost incredibly, the Conservative Party had established a small lead in the polls.

Now, however, on 19 December 1985, the success and security of her government were banished from her mind by an infuriating, niggling little argument. Once again the cabinet had been discussing what she described as 'an insignificant little company in the Southwest with a capitalization of less than £30m'. More than half the meeting had been taken up with a wrangle over Westland Helicopters. It was all most unusual and most irregular: her cabinet hardly ever discussed individual companies like this. Westland was an *ailing* company and Margaret Thatcher's attitude to ailing companies over the years had been simple and consistent. If companies ailed, if they couldn't stand on their own feet, then they would have to go to the wall. There was no room for the lame ducks as there had been in the dark days of the Heath administration of the early seventies. *That* government's slackness towards ailing companies had ushered in all sorts of horrors – strong trade unions, a Labour government. As she had said a thousand times, there would be no 'U-turn' for hers. Market forces, she had repeated, were the only real discipline in a capitalist world.

No matter that Westland made military equipment and was therefore not really subject to market forces at all. No matter that the main market in which Westland dealt was the government market, and that some £750m worth of government orders had been its staple economic diet since the war. Defence industries, too, had to undergo the rigours of the market, and if Westland was in trouble, it would have to find its own way out, as so many other companies had (or hadn't). It was of course a pity that Westland employed 7,000 workers, but not *such* a pity when most of those voted in Yeovil and the Isle of Wight – which had had the effrontery to return Liberal MPs at the last election. If workers were to learn the lessons of unprofitability in a real world, there could hardly have been a more suitable place for them to do so.

These elementary lessons had been automatically applied by the Thatcher government ever since Westland first started getting into real trouble at the beginning of 1985. A mixture of old-fashioned British management and plain bad planning had left this famous helicopter company without any orders for a couple of years at least, and with a main new product – something called the W 30 – which no one, not even the Indian government, wanted to buy. The usual remedies were tried without success. Sir Basil Blackwell departed as chairman with a handsome pay-off. Lord Aldington, a former Tory MP, resigned as president. The colourful Alan Bristow, a helicopter tycoon who had done very well out of flying people to and from the North Sea oil rigs (and by curbing trade unions), made a bid and then withdrew it. By the early summer it looked as though Westland would go bust. Good riddance, as far as the government was concerned. When Westland workers or management lobbied the government – whether the Department of Trade and Industry or the Ministry of Defence – they were lectured about the laws of the marketplace. Good riddance, too, was the message for Westland from the other big helicopter-makers of Europe. Fewer and fewer helicopters were needed, because fewer and fewer people (or countries) could afford them. There was what businessmen call 'over-capacity'. Large firms like GEC in Britain, Aérospatiale in France and Messerschmitt in Germany, were licking their lips at the juicy technology and skilled workers waiting to be gobbled up from Yeovil. The prospect seemed familiar. The company would go into receivership. The banks would move in and flog off the assets to the highest bidder. A few thousand workers would join the vast dole queues of the Southwest, and the other companies would be able to continue for a short while, making profits in a smaller market until one day the whole process would start again, and a new victim would go to the wall.

In the summer, the Bank of England tried a last rescue operation. Sir John Cuckney, a 'trouble-shooter' from the City, was 'put in' as chairman to try to sort out the mess. He discovered before too long that there was an alternative to bankruptcy and receivership. The vast American conglomerate United Technologies, and its helicopter subsidiary Sikorsky, indicated that they would be interested in pumping in money in exchange for a mighty slice of the company and a share in its control. A lot of workers would have to go, of course, but production would at least continue for the two years that Westland didn't have any orders. The probable result would be that ownership and control would be ceded entirely to Sikorsky, but the company would, after a fashion, survive.

As Sir John disclosed this new plan, he ran into instant outraged opposition from the other big helicopter manufacturers in Europe. They had been happy enough to sit around and watch Westland go bust. But the prospect of all that technology and skill going to an American competitor was intolerable. The United States of America spends 280 billion dollars a year on what is laughably called its defence requirements. The vast Pentagon buying power (equivalent to the entire product of about three thousand million people in Asia and Africa) is channelled into the largest and richest companies in the world. The bigger these companies become, the more they merge with one another and the more they expand outside American frontiers. Such mergers and expansion are crucial to their survival. As they grow, they threaten the autonomy of companies everywhere else in the world, especially in Europe. The insatiable appetite of these huge American conglomerates is constantly forcing the European defence industries to become huge conglomerates themselves. In this they have been assisted by their governments, who realize that it is difficult to talk about 'national defence' if all the European armaments and defence systems are being made by American companies.

These fears quickly grew to panic proportions in the European defence firms as they contemplated Sikorsky taking over Westland. They were recognized and acted upon by the European governments, including the British government. Early in October, in letters between the Secretary of State for Trade and Industry, Leon Brittan, and Sir John Cuckney, Brittan made it plain that he supported some kind of initiative from the European defence industries, so that, at the very least, the Westland board would have a choice of courses. These letters (4 and 18 October) have been systematically kept secret by the government, but their basic content has never been in doubt. Brittan, the son of a socialist doctor, was supported in this enthusiasm for a European alternative by the Secretary of State for Defence, Michael Heseltine. Heseltine was an expert in subservience to the Pentagon. He had enthusiastically supervised the deployment of American Cruise missiles in Britain, and had based his British nuclear 'deterrent' policy on the American-made Trident missile. He had just completed negotiations for subjecting pretty well all British defence technology to the Strategic Defence Initiative, more accurately known as Star Wars. But he felt, as Brittan did, that the Sikorsky takeover of Westland could be going too far. He was strongly advised along those lines by his national defence procurement officer, an old friend called Peter Levene whom Heseltine had promoted to high office, in controversial circumstances, at a starting salary of £95,000 a year. Levene had been chairman of United Scientific Holdings, whose recent success had been based to a large degree on the cooperation of the European defence industries.

A meeting of Tory ministers on 16 October brimmed with unanimity on the question: a European alternative to Sikorsky, they agreed, should be put together, and the government should do its best to encourage it. Heseltine was out of the country in early November, but when he returned he set his mind to the task. On 26 November, he met Sir John Cuckney, who from the outset was anxious to proceed with the Sikorsky takeover, and told him he was organizing a European alternative. On 29 November, at a meeting organized by Peter Levene, the armaments directors responsible for government defence buying in

four European countries – Britain, Germany, France and Italy –
issued a unanimous recommendation: that *all* future helicopter
production in European countries should be exclusively restricted to
European firms.

Until this moment, there was no sign of the storm that was to come.
Everyone expected that a European consortium would be formed, and
an alternative scheme put to Westland. Other things being equal, the
government supported Europe.

So Mr Heseltine was rather shocked when he found himself
summoned to two 'ad hoc' informal meetings of top ministers on 5 and
6 December whose only purpose was to lift the recommendation of the
national armaments directors the previous week. It was then that he
noticed for the first time that his fellow ministers, not just Mr Brittan
but the Prime Minister as well, were suddenly extremely keen on
Sikorsky; and, as far as he could see, were out to ditch the European
alternative which Mr Brittan himself had openly preferred. What had
happened in the meantime? No one knew, or has ever known. The
change had taken place, not in the Department of Trade and Industry,
but in 10 Downing Street. At some time in the last week of November
or the first week in December, something happened – perhaps in the
course of one of those famous discussions on the 'hotline' to Ronald
Reagan – which turned the Prime Minister from a neutral and rather
bored observer of the argument into a passionate supporter of
Sikorsky.

Poor Heseltine, who had never got on with Mrs Thatcher, found
himself being treated rather roughly. At an Economic Committee
meeting of the Cabinet, as he saw the Prime Minister and Sir John
Cuckney taking the argument away from him, he begged for five days
to 'harden up' the European proposal. 'Give me till the 13th,' he said
(perhaps not realizing that the 13th was a Friday), 'and then let me
come and argue it out with you again.' He says another cabinet ministers' meeting was fixed for the 13th at 3pm – 'when the Stock Exchange
closed'. Mrs Thatcher said no such meeting was ever organized. At any
rate, Heseltine busied himself all that week organizing the European
consortium.

He had a problem. Only one British company, British Aerospace,
had joined up with other European companies in a rival consortium.
What was needed was a bit more clout from a company not so easily
identified with government orders. On 12 December, Mr Heseltine

entertained a most important delegation in his office. It consisted of Sir Arnold Weinstock and Mr James Prior MP. The former was managing director and the latter chairman of the biggest manufacturing company in Britain, GEC.

Neither man was a favourite of the Prime Minister. The previous April, Weinstock had infuriated her with his evidence to the House of Lords Select Committee on British industry. He had ridiculed her claim that it didn't matter so much if manufacturing industry declined, since the gap would be filled by service industry. If that sort of nonsense was pursued, Sir Arnold said, 'Britain would become a little curiosity.' Sir Arnold had long been sceptical of Mrs Thatcher's Reaganomics. Like many industrialists, he was critical of the laissez-faire approach of the government. Like the others, he was happy to keep his opposition quiet while Mrs Thatcher attacked and humiliated the unions. In the meantime, he provided a haven for Tory ministers who had left the government in disgust. When Lord Carrington, the aristocratic Foreign Secretary in the first Thatcher government, resigned over the Falklands, Weinstock took him in as chairman of GEC. Three years later Jim Prior, a consistent opponent of Thatcherite policies inside the cabinet, decided he had had enough and resigned. Carrington stepped aside and Prior became chairman of GEC. Like so many other 'wet' challengers from the inside who had been cast aside by Thatcher – Mark Carlisle, Norman St John Stevas, Sir Ian Gilmour – Prior was not made of the stuff to fight the leader of his own party. A mild, bumbling man, he preferred not to step out of line. Michael Heseltine was different. Rich, abrasive and ambitious, Heseltine was fed up with Thatcher and her schoolmarm ways. In him, Weinstock, Prior and the 'wet' industrialists they represented saw a real champion, and even a possible Tory leader. They promised Heseltine their support, and before long were lining up their 1 per cent stake in Westland behind the European consortium, which they joined.

If he was pleased with his new allies, Heseltine was quite unprepared for what happened next. As he braced himself for the cabinet meeting which would decide the issue on that Friday the 13th, he heard that it was not going to take place. When he protested, he heard to his surprise that it had never been arranged! When he said he'd been there when it was arranged, he was told he had been working all his five days under a misunderstanding. The matter was now left to the Westland board, which, that same Friday the 13th, rejected the European alternative in about thirty-five minutes. When the European bid was improved on 20 December, it was still rejected. The Westland board prepared to put only the Sikorsky offer to its shareholders. After Christmas and New Year, all sorts of strange things started to happen. When Heseltine went to argue the European case on the BBC's *World this Weekend* on 5 January, he was surprised to hear that there had been a phone call from Downing Street telling the producers that the Minister of Defence did not have permission to take part in the broadcast (he took no notice). The following day, part of the text of a pompous letter from the Solicitor-General, Sir Patrick Mayhew, to Heseltine informing him that he had made a few trivial mistakes in a letter he had written on the Westland business to Lloyds Bank, was mysteriously leaked to the newspapers. Two days later, on 8 January, Sir Raymond Lygo, chief executive of British Aerospace, the British 'leader' in the European consortium, was called to the Department of Trade and Industry, where he met a grim-faced Leon Brittan, his Minister of State, the ardent Thatcherite Geoffrey Pattie, and three top civil servants. When he heard what they said to him he asked in amazement: 'Are you writing this down?' After he left the meeting he hurried back to his own boardroom and told his astonished chairman and fellow directors that he had been told it was 'not in the national interest' for British Aerospace to continue in the European consortium, and that they should withdraw. Sir Austin Pierce, the austere chairman of British Aerospace, fired off an angry letter to the Prime Minister asking what was going on.

The following day, 9 January, Mr Heseltine arrived at the cabinet meeting to be told that any future public comment by ministers on the Westland affair was to be cleared first with the Cabinet Office. It was the last straw. He stormed out of the cabinet meeting, and told a press conference he had resigned in order to argue for the European bid, and in protest at what he called a 'grave breach of constitutional government'.

In the sensation which followed, the government tried to explain it all away as a flamboyant gesture by a disloyal minister. But the more they tried to answer the charges of the outraged and media-happy Heseltine, the deeper they dug themselves into the mire.

On 13 January, in the afternoon (at 3.41), Mr Brittan was asked in the Commons about the letter from Sir Austin Pierce. He said he knew nothing of any such letter to anyone. Later in the evening (10.27), he was back again apologizing to the House. There had been a letter, he agreed, but as it was confidential he'd thought it better not to mention it. What of the charge in the letter that the government, while pretending to be neutral between the bids, had tried to pressurize British Aerospace into abandoning the European one? Well, Mr Brittan explained, his recollection of the meeting was quite different from Sir Raymond Lygo's. He'd *never* asked British Aerospace to withdraw, and *never* said it wasn't in the national interest for the company to take part in the consortium. From this blatant contradiction of Sir Raymond's contemporaneous notes of the meeting, Mr Brittan was suddenly saved by a generous withdrawal from Sir Raymond, who accepted that there may have been a 'misunderstanding'.

No sooner was Mr Brittan out of that, however, than he was entangled once again. The Prime Minister told the House on 14 January that she had set up an inquiry into the leaking of the Solicitor-General's letter about Heseltine's figures. On 23 January, she was telling the House that the leak had been authorized by Mr Brittan, with the consent of 10 Downing Street but without the consent or knowledge of the Solicitor-General. She found it all a matter for 'regret'. A new debate was promised.

The government's apologists (led by the ultra-right Minister of Transport Nicholas Ridley) try to pass off the whole affair as remote. Do the British public really care about a difficult argument between two rival capitalist bids? Do they care about what really was said between ministers and an aircraft industry boss in a room in White-hall? Does it really matter who leaked what letter, when the information was all public knowledge anyway? The answers are all, probably, no. But those are not the real questions. What matters is that the central attractions of the Thatcher government have been attacked at their roots. Where the government claimed to be aloof and non-interventionist between rival firms, it has been exposed as shamelessly partisan. Where it persecuted others for leaking secret documents, it has cheerfully leaked its own secrets. Where it calls for others to return to Victorian values, it has been engaging in a street brawl. Above all, the Great White Rhino herself has taken a roll in the mud.

London Review of Books, February 1986

2. Business as Usual

Mr Clean's dirty business

A company which makes millions from cleaning government offices is seriously in arrears with payments to the government.

Last October, I reported that the big Home Counties Cleaning Group, founded and owned by twenty-three-stone Buckinghamshire businessman Patrick Doyle, was more than £800,000 in arrears with its payments of VAT. At the same time, one of Mr Doyle's companies had won the plum contract to clean the big VAT headquarters in Southend. The article led to anxious negotiations between Mr Doyle and Customs and Excise, who collect VAT.

Home Counties agreed to repay the arrears in weekly cheques of between £20,000 and £45,000. But in the first quarter of this year, one payment was missed. A £20,000 payment due on 10 June was also missed. Mr Alan Thirtle, the company accountant, tells me this was because of new arrangements for delivery of the cheques.

Home Counties still have the cleaning contract in Southend, and Customs and Excise will not comment.

Further inquiries into the company have revealed:

- that Home Counties is behind in PAYE payments to the Inland Revenue, while they are cleaning tax offices all over the country.

- the monthly tax payments were reduced earlier this year when, says Mr Thirtle, 'things got tight'.

- that payments of national insurance for their workers are also in arrears – while they are cleaning offices of the Department of Health and Social Security in Central London, Hackney, Tottenham, Southend and Clacton, to name just a few.

Last week, I visited The Firs, Whitchurch, Buckinghamshire, the luxury offices of the Home Counties group, and its complex of supply companies, Oceana Holdings. Mr Doyle was on the telephone, screaming abuse. When he put down the phone he told me he had been talking to Mr Henry Diamond, the estates manager of the Milton Keynes Development Corporation.

Mr Doyle has twenty-seven contracts to clean buildings for the Corporation. He also owns a company which rented a factory from the Corporation in January but which has not yet paid any rent. In May, the Development Corporation issued a writ demanding £18,000 rent. In June, Mr Diamond wrote to the company saying that unless the Corporation got the rent, they couldn't give contracts to Home Counties any more. On 1 July, the morning I visited him, Mr Doyle had another letter from Milton Keynes cancelling a contract for cleaning a bus station.

Mr Doyle confessed he had gone over the top on the telephone. 'I told them to stick their contracts up their arse,' he reported. 'I think what they are doing is f—— blackmail,' but he soon cooled down. 'We'll pay them the rent,' he said. 'We'll issue the cheque today. We don't want to lose any more business.'

Mr Doyle was quite unrepentant about the huge arrears on VAT last year. He said, cheerfully: 'Taking a couple of quarters or three quarters out of the VAT people to me is good business. If I owe the VAT £100,000 because some stupid little girl in the VAT department is inefficient in collecting her money, our interest bill is less by £2,000 a week.'

Now he claims his company is forced to pay VAT monthly, and is even paying in advance. But the figures he gave me show Home Counties nearly £230,000 in arrears at the end of the second quarter, and £101,000 behind on tax and national insurance payments.

Mr Doyle is a strong supporter of the movement to privatize cleaning of public offices which started soon after the Tories were elected in 1979. Since then, largely through government contracts, his business has nearly doubled its turnover.

'I'm expanding – there's all these contracts coming up,' he said excitedly. 'Big schools. Tremendous work in the hospitals. This morning Cambridgeshire County Council are going private with school cleaning. We've already tendered and we hope to get about a quarter of it.'

Mr Doyle's companies employ about 9,000 workers, half of them part-timers on whom Mr Doyle does not have to pay national insurance contributions, because they earn less than £30 a week.

Mr Doyle's companies should be as 'ebullient' as he says he is. But last month, he faced a shoal of eight High Court writs for money owed by his companies, amounting to £88,000. Last September an accountants' report showed the Home Counties Group had assets of £3.5m and liabilities of £4.5m, including a bank overdraft at £1.7m.

Oceana Holdings are in an even worse plight. Though the firm reported a profit in April 1982 of £202,000, it has run up a £1.8 million overdraft with Lloyds Bank at High Wycombe. Lloyds wrote on 7 June insisting that the Oceana account and overdraft be moved by the end of July.

I put it to Mr Doyle that his property interests in Spain had taken up cash which would otherwise have enabled his companies to meet their commitments.

He agreed that more than a million pounds had been transferred from Home Counties to his Spanish business in 1981: 'Of course, had we not sent that money to Spain we would have had the funds to pay the VAT,' he admitted. Mr Doyle says he feels sorry about the £1.50 an hour or so he pays his cleaners but suggests that this is the order of things.

He occupies the former seat of the Courtauld family, Bulbeggars at Potten End, Hertfordshire. The six-bedroom house plus swimming pool, sauna and £10,000 bath was valued last year at £325,000 to £350,000.

For cars he and his wife make do with a Rolls-Royce Carmargue; a Rolls-Royce Silver Spur, a Jaguar XJS 12, a Cadillac, a Triumph Stag, a Range Rover and a Granada and a Lagonda.

His 207-ton air-conditioned company yacht, *Patrilla*, which has a crew of five, is currently valued at three quarters of a million pounds.

Down to his last company yacht, and to his last two company Rolls-Royces, taking money from the public purse but in arrears with his payments into it, bawling and spluttering at customer and staff alike, Mr Doyle is perhaps the perfect representative of the new entrepreneurial Britain.

Daily Mirror, July 1983

The amazing Mr Doyle

Two things happened on the day of my report last week about the amazing Patrick Doyle, boss of the big Home Counties Cleaning Group.

At a Manchester industrial tribunal, three women who had worked for many years for Home Counties until they were sacked last December sued Doyle's company for their redundancy money.

It wasn't very much. One woman was owed £119, another £134, a third £210.

Home Counties were obliged by law to pay the money last December, but refused. The company didn't bother to attend the tribunal. The tribunal awarded the women the money. Now their lawyers will have the hard job of getting it out of Home Counties.

The other thing that happened was that Mr Doyle left the country. He took a morning plane to Spain.

Daily Mirror, July 1983

Mr Foot, you're a ...

'Mr Foot, you're just one of those nasty little men that goes on and on, not interested in printing any facts, just interested in printing lies and innuendoes.'

The speaker was Patrick Doyle, ebullient boss of the Home Counties Cleaning Group. He rang me on Tuesday all the way from his offices in Spain.

At different times during a conversation which went on for more than an hour, he called me 'a classic example of left-wing perversion', 'a cheat', 'a liar', and 'a twister'. He wanted to know the name of my lawyers so he could issue me that day with writs and injunctions. I gave him the names, and the lawyers are looking forward to hearing from him. Mr Doyle was especially upset that I had been ringing senior members of his company's staff who have left him in the last few weeks. In particular Mr Tony Carey-Wood, a former financial director, Alan Thirtle, an accountant who has been with Mr Doyle since leaving school, and his wife have also left after what I understand were stormy scenes.

Mr Doyle strongly denied this and insisted that all these left because they had found other jobs to their liking.

Mr Doyle returns to England this weekend.

On Monday, auditors from the Inland Revenue are due to visit the offices of the Home Counties Cleaning Group to discuss what they calculate as a tax liability of a million pounds.

Mr Doyle's companies, need I add, clean a lot of Inland Revenue offices.

Daily Mirror, September 1983

Mr Doyle's dirty tricks

When his bank turned him down for a three-quarters of a million pound loan, cleaning tycoon Patrick Doyle had a ready remedy.

He forged a letter from his bank manager agreeing to the loan. Then he went along to another bank and got several bankers' drafts for £7 each. By skilful rearrangement of the figures, he forged a draft for £700,000.

He proudly took the forged letter and the forged draft to the owners of a property he wanted to buy. They agreed at once to sell. But then they found that the bank manager who had 'signed' the letter to Mr Doyle had left for Australia eight months previously. They smelt a rat, and called in Thames Valley fraud squad.

Mr Doyle, boss of the large Home Counties contract cleaning

group, was caught red-handed, his brief case bulging with forged letters and forged bank drafts.

Five days *after* his arrest, he went to yet another bank with a forged letter from his accountants in Gibraltar stating that his Spanish company (which was in desperate debt) had assets of £4.4m.

The police pounced again. Last week, at Aylesbury Crown Court, Mr Doyle pleaded guilty to eight charges of forgery. He was sentenced to fifteen months in prison.

Judge David Morton-Jack suspended nine months of the sentence 'in view of Mr Doyle's past good behaviour'.

Oh dear. Yet another learned judge doesn't read my column.

Daily Mirror, July 1986

Calvi's unbelievable true story

One of the problems about socialists, as everyone knows, is that we don't have any imagination. We always *exaggerate* everything so much that no one ever believes us. An example of this is a novel I've been thinking about writing. It's a satire on contemporary capitalist society.

The plot goes rather like this. After the Second World War the American government got rather worried about left-wing extremism in Italy so they sent over a lot of Italian Americans to 'liaise' with friendly Italians who wanted to make money out of postwar rejuvenation.

Because a fair sprinkling of influential Italian Americans are connected with the Mafia, many of the 'rejuvenators' were involved in organized crime. These gentlemen set up a new lodge of the Italian masons, whose object was to get hold of power and money for its members.

The members were not just politicians, admirals, generals, top civil servants, businessmen and bankers. They were also bishops, some of them very high up ones in the Vatican.

Well, naturally, the new lodge needed money so they took over a very respectable bank, which could borrow money from banks all over the world. They then started systematically to loot the bank through its subsidiaries in important trading centres like Nicaragua, the Bahamas and Panama. Altogether, about a thousand million pounds was robbed out of these subsidiaries.

Even in Italy someone was bound to find out about this some time, and questions started to be asked by the odd magistrate who wasn't a mason. A few judges and magistrates got shot down in the street for asking the questions, but eventually the other banks started to get worried.

The president of the bank promptly went to the Vatican and asked for some money to fill the hole left by the looting.

The Vatican told him to go and jump in the Holy Lake. The banker, in desperation, decided to get his own back by persuading the extreme right-wing Catholic organization, Opus Dei, to raise enough money to buy the whole bank.

Collecting together all the secret documents of his bank, the banker slipped out of Italy and came to London. With him were two 'body-guards' who had been told to 'look after him' by the very masons he was trying to shop. Before he could even start negotiations with Opus Dei, the masons, assisted by their friends in the Vatican, called up one of the most expert killing squads money can buy.

They killed the banker and hung him up under Blackfriars Bridge, without a mark of a struggle. The sign of the masons' lodge, by the way, was the Black Friar.

The documents vanished.

The police of course concluded that the banker had committed suicide. Suitably warned, the other masons closed ranks. The Vatican Bank then did a deal with the creditor banks whereby they paid back some of the money and no more questions were asked.

The biggest bank robbery in world history, in short, turned out to be a triumphant success.

As I say, I can't write this novel because no one would ever believe it. The whole story is just typical of the ridiculous exaggerations of left-wing extremists.

So you will have to read *God's Banker* by Rupert Cornwell instead. It's even more ridiculous, and it's true.

Socialist Worker, October 1983

Hill Samuel's private shocker

Is electricity (including nuclear power stations) next on the list for privatization?

The government says no. A spokesman for the Department of Energy was quite firm. 'We have no plans at all for privatization of electricity,' he said.

But I wonder. A bunch of strange documents have just landed on my desk. They come from the offices of Hill Samuel, one of the top merchant banks in the City of London. They show that as long as a year ago senior executives in the bank were looking forward with great excitement to the possibility of electricity privatization.

A high-level meeting was held in the bank on 27 June last year.

The report of the meeting by Mr Bruce Terry, then the bank's corporate finance manager, lists five areas of 'current privatization involvement' for the bank: water, Rolls-Royce, electricity, British Nuclear Fuels and British Leyland.

In only one of these – water – had there been any mention by the government of possible privatization. Electricity was the jewel in the crown.

The report said:

> MRBG [the initials of Mr Michael Gatenby, a Hill Samuel executive] is to continue to retain overall responsibility for electricity.
>
> HS [Hill Samuel] is already well in with the Electricity Council, but the CEGB is the really important part and we need to get close to the appropriate person there.

A week later, on 2 July, Mr Tim Eggar, Tory MP for Enfield North and then a parliamentary consultant to the bank's stockbrokers, Wood, MacKenzie, was invited to lunch at Hill Samuel's sumptuous headquarters in Wood Street. The lunch was reported in another long document by Mr Timothy Frankland, a director:

> Eggar thought it most likely that electricity would be privatized on an area basis and the CEGB [the Central Electricity Generating Board, which owns the power stations] floated off separately.

Eggar thought we should look most carefully at the South of Scotland – which is a self-contained entity and the one most ready-made for privatization. We should also have a good chance of getting it with Woodmac [Wood, MacKenzie].

Eggar believed it possible that if Malcolm Rifkind were made Secretary of State for Scotland and (Lord) Maude were made Secretary of State for Energy, Rifkind would be keen to press ahead as a means of getting away from his 'left-wing' image.

It does appear that the South of Scotland is something we should look at very closely and that we should begin to make friends with the right people there as soon as possible.

Mr Eggar has been proved right in at least one respect. Malcolm Rifkind is now Secretary of State for Scotland. His promotion led to a reshuffle at the Foreign Office, where a new junior minister was appointed – Mr Tim Eggar. On his promotion, Mr Eggar cut his links with Wood, MacKenzie.

Should we take Mr Eggar's predictions about electricity privatization seriously? Yes, we should.

Another document in the Hill Samuel bundle shows that the then chief executive of the bank, Mr Richard Lloyd, wrote a letter to Treasury Minister John Moore in January 1985, outlining Hill Samuel's 'enthusiasm' for the privatization of water.

A few days later, on 7 February, the government announced it was setting up a study to investigate the privatization of water.

As the old City proverb has it, 'what we say at lunch today is government policy tomorrow.'

Daily Mirror, June 1986

Bank on your MP

If you live in East Berkshire, your MP is Andrew MacKay. If you work for merchant bankers Morgan Grenfell, it seems your MP, even if you don't live in East Berkshire, is Andrew MacKay.

How do I know?

By reading a recent internal memorandum to his colleagues by Morgan Grenfell director David Douglas Home. It goes like this:

> As you are all aware, Andrew MacKay, MP, advises us on our political strategy and it is no small credit to him that we have recovered our political acceptability in Westminster and Whitehall following the problems of early last year.
>
> I do not believe we are using his considerable talents sufficiently as far as our clients are concerned, many of whom are extremely naive as to how to work with and use their MPs to advantage.
>
> Many companies underestimate how much their MP can do for them and many companies don't even know who their MP is. I think we all ought to give some thought and discuss with our clients how Andrew can assist us.
>
> Once you have a chance to think about what Andrew can do to help, perhaps you could let me know and I can introduce you to Andrew (if you don't already know him).
>
> He comes into the bank once a month at times of which you will be advised.

Don't write off this chap MacKay, by the way. Unlike most Tories, he's against David Alton's reactionary abortion bill.

And he was first elected to parliament in a by-election in Birmingham eleven years ago. When the votes were counted, the following figures stood out:

MacKay, Andrew James, 15,371 votes, elected.

Foot, Paul Mackintosh, 377 votes, not elected.

Postscript: A Commons debate was demanded yesterday over *Daily Mirror* revelations linking Tory backbencher Andrew MacKay with merchant bankers Morgan Grenfell. Labour MP Bob Cryer said the story by Paul Foot 'seems to suggest some MPs are operating a Handy Andy service for clients that pay them'.

Foot revealed that the bank – advised on 'political strategy' by Mr MacKay – wanted its clients to make greater use of his 'considerable talents'. Mr Cryer added: 'Morgan Grenfell are actually inviting clients to have him representing them. This is clearly a very serious undermining of the job of an MP.'

Daily Mirror, March 1983

3. Keeping Secrets

An enemy within*

Which is the more subversive: a group of senior people in the security services who are giving secrets to the enemy, or a group of senior people in the security services who are working systematically to bring down the elected government here? The question would worry most democrats, but for the authors of books about the security services it is no worry at all. To a man, they are absorbed with the first danger. The second danger, they protest, does not exist. Or rather, if it does exist, it is best not to mention it.

Security service bosses, they tell us, have been agents of the enemy. The first difficulty here is that enemies change. From 1940 to 1945, for instance, the enemy was Germany, Italy and (to a slightly lesser degree) Fascism. Russia (together with the Communism which that country purported to represent) was an ally. The small group of university-educated Communists, who thought that the best way to advance the cause of peace and socialism was to infiltrate the British security services in the interests of Russia, naturally did very well in those years. They did not even have to tell lies. They devoted themselves with energy and skill to undermining the enemy (Germany, Italy, Fascism) and building links between the British state and the Russian state. In those years they flew high over the more typical officers of British Intelligence at home and abroad, whose natural sympathies were right-wing, and who tended to side politically with Hitler and Mussolini rather than with anything which stank of Communism.

Surprisingly quickly, after the war, the enemy changed. Suddenly Germany and Italy were allies; Russia and Eastern Europe enemies. In

---

*Review of *Molehunt: The Full Story of the Soviet Mole in MI5* by Nigel West.

the security services, the balance of power changed too. The old reactionaries came out of their caves, dusted themselves off and set out in hot pursuit of the Lefties who had had it so good for so long. In the McCarthyite atmosphere which spread across the Atlantic, and with the demise of the Labour government, the Communist culprits were hunted down. Guy Burgess and Donald Maclean fled to Russia in 1951; Kim Philby was finally exposed in 1963; Anthony Blunt in 1979. The first three took refuge in Russia. Blunt died in disgrace, deserted both by the Leftist friends of his youth and by the Royal Family and his colleagues in the Establishment, who had patronized him in his prime.

All through this period the Right grew in confidence and determination. The hunting of Communists in their own ranks became an obsession. Many top men in MI5 (always more paranoid than MI6, which had to deal with foreigners and therefore could not regard them all as one big rabble) became convinced that the Communist cancer had spread far higher even than the agents who had been exposed and deposed. 'Soviet penetration of the security services', it was suggested, had gone right to the top.

What was the evidence for this? The hardest and toughest piece of evidence is laid bare (for the millionth time) at the beginning of this latest book on the subject. In January 1963, a former SIS officer, Nicholas Elliott, was sent to Beirut to denounce Kim Philby to his face as a Russian agent. As soon as he did so, Philby confessed, and gave Elliott an extensive though not complete account of his work for the Russians. Elliott went on his way and Philby promptly cut and ran for Russia.

Nigel West, like many other spy-writers before him, is intrigued by this episode. Most significant of all, he believes, was a remark Philby is alleged to have made to Elliott on the latter's arrival. This remark, described by West as 'ambiguous', was as follows: 'I had not expected you so soon.' Nigel West concludes: 'Philby's disappearance from Beirut, and his unexplained comment to Elliott, suggested that the KGB had been in control of the episode; and they had known of Elliott's offer of immunity and had enabled Philby to prepare a cover story.' Moreover, '*the logical conclusion* of this viewpoint was the existence of another highly-paid source within the small group of counter-intelligence experts privy to Elliott's mission. The only question was the name of the culprit' (my emphasis). This 'logical conclusion' set off the 'molehunt', which absorbed the time and effort of a substantial section of the security services for a quarter of a century.

The Philby incident, therefore, deserves a closer look. Kim Philby had endured several tough interrogations during the fifties after the flight of Burgess and Maclean. He had fooled his rather dimwitted interrogators, and had convinced them of his loyalty. But he must have known that he could not last for ever. There was, for him, a constant danger that he would be unmasked. No doubt he had his instructions from the KGB that as soon as he was uncovered, he should confess to his activities on behalf of the Russians, and buy time for his flight to Russia.

That is exactly what happened, and what anyone with a grain of common sense might have expected to happen. One day Elliott arrived with the news that Philby's role as a Russian agent was now so obvious that it was futile to deny it. Philby at once agreed, provided Elliott with an account of his work for the Russians, waited for Elliott to go on his way, and then fled to Russia. Nothing could have been more rational or predictable. Now consider the allegedly sinister remark of Philby to Elliott: 'I did not expect you so soon.' That could have meant that a plane had arrived early, or that a taxi had made rather good time from the airport. At its most sinister, it could have meant that Philby had been expecting, before long, to be denounced but had such a low regard for his colleagues in the security services that he had imagined it would take them rather longer than it did.

To most people who put two and two together and make four, the remark has no significance whatever. But to the wild men of MI5 it *proved* that Russian agents were sitting at the top of the British security services. From that moment started the long MI5 campaign to root out the traitors in their midst. The finger of suspicion was pointed at Sir Roger Hollis, the hard-working, conventionally minded former head of MI5, and his deputy Graham Mitchell. Mitchell, Nigel West tells us, had, at some time in his career, 'gained something of a reputation as a Leftist'. This was a remarkable achievement, since Mr Mitchell had spent a slice of his early life as an enthusiastic assistant at Conservative Central Office.

This book, like all the others, drags on through the interminable committees and inquiries which were set up to investigate Hollis and Mitchell and any other moles who might at any time have gained something of a reputation as Leftists. The two officers at the centre of this molehunt were Arthur Martin and Peter Wright. Wright was a

brilliant scientist and a grammar-school patriot who always doubted
the patriotism of his public-school superiors. He held extreme right-
wing views. His devotion to rooting out Lefties at the top placed him at
the head of the Fluency Committee, the team which investigated
Hollis, and allowed him to move freely round MI5 and to establish
contacts among officers who shared his views. Thus, by the mid-seventies, Wright was in a position of great power inside the security
services. His devotion to sniffing out the Left inside the service was
matched only by a devotion to hounding the Left in society at large. He
shared Mrs Thatcher's view that socialists *because they are socialists* are
traitors.

In the early and middle seventies, when the Left took vast strides
forward in the industrial and political field, Wright and his supporters
in the security services threw their considerable influence and energies
into the domestic political fray. Caution was thrown aside in March
1974 after a minority Labour administration was elected in the middle
of an unstoppable miners' strike. In the interregnum between the two
elections of that year, and in the months following Labour's second
victory in October, the Wright faction used all their information and
their skills, not just to disorientate the Labour government, but also to
ensure that a new, 'more resolute' leadership was established over the
Conservative Party. At its mildest, this campaign took the form of leaks
to the media, 'catching out' ministers in lies which were prepared for
them, feeding foreign journalists with fantastic notions of the
'extremism' of Labour ministers, leaking secret government plans so
that they could be 'neutralized' before they were announced. It involved burglaries and break-ins at the homes of senior ministers (even
the Prime Minister) and their staffs, and even, as has recently been
revealed, inspiring 'disorientating events', the most important of which
was the Protestant Workers' strike in Northern Ireland in May 1974.

By 1976, the back of the Labour government had been broken.
Harold Wilson resigned, and begged his successor, James Callaghan,
to carry out a full-scale investigation into what he felt had been the
subversion of his office by the security services. Callaghan refused.
Although Wilson continued with his allegations, the security services
felt reprieved. Wright's offensive had been successful. Not only was
the Labour government a pale shadow of what it had seemed in 1974.
The Conservative Party now had a 'resolute' leadership. The whole
political and industrial atmosphere was moving sharply to the right.

Peter Wright was still not satisfied, however. His indignation had outlived the causes of it. He was still furious: the men who had been his masters in the fifties, sixties and even seventies had been Communist traitors. He wanted to go on burgling and bugging Labour ministers, to continue with his dirty tricks and his invasion of private lives. But he found all this much more difficult. His colleagues warned him off, told him to cool it. In a high sulk, he retired to start a stud farm in Tasmania and prepare his Great Indictment.

He was a thorn in the flesh of the security services, who watched him warily. They were no less right-wing than before, but they found they could get on well with Callaghan and, even more so, with his successor in Downing Street, Margaret Thatcher.

The Prime Minister's declared intention was to destroy British socialism for ever, so what reason was there now to 'disorientate' the elected government? Of course the buggings and the burglaries continued, but this time against 'legitimate targets' – against enemies of the government (Sara Keays perhaps, or Hilda Murrell) – not against the government itself. The security services could now bask in their respectability, which would be sadly compromised if any of the unfortunate behaviour of the Wright gang in the mid-seventies was exposed. The only person who might expose them with any credibility was Wright himself, who was still sorting out the notes and secret documents for his Great Book.

How to spike Wright? That was the awkward problem which dogged the MI5 bosses. In late 1980, they came up with a solution. Peter Wright in Tasmania was astonished to get a letter from a former MI5 colleague, Lord Rothschild. The peer enclosed a first-class air ticket to London and begged Wright to use it.

Before long Wright found himself being introduced to Chapman Pincher, the celebrated spy writer from the *Daily Express*, who, Rothschild suggested, might be just the person to get Wright's ideas across. Pincher agreed with Wright that Sir Roger Hollis, who had conveniently died, was a prime suspect as a Russian agent. Rothschild suggested that Wright hand over his material to Pincher, and that Pincher write a book. Wright agreed. Pincher travelled to Tasmania in October 1980, got all the material, returned to England, and signed a contract with Sidgwick and Jackson for a fantastic £60,000 advance (the envy of us Sidgwick authors ever since). £30,000 of it went straight to Wright.

The contract was signed in December and the book, with the glamorous title *Their Trade is Treachery*, was ready the following month. Hardly were the page proofs printed than they were being read by MI5, and its shadowy legal adviser Bernard Sheldon. As expected, the book was just the job for MI5. It concentrated almost entirely on Sir Roger Hollis, who, being dead, did not matter. It whipped up a nice anti-Communist froth. It did not demand a public inquiry.

MI5 were delighted. Bernard Sheldon persuaded a slightly hesitant Prime Minister and Home Secretary (the ever-persuadable William Whitelaw) that there was no need to prosecute the book under the Official Secrets Act, although it was brimful of official secrets. The government's law officers were not even consulted. Mrs Thatcher formally cleared Sir Roger Hollis. And the main outcome as far as MI5 were concerned was that Wright's sting had been drawn.

But had it? The irascible old maverick was not at all pleased when he read Pincher's book. He felt, as he put it later, that he had been sold down the river (though for a good price). He had wanted the book to campaign for a full public inquiry into the pinkos who had ruled MI5, but Pincher's book hadn't even *asked* for an inquiry. Wright realized he had been duped. He had handed over the bulk of his material, but he hadn't got what he wanted. He put it around that he would be writing his book anyway, and he would publish the whole lot, including all the bugging and the burglaries and the disorientation of the Wilson government.

The 'Pincher plan', alas for MI5, had not worked. *Now* who would rid them of this impudent pest in Tasmania? Who would rubbish Wright, and in the process rubbish Pincher?

Step forward another 'expert' in the spy field, Mr Nigel West, who writes almost as dreadful prose as does his rival Pincher. Mr West is another right-winger, the son of a Tory MP, and now Tory candidate for the safe seat of Torbay. On page 128 of this latest book, Nigel West is quite frank about how his earlier book, *A Matter of Trust*, came to be written. It was, he discloses, 'an unorthodox method' of exposing the real mole-in-chief. This was not Sir Roger Hollis after all but his deputy, Graham Mitchell, the man from Conservative Central Office. Nigel West's main source was the obsessive 'molehunter' Arthur Martin, probably the only MI5 officer more right-wing and more worried about Reds in High Places than Peter Wright. Wright had furnished the material for Pincher's book; Martin did the same for

West's book, and in the process poor Pincher (and Wright) got a bit of a hammering.

Pincher promptly wrote another book, entitled *Too Secret Too Long*, in which he restated the Wright thesis that Hollis was a spy. West now writes another one too, which restates Martin's thesis that Mitchell was. Now that Mitchell, like Hollis, is dead, the thing can be said out loud, without fear of a libel writ.

Needless to say, the evidence that Mitchell was a spy is laughably thin. Mrs Thatcher has been obliged publicly to dispense with that allegation too. But the real purpose, from MI5's point of view, of both West books was to discredit Pincher and Wright. For someone like me who has no time whatever for Chapman Pincher, it is pleasant enough to read about his inconsistencies and contradictions. Nigel West, like all sectarians, does not mince his words. Summing up Pincher's relationship with Wright, West writes: 'At long last, at the end of his career he had stumbled across a source that undermined all his previous observations about MI5 and its brilliant efficiency.' *Molehunt* is the latest shot in a silly if profitable war between authors who would seem to be without the wit or resources to find and sift information themselves, and to have become dependent on their sources – and, more relevantly, on those who put their sources in touch with them. The result has been that although these authors, and others like them in the past, pretend to be independent observers of the security services, their books manage to leave out any reference to the most controversial activities of the security services in recent years: the disorientation of the Wilson government and the hounding of dissenters. Book after book has poured off the presses, each one challenging the other in circulation terms: *Their Trade is Treachery, A Matter of Trust, Too Secret Too Long, Molehunt* – all of these are about the subversion *of* the security services, not one of them has a single word to say about subversion *by* the security services. That is why none of them has been prosecuted. It is also why the one book which does tell some of the real story is the only one against which the British government has thrown the full weight of its legal powers.

The government is prepared to risk any amount of humiliation in the Australian courts in a desperate fling to stop Wright's book. As their tolerance of Pincher and West in the past has proved, this has nothing to do with any principle about the trustworthiness of MI5 officers. On the contrary, MI5 officers can say what they like, and get it published, provided MI5 and the government like what they say. The very idea that a representative of the loony Right should be allowed to tell how his secret gang, armed with all the information and powers of the state, conspired in the humbling of a Labour government, and in the election of Mrs Margaret Thatcher as leader of the Conservative Party, is obviously unthinkable.

London Review of Books, April 1987

Whitehall farce*

Hardly a week goes by without the enemies of official secrecy having good cause to sing the praises of James Rusbridger. From his Cornish retreat he sprays the correspondence columns of newspapers with volleys of good sense and good humour. This bluff, meticulous man spent much of his youth as a British businessman in Europe, where he worked in a dilatory sort of way for MI6. Since his 'retirement' (he is a prodigious worker who never seems to be at rest) he has become a journalist whose main ambition is to put to flight the sycophantic writers who make fortunes from what he calls the 'intelligence game'.

The writers' success depends on their game being taken seriously. Unless the public thinks it important whether or not there was a fourth or fifth or sixth Russian spy in British Intelligence; unless they worry about what the latest defector from Prague has to say about a senior Labour politician; unless it is a matter of life and death for all of us what codes are being broken at GCHQ – there would be no reason for hundreds of thousands of them to buy books called *A Matter of Trust, Their Trade is Treachery, Too Secret Too Long, Molehunt, Conspiracy of Silence* or, for that matter, *The Spy who Came in from the Cold.* Most of these books parade the obsessive belief of MI5 officers that their failure to do anything worthwhile over a quarter of a century was a conse-

---

*Review of *The Intelligence Game: Illusions and Delusions of International Espionage* by James Rusbridger; and *The Truth about Hollis* by W.J. West.

quence of there being a Russian spy in MI5. Some say the spy was Sir Roger Hollis, the director. A man called *Nigel* West wrote a whole book saying the mole wasn't Hollis: it was his deputy, Graham Mitchell (a former official of the Tory Party). Now we have another equally boring and unimpressive book by *W.J.* West, who says it was Hollis after all. This last book costs £14.95 – compared to £12.95 for Rusbridger's, which puts the whole lot to the sword.

James Rusbridger's great contribution is to raise British Intelligence to the element which best suits it: farce. At one level this book can be read as a series of Hilarious Tales. It describes, for instance, the elaborate plan by the CIA and MI6 in the early fifties to tunnel into the Russian sector of Berlin, so that communications from there could be 'monitored'. The plan was called Operation Gold. There was really nothing wrong with it, except that the secretary of the committee which planned it was the British MI6 officer and Russian spy, George Blake, who passed details of the entire operation to the Russians two years before the tunnel was completed. Here, too, is the story of MI6's courageous decision to order Commander Lionel Crabb to swim under a Russian warship in Portsmouth to take photographs of the propellor design. The Russians were waiting for the unfortunate Commander, of course, and he was never seen again. Rather more expensive has been the unimaginably complex listening-post at Cheltenham's GCHQ, where thousands of experts listened to communications from the Russians and Eastern Europe for years and years using devices which they imagined to be wholly secret until one of them, Geoffrey Prime, was unmasked as a Russian spy who had sold the Russians everything they wanted to know about GCHQ. Prime, by the way, was not caught by some scrupulous spycatcher. The army of spycatchers which is MI5 has never by its own devices caught a spy in its entire history. Prime was caught as a result of a police inquiry – this expert 'listener' to enemy secrets was also a persistent child-abuser. It appears that he had been 'positively vetted' six times.

James Rusbridger paints a vivid picture of the man whose character and career epitomize the postwar triumphs of MI5: Michael Bettaney. Poor Bettaney was off his rocker from an early age. Though he was clever enough to go to Oxford University, he could not contain his twin obsessions: Adolf Hitler and alcohol. Observers in Oxford pubs would ask him to be quiet when he clicked his heels to attention at the bar or broke into not very tuneful renderings of the 'Horst Wessel'. As an obvious fascist and loon, Bettaney had no trouble at all being recruited to MI5, or being promoted in it, in spite of an arrest for drunkenness and in spite of his shouting at the arresting officer: 'You can't arrest me, I'm a spy.'

Twice positively vetted, Bettaney was duly converted, by means which are not exactly clear, from Fascism to Communism, which conversion he shared at once with his ultra-right friends in MI5. They thought it frightfully funny and promoted him to the Russian desk. There he stole a huge library of MI5 secrets which he stored in his home. He was only caught when he tried to stuff some of the juiciest of these into the letterbox of the Second Secretary of the Russian Embassy. Confused by this latest excess of British Intelligence, the secretary immediately shopped Bettaney to his superiors. The wretched Bettaney became one of the few spies actually trapped by the person he was trying to leak secrets to.

'Anyone who works in intelligence for more than ten years becomes slightly crazy,' concludes James Rusbridger, whose Hilarious Tales suggest that the time-span might be rather shorter. But his book is much more than a catalogue of Bettaney-style fiascos. He reminds us that the British Intelligence services are not just a joke. Most men and women who work there hold extreme right-wing views. The man who took over the major intelligence role in Germany after the war – he worked for the CIA, MI6 and later for the new state of West Germany – was Reinhard Gehlen, an anti-semite of the most disgusting variety who had been military intelligence chief of Hitler's armies in the East. Such extreme views are inclined to deflect the intelligence effort from what one would normally think of as their legitimate purposes. Rusbridger reminds us that the Italian government recently asked for the extradition of four men suspected of a connection with Fascist bombings and shootings in Italy. The British courts, after advice from MI5, refused the extradition. The Italian Fascists are still here, protected by MI5 officers, and according to the magazine *Searchlight*, regularly assisting them in their crusade against subversion.

The crazy gang is possessed of the most extraordinary powers. They can (and regularly do) tap people's telephones, burgle their houses, intercept their letters, engage in dirty tricks to disorientate their lives. Their targets are people they believe to be 'subversive', the definition of which, to an average MI5 man or woman, can be anywhere to the left of, say, Sir Geoffrey Howe.

Who controls these 'controllers'? That question is answered very forcefully by Rusbridger. In 1963, Lord Denning wrote (apparently meaning it): 'The Security Services (MI5) are, in the eye of the law, ordinary citizens with no powers greater than anyone else.' That view was recently put in perspective by the Master of the Rolls. 'It is essential in the public interest for MI5 officers to break the law in some ways and such breaches can, or will, never be prosecuted,' Donaldson said in January 1988. But 'murder is an entirely different matter'.

In other words, the Master of the Rolls says that MI5 can do what they like in the public interest, even if what they like is illegal. They are expected, rather squeamishly, to stop short of murder. If you are relieved by that, you had better read what James Rusbridger has to say about the murder in March 1984, just outside Shrewsbury, of Hilda Murrell, an 82-year-old rose-grower. Miss Murrell was taken out of her home in the middle of the day, driven as a passenger in her own car through the streets of Shrewsbury, and later found dead from exposure with multiple stab wounds to her lower stomach. The West Mercia police, who did nothing at all when her car was reported empty and damaged by the side of the road near where she was killed, immediately announced that the rose-grower had been killed by a 'common burglar' (perhaps the first burglar in history to have taken a householder out of the burgled house and murdered her in fields several miles away). James Rusbridger says her murder 'had all the hallmarks of a botched MI5 operation using freelance burglars'. He takes the view that her house was entered – at a time when she was expected to be out to lunch – by 'contractors' working for MI5 who had her down as a 'subversive' because she was a prominent and articulate opponent of the nuclear power station at Sizewell. When she came back to the house unexpectedly, the 'contractor' probably panicked, and decided that it would be better for his employers if Miss Murrell did not live to identify her intruders and tell the tale. (The peculiar nature of this murder, which had all the marks of a Satanist ritual, also fits the dark sub-world of intelligence 'contractors', with their fanatical religions, incantations, uniforms and insignia.)

If the law, even according to those in charge of it, has little or no control of these freelance 'operatives', who does control them? Certainly not parliament. No one even suggests that parliament has any say whatever over what goes on in intelligence. There are no accounts, no reports, no cases to answer. The Home Office speaks for the security services, but will answer to parliament for none of their activities. The Prime Minister, we are assured, has overall control over intelligence. Yet one of the most striking stories in the book – that of Commander Crabb – shows exactly how seriously the intelligence gang takes prime ministers. Anthony Eden, who was then prime minister, gave specific instructions that there was to be no intelligence surveillance of Bulganin and Khrushchev, in the course of their celebrated visit to Britain. At once, MI5 ordered the bugging of the suite at Claridges where the Russian leaders stayed (apparently this did not involve much extra work, since Claridges is bugged anyway). MI6 then ordered the Commander on his last ignominious underwater voyage. It was as though the instructions of the Prime Minister had been given in order to be broken. Eden was so angry that he sacked the head of MI5. So devastated were MI5 by this rebuke that they systematically plotted against at least two of Eden's successors: Edward Heath and Harold Wilson. According to the evidence of three people who worked in or close to intelligence in the mid-seventies – Peter Wright, Cathy Massiter and Colin Wallace – a substantial section of MI5 was working almost full time to disorientate the office, and subvert the political achievements, of Prime Minister Wilson, allegedly the one man in the country who could control them.

What about the free media? Surely, if all else fails, an independent press and television ensure some sort of control over intelligence excesses? James Rusbridger answers this point in a special chapter. He chronicles, first, how much of the media themselves are absorbed into the intelligence game. He cites the *Daily Express* journalist Chapman Pincher as a perfect example of how officers in MI5 and MI6, assisted in one shocking case by the deputy leader of the Labour Party, George Brown, get their side of the story into newspapers. They simply 'leak' to Pincher. Pincher finally got his come-uppance when he was set up by Lord Rothschild to publish Peter Wright's obsessions about Roger Hollis. But there are many other less famous conduit pipes for intelligence 'stories'. Finally, Rusbridger reminds us, the government has after seventy-seven years repealed and replaced the Official Secrets Act. They were not of course inspired to do so by any discomfort about secrecy, but because they wanted to stop anyone in intelligence saying a single word in public about what goes on in their crazy gang. The 'inspired leaks' will continue, but the critical leaks are effectively plugged by Hurd's new Act.

James Rusbridger, for all his jolly choice of adjectives, is a serious man with a serious purpose. He takes head-on the familiar argument by which all the bungling, burgling and bugging is justified: 'We must have a secret service, and it must be secret.' The whole of James Rusbridger's book argues the opposite. Secrecy in government, he says, is the real enemy of democracy: a far greater enemy than the Russian Army, whose shortcomings and incompetence are as legendary as those of MI5 or the CIA. Secrecy turns otherwise rational people into fascistic nutters; secrecy allows untold billions of pounds and endless energies to be wasted in unnecessary intelligence; secrecy pollutes the political process, muzzles what is left of the independent press and makes a mockery of parliament and elections. In an impressive climax, Rusbridger tells the story of Chevaline, the last Labour government's attempt at a defence policy. Chevaline was a sort of updated Polaris nuclear submarine. It formed the basis of Labour's defence policy from the late sixties. But no one in the Labour Party outside the cabinet knew about it. It was authorized by the Prime Minister (Wilson) without parliament ever being told. The Labour government returned to it, again in total secrecy, in the seventies. No one knew about it until Labour lost the 1979 election. The Tory Defence Secretary then disclosed that a billion pounds of public money had been spent on a project which neither parliament nor the Labour Party membership had ever even heard of, let alone approved. All this was done in the interests of national security – and so was kept secret.

What, after all, *are* the benefits of our intelligence service? This is James Rusbridger's answer:

> Whether any intelligence does much good or actually enhances a country's security is doubtful. After all, despite the success of Mossad, Israel still lives in a perpetual state of fear and terrorism. But the intelligence game is now an international affair where winning and point-scoring is the most important thing.
>
> No one dares ask whether any of it is worthwhile or could be done far more cheaply. The king must not be seen without his clothes.

London Review of Books, October 1989

The scandal that never was*

Profound embarrassment has greeted the publication of R.W. Johnson's book on the shooting down of a Korean airliner over Russian airspace. Even its serialization in the *Sunday Telegraph* showed signs of embarrassment, as though the editors had not realized what they were commissioning. 'Experts' with strong connections with the Central Intelligence Agency have been hired to 'dispose of' the book in important people's newspapers, and most of the media have responded with their most deadly weapon: silence. This embarrassment is not surprising. It is a tribute to the blow which Mr Johnson has struck at the heart of the politics which have dominated the 1980s on both sides of the Atlantic.

The shootdown of KAL 007 on the night of 31 August/1 September 1983 gave a boost to President Reagan's administration. At once, a set of cold war measures which had previously been threatened passed through both elected Houses. Disarmament talks faltered, and the arms race quickened.

On all sides, people believed the story which was circulated with much panache by Reagan's team. An airliner with 269 people in it, many of them children, had strayed by accident over Russian airspace on a routine flight from Anchorage in Alaska to Seoul, South Korea. Without warning, Russian fighters shot it down: 269 innocent people had been murdered by a barbarian power. What more proof was needed of the old maxim that good and democratic people must arm themselves against the forces of lawlessness and terror? Anyone who suggested otherwise was plainly an agent of the barbarians.

R.W. Johnson was one of the few people on either side of the Atlantic to resist. His articles in the *Guardian* drew a message from a Tory MP (generously not named in this book) to the head of Magdalen College, Oxford suggesting that Mr Johnson was 'not a fit person' to be a don there. He stuck to his sceptical view, however, and enriched it with meticulous research. The result is not only a terrifying story – far more terrifying than any work of fiction could ever be – but a political exposé of the highest order.

---

*Review of *Shootdown: The Verdict on KAL 007* by R.W. Johnson.

The story starts with the facts about the last flight of KAL 007. The aircraft was equipped with the most sophisticated, computerized navigational aids. The route from Anchorage to Seoul goes so close to Russia that it is dotted with signals waypoints, all equally well equipped. If the equipment works, an airliner *cannot* stray off course. If it doesn't work, the warning mechanisms in the plane and on the ground are certain to alert the pilot within seconds. Yet almost from the moment it left Anchorage, KAL 007 strayed northwards off its proper path. It was 365 miles off course when it was shot down: further than any other plane had strayed in the history of civil aviation.

Somehow, none of the waypoints were warned of this deviation. Somehow, no one on board noticed. Somehow, before he set off from Anchorage, the aircraft's captain had sketched a route very similar to the one he actually took. Somehow, he had taken on extra fuel, though he logged *less* fuel than his proper complement. Somehow, when the Russian fighters swarmed around him firing tracer bullets, he seemed to try to dodge the Russian fighters with changes of course and altitude which were not notified to ground control. R.W. Johnson makes an effort at the end of his book to reckon the odds on all these things happening by accident on one night. He gives up at 'literally billions or trillions to one'.

If the plane did not stray by accident into Russian airspace, however, it must have done so by design. Here, incredulousness vies with probability. For what conceivable reason would a civil airliner deliberately fly with more than two hundred passengers into some of the most sensitive and dangerous airspace on earth? Could it have been on a surveillance mission? R.W. Johnson convincingly rejects the notion that KAL 007 carried its own surveillance equipment – so how could it have been spying?

One good answer to that comes from Ernest Volkman, editor of the American *Defense Journal*. He was interviewed in July 1984 on the British current affairs programme *TV Eye*. 'As a result of the KAL incident,' he said, 'United States Intelligence received a bonanza the likes of which they never received in their lives. Reason: because of the tragic incident it managed to turn on just about every single Soviet electromagnetic transmission over a period of about four hours and an area of approximately seven thousand square miles, and I mean everything.' In particular, the Russians turned on all their air defence radar systems. They were allowed to do so under a 1982 agreement between

Russia and the United States which granted an exception to the general rule that air defence radar systems must be turned off. The exception was where 'an unidentified aircraft' was spotted over either country.

Air defence radar had been much in the news in the United States in the weeks before the Korean airliner disaster. In June 1983, a satellite had spotted the construction of a huge new Russian radar system at Krasnoyarsk. At once the American Far Right, which was anxious to prevent any further progress in the disarmament talks, seized on the new radar system as a clear breach of the SALT 2 disarmament treaty. The Heritage Foundation – so often the leader in right-wing propaganda offensives of this kind – was fed top-secret information by the security services, and immediately orchestrated a campaign across the whole of the United States to the effect that Krasnoyarsk was clear evidence of Russian treachery. The cry was taken up enthusiastically by Republican cavemen in the Senate.

The President's advisers wavered. None of them were keen to continue with the arms talks, but public opinion in the States and Europe was strongly in favour. Did Krasnoyarsk provide a good enough excuse to denounce the Russians for breaking past treaties? To answer that question, more information was needed about the state of the radar systems in Eastern Russia. Was there, perhaps, a gap in the system which was being filled by the new station at Krasnoyarsk? If so, the new station could be said to be directed against anti-ballistic missiles, as the Heritage Foundation claimed, and could therefore be said to be in breach of SALT. R.W. Johnson concludes: 'Just a month before its fatal flight, the US had developed a very powerful motive for testing the Soviet radar network in Soviet East Asia.'

The airliner appeared on Russian radar screens as a mysterious intruder, an unidentified aircraft which could be hostile. As a result, it achieved what the vast array of United States radar systems ranged round the East Russian coast could not do: it turned on every available inland radar system for five thousand miles. All these systems were duly recorded and photographed by a US 'Ferret' satellite which just happened to be passing overhead and whose range and sophistication were such that it was 'bound to pick up enough data to keep US analysts busy for a long time'. Indeed, KAL 007 was delayed in Anchorage for forty minutes, just the time necessary to place its flight path over Russian airspace in range of the satellite as it passed overhead.

If the reader's mind is not yet made up, R.W. Johnson clinches the matter with his account of the most mysterious episode in the whole mysterious story. Six and a half hours after the shootdown, as anxious friends and relatives at Seoul Airport clamoured for information about the missing plane, the Korean government announced the 'news' that 007 had been forced to land by the Russians and that all passengers and crew were 'safe on Sakhalin Island'. The distraught families gave a cheer and went home to bed. The story was promptly carried by the media throughout the world. It was completely, cruelly false, and can only have compounded the grief of the families when they were told the truth the next day.

Johnson has little difficulty in proving that the source of this false story was the CIA: the Korean government admitted it. He has even less difficulty in showing that the shooting down of the airliner must have been recorded in the closest possible detail by the battery of US radar systems in the area. He tells us, for instance, that on Shemya Island a vast radar system called Cobra Dane is 'able to monitor 200 objects simultaneously and pick up a baseball sized object 2,000 miles out in space'. The US authorities must have known within minutes that the airliner had been shot down. Why did they sent out a false report that it was 'safe on Sakhalin'?

If the plane had been shot down by trigger-happy Communists as the result of its pilot's own genuine mistake, what cause was there for a false report, and a delay in making the outrage public? Why should the truth not have been blazoned abroad at once, to the certain horror of the whole world?

On the other hand, if the shootdown meant that a crazy plan to get sensitive information had gone dreadfully wrong, there *was* a very strong motive for delay. The planners would need time to get the tapes from the computers and doctor them so that the best possible picture could be presented to the world. They needed what Johnson calls 'a holding operation' – which is exactly what the 'safe on Sakhalin' report provided.

Even when all the arguments pile up on one side of the scales, the rational mind hesitates. Whatever the facts about the technology and the signals, whatever the odds against an accident, is it really possible that responsible people in a democracy could behave in such a reckless way? Anything can happen in a country where there is no democracy and no accountability. But the United States of America has both. Is it conceivable that people in the public eye, people who have to answer questions on television, could send 269 passengers to their death, like guinea pigs to the scalpel?

It is here that this book is at its most revealing and persuasive. Behind the aircraft thundering through the night to its doom, behind the complicated analysis of signals, radar and military technology, Johnson paints in the essential background. He introduces us one by one to the wild bunch ushered by the old cowboy Reagan into the highest reaches of the most powerful government on earth. They came from the backwoods, from the Moral Majority, from the ranches of the Sunbelt, and from the phoney institutes where the doctrines that the only good Russian is a dead Russian and that it is better to be dead than red are taught as religious dogma.

At the centre of the stage, swaggering in stetson hat and cowboy boots, is William Clark, National Security Adviser, who had been nominated by Reagan to the Californian Supreme Court of Justice though he'd never made it out of law school. When appointed to take charge of all foreign policy, he cheerfully admitted he knew nothing about it, and was not at all embarrassed when he couldn't name the president of South Africa or the leader of the British Labour Party. He did not give a damn about anything except zapping Communists. Nor did his chief supporter, Richard Perle, nicknamed 'Prince of Darkness', for his single-minded obsession with avenging his ancestors for what the Russian Reds did to them. Perle's high moral tone reached its zenith when he recommended arms purchases from an Israeli firm which had paid him 50,000 dollars before he took office.

William Casey, the hustler and PR man appointed by Reagan to head the CIA, was seventy and forgetful. He forgot, on taking office, to list seventy of his former clients, who included the South Korean government. Forgetfulness was a problem, too, for Edwin Meese, Reagan's choice as Attorney-General. Meese forgot to mention a number of personal loans to himself and his wife from benefactors who later got Federal jobs. But Meese had a sense of humour. He made all Washington hoot with laughter when he announced that Scrooge had had a bad press. Scrooge's chief problem was that he did not have showbiz agent Charles Z. Wick in charge of his publicity. Wick also rose high – but was caught paying 32,000 dollars of government money to install a complicated burglar alarm system in his private house.

These were the 'boys' whom the President trusted absolutely to 'get on with the job' and leave him to his afternoon siestas and his evening horseback rides on the range. It was not simply that they were fanatical right-wingers, without intellect and without even a twitch of social responsibility. They were all infected by *Fingerspizengefuehl*, a 'feeling for the clandestine'. They were fascinated by covert operations, code-names, disguises, stunts. Senator Barry Goldwater, the wild man of the American Right in the sixties, summed them up: 'Some of the conservatives are crazy as hell.'

Even crazier were the hell-raisers of the KCIA, the mirror of the CIA in South Korea. In that country, of course, no one has to bother with elections. The CIA *is* the government. The President and the Prime Minister are both former bosses of the KCIA. The KCIA was often used by the CIA for 'operations' in the United States. One of their most useful fronts was the Moonies, whose high priests used KCIA money (and a Washington daily newspaper) to persuade the young of the spiritual cleanliness of the anti-Communist way of life. No one was closer to the stetson-hatted, cowboy-booted, clandestine world of martial arts and red-baiting than the daredevil pilot and captain of KAL 007, Chun Byung-in.

Men like these were perfectly capable of the plot which R.W. Johnson presents, carefully, as a 'scenario'. The disarmament talks were showing dangerous signs of success. Information was necessary to stop them. The only way to get the information was to persuade a civil airline captain to pretend to lose his way, to stray into Russian airspace and to spark off the radars. If the airliner survived and was brought down, there would be an embarrassing incident, but it would quickly be smoothed over. If the airliner was shot down, there would be plenty of opportunity for international indignation. Either way, the information would be in the bag. Heads, the CIA won. Tails, the Russians lost. In these circumstances, what tough cowboy from the Sunbelt could afford to be squeamish about 269 passengers, most of whom were foreigners anyway?

R.W. Johnson's book deals in facts, not assertions. Though his contempt for Reagan and his circle is quite obvious, he never allows it to mask the facts. He is still short, he explains, of the vital information which could turn his 'scenario' into unquestioned fact. Nor is he in the least impressed with the Russians' handling of the affair. There was, he insists, 'no excuse' for shooting down a civil airliner, however great the doubt or the provocation. The Russian authorities, moreover, matched the United States lie for lie. It was almost as though both sides expected the other to lie, and lied instinctively even when it was better to tell the truth.

If the President's men were responsible for a plot to send KAL 007 into Russian airspace, they got away with it. The only casualty was William Clark, who beat a retreat into the Ministry of Interior six weeks after the shootdown, and, soon after that, retired to Californian pastures for the last time.

The comparison with Watergate is irresistible. The last Republican president before Reagan was hounded from office after a minor break-in at the Hotel Watergate. This small crime and its cover-up released a great tide of indignation. The grand traditions of American rationalism and scepticism were tapped to the full. Investigative journalists wrote best-sellers about their own triumphs. Films were made about them. They were joined by congressmen and senators disturbed about the rule of law. Together, they drove the President from the White House.

The skills and powers of such investigators and politicians are still there in the United States today, as the unfortunate officials of NASA are finding to their cost. When the scandal is domestic, as in the case of Watergate or Challenger, there is no more effective force than American liberalism at its most outraged. But as soon as the cold war looms over the scandal, the scandal vanishes. As soon as anyone who probes the misdeeds of government can be branded a crypto-pink, the investigators and the liberal politicians scatter in silence. I don't believe that anyone can read this book without believing that it is at the very least highly probable that the closest advisers to the President of the United States plotted with their allies in South Korea to send an airliner on a surveillance mission over Eastern Russia. Predictably, the plane was shot down and 269 people were killed.

A more appalling charge is hard to imagine. Yet the great engine of investigation which has achieved so much in the past never left its shed. The *New York Times*, champion of the Freedom of Information Act and of investigative journalism, refused even to accept an advertisement putting the case against the government over KAL 007. Congressional and Senate Committees whose public hearings are celebrated everywhere as the apotheosis of open government found other things to look at. The public bodies whose job by law is to investigate air disasters responded to what was arguably the most notorious air disaster in world history with the blandest of cover-ups or by obeying orders from the White House to shut up. The whole façade of Western liberalism and open government collapsed.

Completely? Not quite. For now we have this fine book, easy to read and easy to understand. We have Chatto and Windus, who had the guts to publish it in spite of what must have seemed insurmountable libel problems. It should be published again, soon, in paperback, and read high and low on both sides of the Atlantic. It is not just an exposé of a single atrocity. It helps to explain other atrocities from the same source in other parts of the world, from Managua to Tripoli. It is also a warning. For if the New Fanaticism in the United States, unrestrained and unexposed, can play cynical spy games with 269 lives, then it can go much further. Like the Reaganite loon in *Dr Strangelove* who whooped his way to freedom sitting astride a hydrogen bomb as it hurtled to Communist earth, the New Fanatics will yell three cheers for God and Property as they blow us all to pieces.

London Review of Books, July 1986

Nuclear nightmares*

When something awful or unexpected happens in public affairs, we are usually referred to the 'cock-up theory of history'. This is preferred by realists to the 'conspiracy theory of history'. That strange or shocking events should be ascribed to mistakes, accidents or coincidences is very much more comforting than the notion that they are part of some sinister plot. Take the example of Hilda Murrell. In 1984, Miss Murrell, a rose specialist who lived in Shrewsbury, was taken out of her house in her own car, driven to a field outside the town and systematically, apparently ritualistically, stabbed. She was left unconscious in the field, where she died of exposure. The Shrewsbury police announced that the murder was the result of a burglary gone wrong.

---

*Review of *Britain's Nuclear Nightmare* by James Cutler and Rob Edwards.

Their suspect, they were convinced, was a 'common burglar'. He had, we were told, been surprised by Miss Murrell returning to her home, and had panicked. This was perhaps the first common burglar in the history of petty crime who 'panicked' in such a way that he took his victim out of the house, where he and she were relatively unobserved, and in broad daylight drove her through crowded streets to a place where he carried out a ritual murder. There were those at the time who challenged the police assumptions. There were even some conspiracists who observed that Hilda Murrell had been an objector to the proposed new nuclear power station at Sizewell; that the surveillance of all such objectors had been put out to contract by a high-powered London security firm; and that the contract had been won by an Essex private detective, Victor Norris, whose main credentials were that he was a Satanist, a fascist, and had been sent not long previously to prison for six years for hiring out his own small daughter for the sexual gratification of his associates. Norris wasn't Hilda Murrell's murderer – who, everyone agrees, was a man half his age – but the choice of someone like him to carry out this kind of surveillance is an interesting indication of the characteristics required of a nuclear spy.

With the help of the *Daily Mail*, the realists – or 'cock-up' theorists – prevailed in the argument over the Hilda Murrell murder. In the end, most people were inclined to adjudge it beyond belief that an old woman should have been so foully murdered as part of a conspiracy about a nuclear power station on the other side of Britain. The police relentlessly pursued the 'common burglar' theory. They rounded up all the common burglars in the area and questioned them. They pursued the matter with 'the utmost rigour' – and never even came up with a suspect.

If something so extraordinary happens once, most people will think it a cock-up or an accident or a coincidence. But what if something rather like that happens again? What if William McRae, a radical Glasgow solicitor, and a prominent objector to the dumping of nuclear waste in the Galloway hills, is found shot dead in his car with the revolver some twenty yards away in a stream? Are we to assume, as the authorities in Scotland did, that the solicitor had shot himself? How did he manage to hurl the gun that distance before his (instant) death? 'There are no circumstances to justify a public inquiry,' said the Procurator Fiscal. And thanks to the rather quaint Scottish habit of not holding inquests, there *was* no inquiry of any kind into this strange death.

As in the Murrell case, the very idea of a conspiracy connected with the nuclear power movement seemed grotesque. But then there is the story of Pat Davies of Slough. She was married to a sailor on the *Resolution*, a nuclear submarine, based at Faslane in Scotland. When her friend, whose husband also sailed on *Resolution*, had a baby, Pat Davies went to visit her. She was shocked by the baby's hare lip. Not long afterwards, Mrs Davies herself had a baby with a hare lip. Then she heard of a third, and then a fourth wife of a submariner on *Resolution* who had given birth to babies with hare lips. All four babies were born between 1972 and 1975. If the figures for babies with hare lips and cleft palates born to wives of submariners on *Resolution* had been equivalent to those for the country at large, each of the *Resolution* crew would have had to have fathered thirteen or fourteen children over three years. The figures (even the four which are admitted by the Ministry of Defence) are wholly unattributable to chance; and almost certainly connected with a leak of radiation from the submarine.

Pat Davies started a campaign for an inquiry into deformities among children fathered by the crew of the submarine. She wrote letters to the press and contacted journalists. In February 1987 she claimed she was visited one night by two men who beat her up and told her to stop what she was doing. Once again, Mrs Davies's claims are usually written off as ridiculous. There is no evidence that two men went to her house. Perhaps she is a fantasist? Perhaps she is, but when you put her story together with that of Hilda Murrell and William McRae it seems rather more credible.

What about Vera Baird? She was the lawyer acting for LAND, Lincolnshire against Nuclear Dumping, which campaigned against the proposed NIREX site at Killingholme. Her car was broken into and her confidential papers stolen. Or Debbie Ladley. She was eighteen, a nanny, and she had given some help to LAND. James Cutler and Robert Edwards record: 'On 29 September 1986, she was hanging out her washing in her garden at Stragglethorpe near Fulbeck. A man grabbed her from behind by the throat and banged her head against the wall. She suffered a fractured wrist, a cracked rib and injuries to the face.' The men muttered threats which can only have been connected with her anti-nuclear work.

The cock-up theory of history is hard put to it to explain what happened to Hilda Murrell, William McRae, Pat Davies, Vera Baird and Debbie Ladley. As the cases mount up, the conspiracy theory becomes more credible. It suggests that the movement for nuclear power is sustained by secret forces who have orders to stop at nothing to dissuade dissent.

These forces appear all the more ugly when reflected against the background of the industry's ever-smiling and confident public-relations army. I recall with some misgivings my first really 'big' assignment as a cub reporter on the Scottish *Daily Record* in the early sixties. I was dispatched to Dounreay, near Thurso, on the northern-most tip of Scotland, to 'write up' the new nuclear reactor there. I was twenty-five, an unqualified reporter accustomed to being treated with cheerful scepticism by the population of Glasgow. In Thurso I was met by rows of smiling, intelligent and enthusiastic men and women in white coats. With tremendous care and enthusiasm they escorted me round their beloved reactor. They would not rest until I had under-stood the principle of nuclear power and shared their excitement for it. No more digging coal out of the ground! No more dependence on 'finite resources' like gas and oil! Here, in something smaller than a bucket, was a force which could light up every home in Scotland, and fry every egg for every breakfast all the way down to Manchester! It seemed quite wonderful: clean, simple, optimistic. The whole social atmosphere in the area reeked of this enthusiasm. New life had come to Thurso; new, well-off middle-class people had come to boost the impoverished rural economy. Pretty well everything from the chess club to the thriving Scottish reels society was 'sponsored' by the new dynamic power which buzzed away in the bucket.

I shudder to remember what I wrote in the *Daily Record*. I do remember that it went down so well in Thurso that I was summoned again for another mind-bending freebee, which resulted in yet more idealistic claptrap. Somehow, during all those days and all those lectures, no one had ever bothered to ask whether the new energy revolution was safe. In any case, the answer would have been very reas-suring. 'Join Atomic Energy and live a longer life,' Sir John Hill, chairman of the Atomic Energy Authority, said in 1976. Until 1984, even the government went on claiming there had been no deaths from radia-tion inside a nuclear power plant. At Windscale, the nuclear plant in Cumbria which caused some local worries after a massive leak of radi-ation in 1957, the local medical authorities were just as complacent as the company which ran the plant, British Nuclear Fuels. The Medical Officer of Health in West Cumbria announced in 1983 that 'hard statistics' showed you had more chance of not dying from cancer in West Cumbria than in Britain at large. The industry did not quite get round to advertising for people to come to Windscale to get away from the higher rates of cancer in other parts of Britain, but no one who knew their PR department would have been surprised if they had done so. By one of those curious twists of fate which sometimes name people by what they represent, the chairman of British Nuclear Fuels in the company's halcyon years was called Con Allday.

The first stone was thrown into this complacent pool by James Cutler, a television journalist. His programme, broadcast by Yorkshire Television in 1983, set out to establish the true facts about child cancer in the area immediately around the Sellafield plant. It was hard work. There was obstruction from the extremely powerful company, which runs the area as though it were its property; from the workers in the plant; from the local health authorities and from the government. It was not easy to tour the houses of bereaved parents asking how their children got ill and died. But the final result dispelled the notion that there was no link between the plant and child cancer. The figures were so striking that the government was forced to set up an official inquiry. That inquiry (whose statistics have since been cast in doubt) was cautious about the evidence. James Cutler continued with his work. Another Yorkshire Television programme exposed the dreadful catalogue of death and destruction inside and outside Britain's nuclear bomb plants at Aldermaston and Burghfield, in rich, heavily populated Berkshire. Once again, there were arguments about the figures. But when, in May 1988, a government committee produced the results of a long and thorough inquiry into child cancers in and around the Dounreay plant in Scotland, the question which I hadn't asked in 1964 was answered. There *is* a high rate of child cancer in the area, so high that there must be a connection between it and the reactor.

To write this tough and uncompromising book James Cutler was joined by a freelance journalist in Edinburgh, Rob Edwards, one of the few writers to sustain in the *New Statesman* something of that magazine's tradition of combining good writing with informative journalism. Bit by bit, the book dismantles the nuclear industry's case. The chief victim is Windscale/Sellafield, the world's nuclear dumping ground. But there is no part of the industry which is safe from this assault. It ranges from the old Magnox stations to the proposed new pressurized water reactor at Sizewell. It takes us through the harrowing stories of the nuclear power workers, most of them loyal to their employers, who have died, or are dying, from cancer because of their work. Each claim by the nuclear industry is followed by a recital of the facts. Is nuclear power (as the industry would have us believe) cheaper than other sources of power? No, it is not. The Dungeness power station, for instance, produced 20 per cent less electricity than was planned and cost five times more than the original estimate. Is nuclear power accident-free? After Windscale (1957), Three Mile Island (1979) and Chernobyl (1986), who can claim that? Is it likely to be any safer here than in other countries? Certainly not. Indeed, more scrupulous governments send their nuclear waste to Britain for treatment because they know how low the standards are here. For discharging radioactive waste into the sea, for instance, Windscale/Sellafield is the 'worst polluter' in the world.

How is it that so many modern governments (though by no means all – Italy, for instance, will not touch it, and in the United States no new nuclear plants have been commissioned since Three Mile Island) have promoted this monster? How is it that the British government has promoted it more enthusiastically than any other with the possible exception of the French? One answer can be found in a leaked cabinet minute of 1979: 'A nuclear programme would have the advantage of moving a substantial proportion of electricity production from the dangers of disruption by industrial action by coal miners or transport workers.' The miners' strikes of 1972 and 1974 still haunt the Conservative governments of the eighties, and to some extent have dictated their energy policies. But the real reason for nuclear power is more obvious, and more frightening. It is that civil nuclear power is a spin-off from and complementary to military nuclear power. There is, as these authors put it, 'a fundamental and indissoluble link between the civil and military application'.

The absorbing book *Brighter than a Thousand Suns* told the story of the argument among scientists in the first half of the century as to whether or not they should split the atom to process weapons of unimaginable destructive power. The most curious feature of this argument was that no one seriously suggested (as military enthusiasts usually do when they defend military expenditure) that there was a recognizable civilian 'spin-off' from the process. The fanatics who carried the argument for the development of weapons of mass destruction did so on mainly military grounds: they were servants of their governments, and their governments wanted to win wars quickly. The military aim was deadly dangerous, and so were the weapons which were produced. The same dangers haunt the civil nuclear industry.

The book ends with a chilling scenario. In 1997 there is yet another Sellafield accident. The cooling systems have failed, all the waste has boiled away, pouring vast quantities of radiation into the atmosphere. Lancaster and Manchester are worst hit. Soon the experts are (under)estimating eight hundred deaths in a year, and eight thousand cancers in twenty years. The cancers will be duly passed on to future generations. Some might say that this is rather sensational stuff for serious journalists. I think it is a little on the conservative side. Those who really believe that there will not be such an accident somewhere in Britain or France some time before 1997 are victims of incurable complacency. They should look for a job at once in the public relations department of British Nuclear Fuels.

London Review of Books, August 1988

4. All in the Family

The Windsors' family secret[*]

A great many books and articles have been published recently about the possibility that a former head of MI5 was the agent of a foreign power. Could there be anything more horrible, more unthinkable? Well, yes, according to Charles Higham's extraordinary biography, there could. He suggests that not long ago the most dangerous agent of a foreign power was the King; and the second most dangerous was the King's lover. Both were sympathetic to, and possibly active agents for, Mussolini and Hitler at a time when the British government was about to declare war on Italy and Germany.

Mr Higham's book has been greeted with a tremendous shout of fury. 'Universally slated' was how Sidgwick and Jackson described its reception to me. It has been passed over for serialization. Film rights, once assured are now in jeopardy. Writing in the *Spectator*, Frances Donaldson, modestly omitting to refer to her own worthy, if rather pedestrian biography of Edward VIII, could not contain her indignation. 'Nor am I alone in thinking it rather shocking,' she boomed, 'that Mr Higham was able to find a reputable British publisher for his book.'

Lady Donaldson doesn't believe for a moment that either the Duke or Duchess of Windsor were even pro-Nazi. She follows in a long line of biographers, historians and journalists who concede, since it is plainly on the record, that the Duke and Duchess were both opposed to war with Germany, but who dismiss the idea that they were sympathetic to Fascism as a 'mistaken notion' (Brian Inglis's conclusion in

---

[*]Review of *Wallis: Secret Lives of the Duchess of Windsor* by Charles Higham; and *The Secret File of the Duke of Windsor* by Michael Bloch.

his 1966 account, *Abdication*). Lady Donaldson denounces Charles Higham for retailing tittle-tattle, and concludes that if you leave out the gossip and the speculation there is nothing left in his biography which we didn't know before.

What is the picture so gaudily painted by Mr Higham? Wallis Warfield was born (out of wedlock) into a rich and comfortable middle-class family in Baltimore. She went to high-society schools, where she read Kipling to her boyfriends. She married a young air force officer, and became, in her twenties, an important personality in Washington society. Her main male friend outside her collapsing marriage was the ambassador in Washington of the new Fascist regime in Italy, Prince Gelasio Caetani, an attractive and powerful propagandist for Mussolini. While still friendly with Caetani, Wallis forged even closer bonds with Felipe Espil, First Secretary at the Argentinian Embassy in Washington, an ardent Fascist and a representative of the savage Irigoyen dictatorship in Buenos Aires.

Mr Higham, who has certainly done his homework in the American state files, produces clear evidence that Wallis Spencer, as she then was, was hired as an agent for naval intelligence. The purpose of her visit to China in the mid-twenties, where she accompanied her husband, who also worked for intelligence, was to carry secret papers between the American government and the warlords they supported against the Communists. In Peking her consort for a time was Alberto de Zara, naval attaché at the Italian embassy, whose enthusiasm for Mussolini was often expressed in verse. When she moved to Shanghai, she made another close friend in another dashing young Fascist, Count Galeazzo Ciano, later Mussolini's Foreign Secretary. Wallis's enthusiasm for the Italian dictatorship was, by this time, the only thing she had in common with her husband, Winfield Spencer. In 1936, ten years after the couple were divorced, Spencer was awarded the Order of the Crown of Italy, one of the highest decorations of the Mussolini regime.

Ernest Simpson, the dull partner in a shipping firm whom Wallis married in 1928, had close business ties with Fascist Italy. But her feeling for Fascism cannot be attributed only to her men friends. On the contrary, the 'new social order' brayed around the world by the Italian dictator and his representatives fitted precisely with Wallis's own upbringing, character and disposition. She was all her life an intensely greedy woman, obsessed with her own property and how she could make more of it. She was a racist through and through: anti-semitic, except when she hoped to benefit from rich Jewish friends; and anti-black ('Government House with only a coloured staff would put me in my grave,' she moaned when, many years later, her husband was the governor of the Bahamas). She was offensive to her servants, and hated the class they came from.

Her Fascist sympathies stayed with her all her life. When she needed a lawyer to start a libel action in 1937, she chose the Parisian Nazi Albert Grégoire. Even when the war was on, she fraternized with the pro-Nazi French businessman, Charles Bedaux. Perhaps her most consistent British confidante and friend was Diana Mosley, Sir Oswald's wife. As the Windsors and the Mosleys grew old in exile, they took regular solace together, meeting and dining regularly and musing about the great times they could have had if only the British had seen sense and sided with Hitler and Mussolini against the Reds.

Of all the bonds which united this dreadful woman to the glamorous Prince of Wales in the late twenties, none was so strong as their shared politics. Charles Higham's biography sets out the facts about the Prince's fascist leanings and sympathy with the Nazi cause and the corporate state in Italy. The Prince was proud of his German origins, spoke German fluently, and felt an emotional, racial and intellectual solidarity with the Nazi leaders. As early as July 1933, with Hitler only just ensconced as German Chancellor, Robert Bruce-Lockhart records conversations between the Prince and the grandson of the former Kaiser, Prince Louis-Ferdinand: 'The Prince of Wales was quite pro-Hitler and said it was no business of ours to interfere in Germany's internal affairs either re Jews or anything else, and added that the dictators are very popular these days, and that we might want one in England before long.' Not long afterwards the Prince confided in a former Austrian ambassador, Count Mensdorff, who wrote: 'It is remarkable how he expressed his sympathies for the Nazis ...'

Such sympathies were of course common, at least for a while, in London society, but when others began to waver, the Prince of Wales remained steadfast. He asked the Germans to fix up a special dinner for him at the German Embassy, as a special mark of his solidarity with their government. The Germans, on instructions from Berlin, invited Mrs Simpson, who was then his paramour. The company he kept in London burgeoned with keen young supporters of the Nazi 'experiment'. Edward ('Fruity') Metcalfe, one of his closest friends, and the best man at his wedding to Wallis, appeared in the *Tatler* dressed up in

Fascist regalia at a 'Blackshirt' dinner. When the Foreign Secretary Samuel Hoare fixed up a deal with Pierre Laval, the French Foreign Secretary and a Nazi fellow-traveller, to legitimize Mussolini's conquest of Abyssinia, the Duke also travelled to France. Whatever part he played in the Hoare–Laval Pact, he enthusiastically supported it when it was completed.

In all the innumerable versions of the 'Greatest Love Story of the Century' it is assumed that the British Establishment, led by Stanley Baldwin and the Archbishop of Canterbury, could not stomach the idea of a monarch marrying a twice-divorced woman. The objections, it is said, were moral and religious. The truth is, however, that throughout the centuries archbishops and prime ministers have miraculously overcome their moral objections to royal idiosyncrasies in the bedchamber. The real objection to the liaison between the King and Mrs Simpson was that both were Nazi sympathizers at a time when the more far-sighted civil servants, politicians and businessmen were beginning, sometimes reluctantly, to realize that British interests and German interests were on a collision course. As the biographers of Baldwin, Keith Middlemas and John Barnes, observed, 'the government had awakened to a danger that had nothing to do with any question of marriage'.

Charles Higham quotes an FBI file in Washington: 'Certain would-be state secrets were passed on to Edward, and when it was found that Ribbentrop' – the German ambassador in London – 'actually received the same information, immediately Baldwin was forced to accept that the leakage had been located.' Higham then asserts (without quoting the relevant passage): 'The same report categorically states that Wallis was responsible for this breach of security.' Of Sir Robert Vansittart, Permanent Under-Secretary at the Foreign Office and head of British Intelligence, Higham writes (and here he does provide the evidence): he 'was Wallis's implacable enemy from the day he was convinced she was a Nazi collaborator'.

It is this, far more than any moral consideration, which explains the determination and the ruthlessness with which Baldwin and his administration dealt with the King before his abdication. They were prepared to put up with him, as long as he was acting on his own. They bypassed him. By midsummer 1936, Higham writes, 'all confidential documents were withheld from the King'. The prospect of a Nazi king backed up by an infinitely more able and resourceful Wallis Simpson was intolerable. If the King wanted Mrs Simpson, he would have to get out. If he wanted to stay as king, she would have to be banished. The King's choice (the 'woman I love', and exile) came as a great relief to the government. Yet Edward remained a menace as he continued, in his exile, to offer the Nazis solidarity. When war broke out, he was summoned back to England and sent to France on military duty with the rank of major-general. His lack of interest and enthusiasm for the job, which he showed by coolly abandoning his duties to attend some parties in the South of France with Wallis, would, in normal circumstances, have led to a court-martial. The Duke of Windsor was not court-martialled. He was made governor of the Bahamas.

Wherever he went, people noted his Nazi sympathies, which were fanned to fury by the Duchess. As early as 1937, Sir Ronald Lindsay, British ambassador to Washington, wrote to his wife that the Duke of Windsor was 'trying to stage a comeback, and his friends and advisers were semi-Nazis'. A month or two later, Lindsay wrote, officially:

> The active supporters of the Duke of Windsor within England are those elements known to have inclinations towards Fascist dictatorships, and the recent tour of Germany by the Duke of Windsor and his ostentatious reception by Hitler and his regime can only be construed as a willingness on the part of the Duke of Windsor to lend himself to these tendencies.

On that tour, the Duke seemed to take special pleasure in greeting the enthusiastic crowds with the Nazi salute. Years afterwards, he would proudly show his guests the pictures of him and Wallis being greeted by the Führer. David Eccles, then a young civil servant, met the Duke and Duchess in Spain and reported 'The Duke is pretty fifth column.' In Portugal, the German ambassador Oswald Baron von Hoyningen-Heune, relayed to his superiors in Berlin the Duke's conviction that 'had he remained on the throne, war could have been avoided'. 'He describes himself,' von Hoyningen-Heune continued, 'as a firm supporter of a compromise peace with Germany. The Duke believes with certainty that continued heavy bombing will make England ready for peace.'

Many opponents of the view that the Duke and Duchess were active supporters of the Nazis throughout these times point to his interest in workers' conditions and to his visit to South Wales in 1936, when he made the famous (and fatuous) statement that 'something should be done' about unemployment. Yet the provision of good facilities for hard-working people was crucial to the Nazi idea of a 'new social order' and a key to its popularity.

Once they were exiled to the Bahamas, and closely watched by both British and American intelligence, the royal couple's Nazi sympathies were kept in check. Even there, however, they associated with fascist businessmen, in particular the corrupt Harold Christie, with whom the Duke, with the help of the Bahamian taxpayer, went into partnership. As the war swung towards the Allies, the couple's enthusiasm for the Nazis began to lose its fervour, and in their autobiographies, written much later, both Duke and Duchess would take refuge in the familiar excuse that they had underestimated the horror of the Fascist regimes.

Their former adversaries in the British government and Civil Service were among the many people who assisted them in their rewriting of their past. The Duke's brother, George VI, made every effort to ensure that the fact that the King of England had been a Hitler supporter before the war was kept under wraps. Albert Grégoire, the Duchess's Nazi lawyer, was tried for collusion with the enemy and sent to prison for life, without being asked for (or volunteering) information about his role as intermediary between the royal couple and his Nazi masters. Charles Bedaux, who might have been persuaded to trade some such information in exchange for lenient treatment, committed suicide while under arrest for treason. Coco Chanel, an intimate friend of the Duchess, was arrested and charged with treason against the French state. The evidence against her was prodigious. She had worked directly for Nazi intelligence against her own government. After a twenty-four hour interrogation by American intelligence, however, she was released. 'Had she been forced to stand trial, with the threat of execution as an employee of an enemy government,' Higham writes, 'she could easily have exposed as Nazi collaborators the Windsors and dozens of others highly placed in society. Despite the hatred of the Windsors at Buckingham Palace, the royal family would not willingly tolerate an exposé of a member of the family.'

This sense of solidarity prompted the King to send the Keeper of the Royal Pictures on a secret mission to Germany soon after the war to collect from the Schloss Kronberg, family home of the Princes of Hesse, a bundle of documents which exposed the connection between the Windsors and the Nazis. The Keeper of the Royal Pictures and an associate went to great lengths to retrieve these papers, which have never been seen since. The Keeper of the Royal Pictures was Anthony

Blunt, who for nearly ten years had been an active agent of the Russian government. By 1945 Blunt's loyalty to his king had superseded his loyalty to Communism, and he kept quiet about his secret mission. In 1964, when he finally confessed to his KGB past, his interrogator was a middle-ranking MI5 man called Peter Wright. Wright was summoned to the Palace. On the one hand, he was told by Michael Adeane, the Queen's private secretary, that the Palace would do all they could to help, and, on the other, warned that Blunt might mention his trip to Germany after the war, and ordered abruptly not to pursue this parti-cular matter. In the event, despite hundreds of hours' interrogation, Blunt never told Wright (or anyone else) about what he found in Germany. Possibly, like Coco Chanel, he knew that a promise to keep quiet about the papers would ensure his own immunity from prosecu-tion.

Whether intended or not, the refusal to accept that the Windsors were Fascists has gone on and on. The 'Great Love Story' has appeared on television, and in numerous books. Experts argue about the psychology of the King, the ambition of Wallis Warfield, the hypocrisy of the British Establishment, the size of Edward's penis, and whether or not he was a foot-fetishist. All these matters are marvellous for serialization in the *Daily Mail*, which itself enthusiastically supported the Fascists in the thirties. Michael Bloch's *Secret File of the Duke of Windsor*, the latest in this genre (inevitably serialized in the *Daily Mail*), has but four references to Hitler and continues in the traditional view that the Duke was naive. He thought, Bloch suggests, that the Nazis were 'rough but reasonable men', and underestimated their barbarism. Charles Higham has an answer to this:

> The repeated absurdity of journalists that the couple's commitment to Fascism and a negotiated peace in World War Two was based upon a transcendent foolishness stood exposed the moment one entered a conversation with the Windsors. Whatever one might think of their views, those views were not entered into lightly or from a position of blind ignorance.

Wallis did not want to be the Duchess of Windsor. In personal terms, she preferred her tedious and undemanding husband Ernest Simpson to the ever-whining, introspective and hypochrondriacal Duke. She wanted to be mistress to the King, not the wife of an exiled duke. She begged the King to stand by his throne, seeing herself as a modern Mrs Fitzherbert, in charge of the court but not of the court, enjoying all the pomp and influence of a queen without being the Queen. This desire was not inspired by straightforward social ambition: it came from her anxiety to influence the course of political events. The story, in short, is not just soppy sexist trash, as portrayed in the *Daily Mail.* It is a political melodrama of the highest consequence.

One of the weaknesses of modern republican theory is that it tends to concentrate on the personal weaknesses of the Royals. How could anyone, it is asked, support a system which raises on a pedestal people like Edward VIII or George IV or Andy and Fergie? Are they not absurd, ridiculous figures, unfit for anything but a jewellery auction or a hunt ball? This argument always falls flat. The influence of a monarchy which has long ago been stripped of real political power lies precisely in its absorption of people's aspirations, griefs, ambitions and endeavours. Weaknesses, therefore, are as adorable as strengths. Princess Diana has no 'O' levels – so what? Nor have most other people. Fergie is a mindless Sloane with nothing but a cheerful grin – so what? A cheerful grin is no bad thing when most people aren't feeling at all cheerful. Royal idiocies, divorces, selfishnesses, as detailed in the popular press, are not destructive of modern monarchy. On the contrary, they provide a vital link between the monarchs and their subjects.

So it was with the Windsors. The King of England fell for a divorced woman and beastly old Baldwin wouldn't let him have her. How rotten of him! How many others have fallen for unsuitable partners, but have not had their jobs taken away from them because of it? So it was that the people maintained their sympathy for the 'gallant young Prince'. The one quality of the Duke of Windsor which might have broken the spell of the British monarchy – his Fascist leanings – was discreetly buried.

Charles Higham's is an important book. But there is a great deal wrong with it. He has provided his critics with plenty of hostages. Again and again, he quotes the most scurrilous and unlikely gossip, without proving it. It is no good quoting one contemporary hazarding a guess that Wallis was the lover of Count Ciano, and that she even had an abortion as a result. There is not the slightest proof of this, and anyway it is beside the point. It is no good inventing (or guessing at) Wallis's sexual education in the brothels of Shanghai or for that matter entering the royal bedchamber to speculate about what exactly went on there. There are times – far too many of them – when bald assertions are not backed by the evidence they need; the notes and the index are a disgrace; and Higham's biographical method, piling incident on incident and referring only to the day and the month, continually loses the thread of the narrative.

But these are really niggles. Gossip *is* a dangerous commodity, but no biography worth its salt could survive without it. The plain fact is that for all its weaknesses the book is enthralling from first to last and for one central reason. It exposes both its main subject and her royal catch, not as the dim-witted, self-obsessed lovers who have been pickled for posterity, but as nasty, determined Fascists who wanted to preside over a 'new social order' which would do away for ever with all pretence at democracy and consign all opposition to the holocaust.

London Review of Books, September 1988

Prince of dunces

After all the acres of space devoted to telling us what a serious, compassionate, concerned and public-spirited man the Prince of Wales is, it was a profound relief last week to have incontrovertible proof that he is nothing but a ghastly snob.

His 'outburst' (Princes only ever say anything in 'outbursts' – anything said in an agreed statement is usually too anodyne to be repeated) on people who don't speak the King's English and the teachers who don't teach the King's English was generally well received in the Tory press.

Some Tory commentators were a little surprised that the nice and charming Prince should attack his own staff so offensively. But what they all liked was the political consequences of what the Prince was saying: that in the old days of decent, disciplined grammar schools there was at least a section of the lower orders princes could rely on to speak and spell.

Now, with the onward march of the comprehensive school and the dreaded spread of equality (and with most teachers in state schools being obsessed with left-wing politics), people didn't speak and spell the way they used to. It is all part of a plot to subvert the King and constitution by not speaking properly like the King and not even being able to spell constitution.

What facts and figures there are show this notion to be a fantasy. Even after the attack on comprehensive education started by the Mad Monk, Sir Keith Joseph, and carried on so viciously by Kenneth Baker, more people are passing examinations in English than ever before. More people can read than ever before, more people can write than ever before and more books are being read (and written, and even published) than ever before.

The figures are not terribly impressive, and they are tied to dull and enervating examinations. But they do show that there is not and has not been a general deterioration in literacy. Compared with what the Prince of Wales and the Tory newspaper editors who support his outburst mean when they talk of the 'good old days' standards have risen hugely.

What then is it which inspires these outbursts about the stupidity and ignorance of the masses and the incompetence of teachers? It is snobbery. Snobbery arises from the belief in the ruling class that ability is measured by breeding and power. If you were properly brought up, if you went to the right kind of school, if for that matter you talk in the right kind of accent, then you believe you are *better* than other people.

Consider for a moment the Prince of Wales himself. He is a man without any recognizable ability whatever. He has never written more than two sentences which appear to make sense.

When he appeared on television last year to talk about architecture, he talked the most unutterable drivel, lapsing again and again into the insistence that architecture must match up to God's will. (This is, I think, why he so likes the new pavilion at Lords.) He cannot speak without gritting his teeth and grunting through them.

The King's English he adores is a dreadful language of pride, privilege and confusion. No king or queen of England has ever written a single sentence which would bear reproduction.

Good plain language has nothing to do with breeding or riches or even with education. The two best ever writers of English prose in my opinion are Thomas Paine and James Connolly. One was the son of a stay-maker in Thetford, Norfolk, the other of an impoverished carter in Edinburgh.

Both taught themselves to write, and by their writing helped to change the destiny of the people of America, Britain and Ireland. They wrote straight plain language of the type no prince could ever hope to write, since they had to convey a simple message to people who had no time for frills or silly disciplines, but were quick to respond to fine language.

Keats and Shakespeare came from nowhere and Shelley wrote plainly in spite of and almost in defiance of his birth and education.

Nothing could be more ridiculous or illustrative of the nastiness of our divided society than the snivelling sound of this Prince of Dunces pouring stilted and cacophanous indignation over his subjects. He thinks they must be worse than him because they don't sound like him.

Socialist Worker, July 1989

Liberals come out of the closet

The most remarkable characteristic of Liberals is the speed with which they abandon liberal causes.

Time was, for instance, when Liberals were in the vanguard of the fight against sexual discrimination. In the mid-1960s, when liberalism was all the vogue, and you could even be a successful liberal in the Conservative Party, the Liberals led the campaign for reform in sexual matters.

A young MP called David Steel sponsored a bill, which became law, to liberate abortion from the dark superstitions of a rich man's law. Steel and his small band in parliament responded enthusiastically when the Sexual Offences Act struck the fetters of the criminal law from gay sex between consenting adults in private.

This liberal tide flowed on through the 1970s. As long as gay rights were in fashion, liberals supported them with great enthusiasm.

Young Liberals could be detected at parties enthusiastically singing Tom Robinson's songs against sexual bigotry. When asked why they were not socialists, these young Liberals would reply that Labour had a very bad record on subjects which were not strictly economic. They were full of funny stories about the 'basic prejudice' of the working class, and how you could only find real reforming refinement in decent middle-class liberal circles.

Then came the counter-revolution. Thatcher, AIDS, the *Sun* – and the swift capsizing of the liberals. The chanting, 'Glad To Be Gay' types have vanished in a puff of prejudice.

While the *Sun* and its allies attack people at random *because they are gay*, there is a mighty silence from the liberals. Not a liberal can be found to stand up and say a good word even against the gutter assault on people like Elton John or Russell Harty. Or even Maurice Oldfield, the former head of MI6.

MI5 are pursuing an old feud with MI6 so they told the old school sneak, Chapman Pincher, that Oldfield was gay. Pincher obliged with his usual right-wing scoop, and a man who had been a hero when he was alive suddenly was a villain. Why? Because he was gay. Surely there is someone who will speak up for Maurice Oldfield? Here on telly comes a chap who was foreign secretary when Oldfield was head of MI6 (the Foreign Office security arm).

His name is David Owen, and he's a liberal, isn't he? Not a Liberal, quite, but certainly a liberal.

Does not David Owen in his book *Face the Future* (that's the one they cut the word 'socialism' out of after the first edition) go on and on about the 'illiberalism' of Labour's left wing and the trade unions? Does he not whine on about the Kenyan Asians Act of 1968 (which he voted for, by the way) as an example of the 'intolerance' of the Left? Is not his new party the party of the decent, benign, tolerant and above all liberal middle class?

Surely this liberal at least, who had to work day in, day out, with Maurice Oldfield, will spare the old rogue's corpse a little embarrassment?

Surely he will step forward to say decent liberal things, like: 'Look,

Maurice Oldfield did his job as well as anyone did. Look, just because a man is gay, you can't attack him for that. Look, gay people must play their full part in every walk of society, or else the very existence of tolerant, democratic society is in peril.'

Owen doesn't say any of these things. On the contrary, he puckers up his most serious of public faces and denounces his dead colleague for 'lying' about his sexual proclivities.

No wonder Oldfield lied if his employers, even liberals like Owen, denounce him as soon as they find out he is gay. What was the wretched Oldfield to do? Was he to say, 'Yes, I am gay, now will you make me head of MI6?'

Perhaps the old weasel could spot the weakness in British liberals like Owen from a long way off. He knew perhaps that liberals are interested in gay rights only when they are an idea. In practice, however, the liberals revert to reactionary type. They want gay people to be neither seen nor heard, and if ever they are seen or heard they will denounce them for not 'owning up' in the first place!

Socialist Worker, April 1987

Lord Alton of Knitting Needle

There are those who say that Liberals will never stand up and fight. They are wrong. Indeed, there is no more terrifying spectacle in all politics than that of a Liberal struggling with his conscience.

David Alton is a classic Liberal in the postwar mould. No contact for him with the old Whig ruling class. Born of humble parents, he worked as a teacher of handicapped children, many of them from the poorest homes.

He developed a rich Liberal conscience which never forsook him. It was his 'caring for the people' which turned him both against the Tories, whom he saw as keepers of the rich, not of people, and Labour which cared for the poor, not the people.

Preaching 'the middle way', representing everyone and no one, he became Britain's youngest city councillor. He was a champion of the people, whenever they were done down by Labour or Tory Parties.

In the wake of the disastrous Labour government of 1974 to 1979 he was elected to parliament for Liverpool Edge Hill. He was always to be seen where workers were made redundant (as they were, in droves, at Edge Hill) or where people complained about their housing conditions.

He involved himself in all sorts of worthy campaigns. But he never went too far. He was against dumping nuclear waste, but not against the nuclear power which produced the waste, still less against nuclear weapons.

He was for housing cooperatives, but not for council housing. He fought for the veterans of the 1950s nuclear tests in Australasia, but did not oppose nuclear tests in the United States or even in the Pacific in the 1980s.

Every MP champion of 'the people' has a dream: that one day they will come top of the ballot for private members' bills. To choose an Act of Parliament which they themselves can create – that is the aim of every Liberal who ever strutted in the middle of the road!

This year it happened to David! What would he choose? How would he immortalize himself with 'the people' he represented? Which of the thousands of Goliaths which loom over the political scene could be slain by the gallant David with his new catapult?

Would he propose a bill to assist the homeless, as his Liberal colleague Stephen Ross had done in 1977? Would he champion tenants' rights, nuclear veterans, handicapped children? Would he try to clean up some of the filth in the prisons or the police stations?

None of these things moved him. Instead, at the fatal hour conscience struck. David was reminded of the pit from which he was dug and the rock from which he was hewn. He was called back to God.

The result is that he proposes a bill which will not improve by one iota the lot of a single human being! No one alive will benefit at all – though many will suffer.

David's God tells him that it is alright to dispose of a foetus under eighteen weeks old, but a Sin Against the Holy Ghost to dispose of one which is nineteen weeks old, or more.

As a climax to his exciting glamorous career David proposes a whole new bill to drive a handful of desperate, exclusively poor pregnant women into the arms of backstreet abortionists.

Suddenly David (who has occasionally annoyed Goliaths) is the hero of Goliaths everywhere. Lords and ladies, bishops and proprietors, praise his 'courage' and offer him assistance.

If he gets his foul little bill, he knows he will prosper hugely. Everyone else affected will suffer, but David's career will get a mighty boost.

One day perhaps he will be raised half-way to the heaven which beckons him. Dressed in suitable robes and coronet, he will at last have raised his conscience to a position to which it is suited. He will be Lord Alton of Knitting Needle.

Socialist Worker, October 1987

Behind the castle wall

'An Englishman's home is his castle.' This is the theme of the howl of indignation which has gone up after the colleagues and admirers of Marietta Higgs and Geoffrey Wyatt have defended them in the press.

A letter to the *Guardian* from pediatricians and other medical experts in the northeast defends the behaviour of Higgs and Wyatt in what has become known as the Cleveland Child Abuse Scandal. The doctors pointed out that the real scandal was the child abuse, not the methods of dealing with it, and for this they have been castigated almost everywhere with the slogan 'an Englishman's home is his castle'.

The expression betrays its meaning. The home is an unassailable fortress, cut off from the outside world. Manners and behaviour within it are to be determined by the hierarchies which grow up inside it. Laws are laid down by the (self) appointed head of the family and can be enforced by the most savage disciplines without anyone outside having the remotest right to intervene.

In these 'castles' people are constantly being abused in every sense of the word. But because the abuse takes place inside the castle walls, its victims are unprotected. They have no recourse to anyone, but most suffer in fear.

Class society, built on hierarchy and exploitation, vigorously defends hierarchy and exploitation inside the family which it has fashioned in its image. So long as no one in the family disturbs the exploitation or the hierarchy outside the family, 'rights' inside the family are sacrosanct.

Thus politicians of every persuasion, led by a Labour stockbroker called Stuart Bell, agony aunts, gossip columnists, churchmen and government ministers, have poured scorn and threats on the doctors who have risen to defend the Cleveland pediatricians.

There is of course another side to the story. Just as the families inside their castles can be brutal and abusive they also can provide some of the affection, interdependence and love – the 'heart in the heartless world' as Marx once described religion – which is so hard to find outside.

The castles *do* provide some sort of security for people who have precious little of it outside. When the police recently raided an east London housing estate and started to batter down a door, whole crowds collected on the landing to abuse them. There was something vile and oppressive about breaking into people's homes.

The same sort of instinct rises in the gut when we read of some of the Cleveland cases. The doctors too – yes, even the social workers and pediatricians – they too are organized as hierarchies.

They too tend to deal with people bureaucratically, by the book, watching over their shoulders in case they should be spotted and criticized by someone higher up the line. Thus the sheer *bureaucracy* of what happened in some of the cases at Cleveland – the clinical way children were separated from the only people they knew and loved and herded willy-nilly into hospital wings – was offensive in the extreme.

And it is nothing but bureaucratic drivel to say, as some of the pediatricians' defenders have said, that one exposed case of child abuse justifies the enforced care of any number of children. It does nothing of the kind, and it is horrific that professional people who deal with children can say such a thing.

There are two sides in the argument over Cleveland, and whoever ignores the other side ignores the contradictory and conflicting nature of the society we live in. But that is not to say that the two sides of the argument are evenly balanced.

The mighty chorus of the last week has shown what the rulers think. They don't specially go for child abuse, but they are much more prepared to put up with it than to accept the responsibility of society to protect children inside those castle walls. The very notion of social responsibility is so disgusting to them that they plump unhesitatingly for that 'great essential freedom of family life', the right to abuse one's children.

The first task is to argue with them for social responsibility, for the social necessity to defend the weak against the strong and the abused against the abusers.

Socialist Worker, March 1989

5. Media Mendacity

Guardian: spineless as a jellyfish

Two propositions were plainly proved once again in the High Court last week: (1) that the High Court is behaving as though it were a subcommittee of the Tory cabinet; (2) that the *Guardian* newspaper has the spine of a jellyfish.

What happened was this. Some person in an important position who cares occasionally about the prospect of nuclear war sent the *Guardian* a copy of a memorandum from the minister of defence, setting out the way the government should deal with protests when Cruise arrived. The Blonde Bomber (Michael Heseltine) was furious. All his silly plans were suddenly made public!

Most ministers would take such a thing in their stride but so conceited is Mr Heseltine that he determined to take action to bring the guilty party to book. He and the attorney general sued the *Guardian* for the document, which, they said, would disclose the identity of the leaker. Instead of saying that they had burnt the thing long ago, the *Guardian* pathetically admitted they still had their copy in the office safe.

Anyway, the *Guardian* were quite happy that they were protected by the law. A new Contempt of Court Act had been passed in 1981, which specifically allowed newspapers not to disclose their sources to the courts. The only exceptions were when national security or law and order were affected. The document quite obviously had nothing to do with security or law and order, so the *Guardian*'s case was assured.

But no. The judge found that the document was Mr Heseltine's property (even though it was a copy of the real one). This seemed a bit fatuous, so the *Guardian* appealed.

Presiding over the Court of Appeal was Lord Donaldson, a former

Tory councillor in Croydon and boss of the National Industrial Relations Court in the early 1970s.

He and his fellow judges came up with the most incredible judgement. The issue, they said, *was* national security.

Why? Not because there was anything about national security in the document, but because there might have been! The person who leaked the document had to be exposed, in case he went on to leak something affecting national security!

You will laugh, and say I shouldn't write such exaggerated things in an extremist newspaper. But I promise you that is what Lord Donaldson said.

The position now is that anyone who leaks anything to newspapers is a potential national security risk, and therefore the papers must disclose *all their sources*. The Contempt of Court Act 1981 offers no defence at all.

The law, in other words, faced with a choice between the words of a statute and soothing the wounded pride of a Tory minister chose the latter course.

There's nothing surprising about that, of course. Anyone with a moment's experience of the High Court in general and Lord Donaldson in particular would predict it. But the fact that the law huffed and puffed should have made no difference at all to the outcome. The tradition among journalists is that they do not disclose their sources even if the law demands that they do so.

Journalists do not demand any privileged position from the law. They realize simply that they cannot survive as purveyors of information if people who offer them information are to be exposed to their bosses.

In 1963, two journalists on the Tory *Daily Sketch* and *Daily Mail* of no special repute or courage went to prison rather than disclose sources in the Profumo affair.

In 1983, the editor of the radical *Guardian* humbly handed over his secret document to the government. His own Christmas was safe.

The sanctity of the law was preserved. But the business of journalists is made a million times harder, and the secrecy of one of the most secretive governments in history is safer than ever.

Socialist Worker, December 1983

Libyan bombing: people and papers

Even in the heat of the battle, the polls were adamant. Sixty-six per cent of the British were against the American invasion of Libya; 29 per cent for. What about the newspapers? Six national daily newspapers whose circulation is 86 per cent of the total, supported the invasion. Four, with 14 per cent of the circulation, were against.

The *Sun* rejoiced. Aliens were being killed, and the bloodlust was higher than at any other time since the Falklands. THRILLED TO BLITZ was the *Sun*'s headline, followed by five pages of jubilation. Even the Page 3 nude took second place to the glories of the United States airforce in top killing form.

The *Daily Express* called the raid 'a Vital Blow For Freedom'. Whoever wrote the leader modestly assumed he was speaking for his country. 'Most of the British public will applaud her courage and wisdom,' he wrote of Mrs Thatcher. The *Daily Mail* hailed the Prime Minister's 'debt of honour' to the President of the United States.

Mr Reagan, declared the *Mail* leader, had been killing children 'in defence of the civilized world'. The *Daily Star*, which started as a radical Labour paper (as did the *Sun*), plastered all over the front page: REAGAN WAS RIGHT. BRITAIN IS WITH YOU – MAGGIE. The article was written by Anthony Smith, the *Star*'s political editor. The purpose of the headline was not clear, but it came across as a statement of the paper's policy. The editorial, on page 8, was slightly more doubtful. 'Only history will tell whether they were right or wrong,' it hedged. But the *Star*'s front page support was in the bag.

The same effect – a huge front page headline which appeared as a statement from the paper – was achieved by *Today*. 'WE MUST NOT CRINGE BEFORE THE TERRORIST' was the headline, in quotes. Putting a headline in quotes without saying who said it is very popular nowadays. It has the intended dramatic effect, without tying the paper to it. The quotation came, in fact, from Reagan, but it looked as though it came from *Today*. *Today*'s coverage was all Thatcher and Reagan and Rambo, and you had to wait until page 6 for a '*Today* Comment', entitled: 'Making the World a More Perilous Place'. The editorial spelt out a cautious opposition to the raid.

This double-act, aggressive news and pacific editorials, reminded me rather of the *Daily Mirror*'s coverage of the Falklands war. The editorials were consistently rational, calling for a negotiated settlement, and opposing the use of force. The news coverage was swept along on the tide of combat and victory.

On the Libyan raid, the *Mirror*'s line was reversed. The front page on the day after the raids was a *Mirror* special, in the paper's best tradition of outraged propaganda. Reagan's ridiculous quotation 'WE DID WHAT WE HAD TO DO' was printed in huge type around a picture of a wounded child crying in agony. But the effect of this was tarnished by a page 2 editorial which *supported* the action (and an editorial before the raid which practically invited it). In the Falklands war, the *Mirror*'s line was to oppose the war, but report it aggressively. Over Libya, the *Mirror* seems to support the military action, but report it pacifically.

The 'quality' papers put up a slightly braver show. Murdoch's *Times*, of course, grovelled with the rest ('The justification for the US raid ought not to have been in doubt'), but the *Telegraph* was opposed. Its editorial was headlined 'a bad decision'. Much of its reporting reflected this view. Max Hastings had heard far too many times for his liking the famous remark on Lord Camrose's deathbed – 'You can be as rich as I am if you don't liven up the *Daily Telegraph*.' He may find it even more disastrous to inject the *Daily Telegraph* with shock doses of common sense, though so far it seems to have been in line with its readers. The *Guardian* leader started: 'They were wrong to do it, and we were foolish to help them.' From then on it apologized and prevaricated with its usual smudge.

Was there really not a single national paper prepared to indulge in a moment's polemic against one of the nastiest international incidents since Suez? Yes, there was. I quote: 'Yesterday's bombing of Libyan targets by US aircraft was futile, deplorable and almost certainly counter-productive: not merely is it unlikely to halt Libyan-sponsored terrorism; it will leave in its wake significant political damage both to the US and the UK.' On and on this went in a rising crescendo of fury.

Am I seeking publicity for some far-left tract? Not at all. This was the *Financial Times*, the national quality paper with the smallest circulation, which does not rely on bluster and claptrap to hold on to it. It tells the truth to its class. The truth is that the Libyan invasion is bad even for the ruling classes (as the collapse of share prices quickly proved).

The *Financial Times* could see that. Most of the other papers are now so lost to militaristic hysteria they cannot see anything. I suppose we should be grateful that the British people – most of them – are a good deal more sensible and decent than the newspapers they read.

New Statesman, April 1986

Wapping greed

When the Wapping dispute started at the beginning of the year, there was a tremendous howl in all the other newspapers about greedy print-workers.

In the greatest detail, the enormous riches of printworkers were set out for all to see. It was hard to meet any journalist in Fleet Street or anywhere else who wasn't delighted that the greedy printworkers had got their come-uppance at last.

Quite decent, reasonable people would fulminate against the 'restrictive practices' which led to people with only minimal skills hoarding cottages in the country, basking on holidays abroad, and even leaving something to their children.

The striking printworkers had one reply. They pointed out that the only real effect of the Wapping switch would be that money which had previously gone to them would go instead to Rupert Murdoch.

Scanning the *Financial Times* the other day (11 October) I found, right at the bottom of an article about the newly launched *Independent*, a couple of astonishing facts:

- In the year to June 1986 the *Times* and the *Sunday Times* made 34.49 million dollars profit. In the previous year the profit from these two papers was 7.8 million.
- In the year to June 1986 the *Sun* and the *News of the World* made 78.9 million dollars profit, compared to 29 million last year.

In the first case, profits were up more than 400 per cent, in the second 150 per cent. I doubt whether you would find a substantial company in the country with a record even half as good as that.

What is the reason for this fantastic increase in profits? Is it perhaps that the newspapers have been outstandingly successful?

No, they have not. Three of the four papers – the *Times*, the *Sun* and the *Sunday Times* – have *lost* circulation over the period, the *Sunday Times* quite drastically.

Everyone agrees that all four papers are incomparably worse than they were even a year ago. The decline in the standards of the *Sunday Times* in particular is the talk of all newspaper buffs.

The product is much worse. In the case of three of the four newspapers, less people are buying them. The price of raw materials, notably newsprint, has been going up. By all that's rational, profits should be going down.

But here is the rub, from the *FT* article. 'The profits were boosted by five months of savings from publishing the four national titles at Wapping.'

The 'savings' here, of course, were in the wages and salaries of the sacked workers, and in the breaking of effective trade unions. And these 'savings' are only for five months of the year. The profits next year, if production continues without interruption, will be absolutely astronomical.

The capitalist argument is that when 'savings' of this kind are made, the economy generally will benefit since the money thus 'saved' will find its way into other profitable investment and not rot away in workers' pockets, cottages, holidays etc.

But what is the reality in this case? The profits will enormously increase the power and greed of one of the most powerful and greedy men on earth. They will enable Rupert Murdoch to tighten further his monopolist's grip on the American media, and to continue his campaign against the BBC and all standards and regulation over the media anywhere on earth.

Instead of the comparative distribution of these vast newspaper fortunes among people who were members of trade unions (and made a lot of what they earned over to other trade unionists in trouble), the wealth previously spent on thousands of families is now concentrated in the hands of one man who is already so rich that he cannot possibly spend any of it on anything he needs.

Margaret Thatcher said in a recent interview: 'We have even

brought sanity to Fleet Street.' What she means by 'sanity' is now clear. It is a world in which contented, well-off workers who cooperate both at work and in trade unions to increase their wealth, are no longer tolerated. In their place are reactionary newspaper magnates whose single aim is to produce more and more newspapers with lower and lower standards so that their vast piles of wealth and power can grow still higher.

Socialist Worker, October 1986

Rushdie and the liberals

I think it was Peter Jenkins, when he wrote a column for the *Guardian*, who invented the phrase 'the paperback Marxist'. How appropriate then that the perfect foil to this foul creature should now have been created by the most liberal and rational of *Guardian* columnists, Hugo Young. Hugo now presents himself to his readers as a hardback liberal.

Hugo Young is a British liberal and he therefore found it disgusting when people burnt books in the streets. But he soon became shocked by his own proposition. A crude slogan like 'books should not be banned' is open to all sorts of counter-arguments. Fellow rationalists rise up and say, in chorus, 'Er ... but.'

So Hugo, after much rational thought, refined his proposition, and restated it like this. To burn a hardback is a defiance of free speech, but to ban a paperback is its very essence.

The subtlety of this epigram appealed to him enormously, and he published it in the *Guardian*. He defended the right of Salman Rushdie to publish *The Satanic Verses* in hardback, but suggested that the author, in the decent English public school spirit in which he and Hugo (and I) were brought up, should instruct his publishers (to their intense relief) not to publish the paperback. Thus, says Hugo, a lot of violence will be avoided, and honours will be even in the great battle for free speech.

This characterizes the *Guardian*'s (and Hugo Young's) approach to all the great freedoms for which they stand. They are in favour, for instance, of freedom of the press from government laws banning newspapers from printing official secrets.

But then ... er well ... but. What happens if someone leaks you an official secret and the government wants the document back? Here indeed is a clash of freedoms, the freedom of the press to publish and the freedom of the government to protect its information.

The *Guardian* solved the problem by giving the document back. When the young woman who leaked the information was identified and sent to prison the *Guardian*, in a courageous leader, denounced the authorities.

For Hugo Young and his liberals, freedom of the press means freedom of unelected editors and unelected columnists to say what they want. If the government interferes it is wrong. If trade unionists do it, they are wrong. But if monopolists and millionaires who own newspapers interfere, they have every right to do so.

The trick is to make a proposition and then cut it in half; to qualify it in such a way that freedoms are preserved only for the cultured minority of which the *Guardian*, its writers and its readers are part.

Hugo's qualifications on the Salman Rushdie affair have an excellent pedigree. In 1793, at the outset of the post-revolutionary war between Britain and France, William Godwin published *Political Justice*, a sustained attack on the received political, moral and religious notions of the day. The Tory cabinet urgently discussed whether or not it should be prosecuted.

Prime Minister Pitt asked one question: how much was the book? Back came the comforting reply – one pound and sixteen shillings (worth at that time at least twenty times what it is today). Pitt heaved a sigh of relief and proposed no action.

At the same time, the cheap, widely distributed *Rights of Man* by Tom Paine was banned with penalties of death for all who sold it, bought it or read it.

Like Hugo Young today, Pitt and his friends could cope with their own class reading subversive or atheistic literature. When such ideas started to spread among the masses, it was time to shelve those liberal principles and engage in a little polite, fair-minded and even-handed repression.

Socialist Worker, January 1990

Hiding his light under a Bushell

I am recovering from a vicious attack on me by Garry Bushell, who writes about television for the *Sun*.

'Next time upper-class twit Foot is invited to appear on TV,' Garry writes, 'they could flash up the sign: Warning! Loony!'

Not a bad idea, is it? But there's always a danger with that sort of label. I remember a sunny morning about twelve years ago when I was working full-time on *Socialist Worker*.

Into the office strode a young man who wanted to change the world. He was brimming over with rage at capitalist society. We calmed him down a bit and set him to work. He wrote beautifully and passionately for the revolution, and we loved him.

I imagine you've guessed his name by now: Garry Bushell.

And I expect you'll agree with the old socialist proverb: Better a loony Leftie than a sane renegade on the *Sun*.

Daily Mirror, November 1989

Bias on media bias

How should you headline a news story which is based on hearsay and is probably wrong?

The traditional answer is to surround the headline in inverted commas. Thus, if a crackpot psychiatrist was to suggest to a newspaper that Tony Benn was mad, this 'fact' would be reported with the headline 'BENN IS MAD' SHOCK. The inverted commas are the newspaper's defence if anyone protests to the Press Council. 'We were not reporting that he is mad,' is the excuse. 'We were merely reporting that someone said he is mad. Proof of that is the punctuation.'

Mrs Thatcher tells us that her government has brought sanity even to Fleet Street and the 'inverted commas' trick now seems to be dying out. On Tuesday 18 November, for instance, the *London Standard*'s headline read: YES, THE BBC IS BIASED.

No doubt about it. Absolutely no inverted commas. The headline shifted a little with editions, and ended up as LEFT BIAS ON BBC AND ITV. Slightly more moderate, but still no inverted commas.

Instead, there was a 'strap' (that is, a smaller headline in much smaller type). The strap is mainly a technical device to make the page look better. I doubt very much whether anyone ever reads the strap, but if they did in this case it said: Report Accuses Current Affairs Programmes.

The long report below the headline indicated that 'a report' had found left-wing bias on almost all television programmes. The report had been issued by an 'independent media research group', the Media Monitoring Unit.

The editor of the report, Mr Simon Clarke, was quoted as saying: 'We are not in favour of bias of any sort.' But he and his colleague, Dr Julian Lewis, had found 'over-representation of fashionable left-wing views' throughout television.

Who is Simon Clarke? According to the *Standard* story he has 'centre right' views. What about Dr Lewis? The *Standard* reported that he is a former Tory candidate. If you think that that line-up is a little unbalanced, don't worry. The *Standard* continued: 'The report was conceived by Lord Chalfont, a former Labour minister.'

That's all right, then. A former Labour minister, a Tory candidate and someone from the centre right. What more balanced team could be imagined?

In case you think the *Standard* had a scoop, by the way, you should know that the story was taken from that morning's *Daily Express*. That paper 'leaked' the result of the report of the Media Monitoring Unit in a huge page 2 report whose headline reverted to inverted commas: TV RAPPED OVER 'LEFT' WING BIAS.

Indeed, a few pages later on, on the main feature page, a regular *Daily Express* columnist had had so much advance warning of the report that he was able to write a trenchant article demanding: GIVE US THE FACTS – NOT BBC FICTION.

The columnist was Lord Chalfont, who referred modestly to the report by an 'independent monitoring unit', without disclosing that he himself had founded the unit, and even written a foreword to the report.

Lord Chalfont's left-wing credentials were remarked upon in the next day's *Sun* (19 November), which described him as 'a Labour peer'. Lord Chalfont is *not* a Labour peer, and has not even pretended to be one for at least twelve years. When he was elevated to the peerage so that he could become Minister of Disarmament in Harold Wilson's 1964 Labour government, most people thought of him as a Liberal. During the 1970s he moved steadily to the right, and publicly broke with Labour in the autumn of 1974, just before the second election of that year. He is now, by my reckoning, very far to the right on almost every issue, including that of South Africa, where he jovially sponsors British sportsmen.

A closer and more accurate examination of the 'independent' Media Monitoring Unit was made on 19 November by Francis Wheen, who writes a marvellous (and biased) column in the *Independent*. He found a contact between Simon Clarke and the ultra-right Adam Smith Institute. He exposed Dr Lewis as one of the leading right-wing propagandists for nuclear weaponry, and found that the 'moneybags' behind the unit is Sir Peter Tennant, Lord Chalfont's chum.

What has happened here is that a group of very right-wing people, financed by money from the City, have done some research and come up with conclusions which are intensely satisfying to right-wing people, and especially to right-wing newspapers who are quick to report their findings as fact, and their source as an 'independent unit'. The most outrageous bias had been applied to reporting a report which alleges outrageous bias.

In a letter to his friend Sir Richard Rees, some forty years ago, George Orwell mused on this curious British obsession with lack of bias, or objectivity as an asset in politics or journalism. He wrote that pretty well anyone who writes anything about current affairs is almost certain to be biased in one direction or another. The way to deal with this was not, he said, to try to cut out opinions or bias, but to admit them. Those who were frank about where they stood on the whole wrote more honestly and informatively than those who pretended to be objective when in truth they were not objective at all.

The real credibility test, it seems to me, is not in the political bias of a story, but in the accuracy and sweep of the information it conveys.

Our newspapers are heavily biased to the right, by any standard. Three out of four national papers openly support the Tories at election times, and at most times in between. In itself, however, that is not the point. The real charge is that this bias cuts down and distorts the information newspapers convey.

In their fascinating book, *The Zinoviev Letter* (a deliberate Tory forgery with which the Conservative Party deceived the entire press and radio in 1924, and, as a result, won an election) Lewis Chester, Stephen Fry and Hugo Young wrote: 'The newspapers of the time were in the most unfortunate sense organs of opinion, and provided an instructive example of the absurdity of the argument that the health of the press depends on its ability to reflect a broad spectrum of views. The health of the press, now as then, seems to us to depend on a simpler, more demanding function – its ability to find out and present facts.'

Hear, hear to that – and what stunning proof of it comes from the media's coverage of a so-called independent report on its own bias.

UK *Press Gazette*, November 1986

Soaraway, servile *Sun*

Tony Miles, former editor, chairman and editorial director of the *Mirror*, used to talk a lot about the success of the *Sun*. In one conversation I remember being rebuked for suggesting, as do many *Sun*-haters, that the huge circulation of that newspaper was simply a matter of plumbing the depths; of starting from the lowest common denominator; of tits, bums, and high morality; and of a contempt for journalistic standards.

Tony disagreed. He had studied the matter closely while the *Mirror* was knocked off its perch at the top of the tabloid tree. He had, after all, every reason to agree that base journalism was the reason for the

Sun's success, and, conversely, that the relatively high standards of the *Mirror* explained its relative failure.

But he didn't. Perhaps out of blind faith for the profession of popular journalism (he was a first-rate chief reporter in his time), Tony refused to accept that any amount of filth churned out in a newspaper would increase circulation. Nor did he agree that debased journalistic standards in themselves can sell four million copies a day. He argued that for all its terrible faults, for all its unforgivable tricks and subterfuge, the *Sun* did have a certain quality which explained its extraordinary success. That quality, he argued, was a brashness, a 'devil-may-care' populism, an earthy, vulgar (in the proper sense of the word) contempt for irrelevant 'values' which mean nothing to the man in the street. Who cares about polite rules of polite society – who cares about professors on Press Councils, bishops in the House of Lords, 'poofy' judges who don't understand the common man? They are all part of an Establishment conspiracy to tell the ordinary chap in the street what's good for him. Your average punter in the pub loves to goggle at a Page 3 nude. Who are the lefty killjoys to tell him he can't?

These notions, Tony would point out, had about them a certain challenge. 'Ordinary' people (if such these be) aren't very interested in formal party politics – they don't study leading articles very carefully. They like a crude paper, easy to read, which sticks up for them against anyone who dares to tell them what's good for them. Tony Miles thought that the 'cheeky chappy' image of all the *Sun*'s ingredients, was the one which most explained its success among the lower orders.

The most recent circulation figures seem to support him. The most interesting figures of course are not those for the *Sun* nor for the *Mirror* but for the *Star*. For if it really is true that journalistic quality has *nothing* to do with circulation, then Lord Stevens and his advisers were absolutely justified in putting Michael Gabbert in as editor of the *Star* with orders to plunge downmarket, filling the paper with soft pornography.

It didn't work. In fact, it was a shattering failure. In a few weeks it came very near to destroying what had been a relatively successful popular newspaper, which had (against enormous odds) built up a sizeable circulation of nearly 1.5 million copies a day. The universal tits and bums drove out most of the few good journalists the *Star* employed. The paper reached rock bottom, and the circulation took a dive the like of which few newspapers have experienced since figures were started. There were many, including I think the UK *Press Gazette*, which breathed a sigh of relief, and produced the Falling *Star* as proof of the necessity of some sort of quality in order to get a high circulation. Once more, the 'brashness' of the *Sun*'s journalistic mix was cited in its support.

I was always a little sceptical, however, of Tony Miles's opinion, and the scepticism survives the collapse of the *Star*. It seems to me that the 'brashness' of the *Sun* is, essentially, the brashness of the braggart and the bully. Braggarts and bullies are bad enough when they are bragging and bullying, but they are worse when they reveal themselves for what all braggarts and bullies are at heart; cowards.

There was an excellent example of that over the New Year. On 30 December, on the *Sun* front page, a story by-lined John Kay, 'revealed' that two heroes of the Zeebrugge disaster had been awarded the George Medal. John Kay was able to 'reveal' this fact because he had attended an unofficial briefing for journalists in which the names of those winning New Year's Honours were announced, and embargoed for 1 January.

The embargo for such meetings had mostly been scrupulously observed in the past, and the papers of 31 December and New Year's Day were full of official outrage that the *Sun*, for the sake of a front page 'exclusive', should have so crudely broken the rules. Even Mrs Thatcher made her outrage publicly known, and the halls of the Establishment rang to unanimous indignation.

Such upper-class politeness, it might be thought, was nothing to the *Sun*. Was this not the same old rubbish about obeying rules made for the advantage of a few lazy journalists in the know? Why shouldn't the *Sun*, in its pact with the common man, tell him what he ought to know without waiting for some footling official to give the nod? Was this not just another professional conspiracy to muzzle the great *Sun*? Could not the Archbishop of Canterbury be somehow held responsible?

At the very least, you might have thought, the brash *Sun* might have ignored the hullabaloo, loftily passing on to matters which more plainly absorb the man in the pub. Not, however, so. The *Sun* editor at once wrote a letter to 10 Downing Street. Did his prose resound with the usual 'cheeky chappy' chirruping of the Beast of South London? Was there a sign of the swagger with which the *Sun* sticks up for the common man against authority?

Not at all. From the first word, the letter crept and grovelled like a puppy which has done its business in the lady's parlour, and tries to whine its way into her favour to avoid a smacking. First, there was the schoolboy excuse. The reason the embargo was broken, whined MacKenzie, was the '*Sun's* strong feeling' that the awards had been 'too long in coming' and therefore should have been announced 'separately from the New Year's Honours list'.

This was tripe. Mr MacKenzie could not point to a single word in his newspaper, either on the day the embargo was broken, or at any other time, to suggest that these George Medals should have been awarded outside the normal lists. Indeed, there was no conceivable reason why they should have been. The excuse was not worth the paper it was written on. It was in the very worst 'Please Ma'am' tradition of whine and crawl. It was followed, by a 'categorical assurance' that this would never happen again. On 1 January the *Sun* published a spine-chilling leading article declaring in brash, vulgar, populist tones that Mrs Thatcher was probably the best thing that had ever happened in the entire history of the world.

Brash? Vulgar? Populist? Maybe the *Sun* is all these things. But with all three qualities goes another which puts the lot of them to flight: servility.

UK Press Gazette, January 1988

US

6. Socialism

What would you put in its place?

The capitalist disaster is all around us, clear to see. But for most people capitalism is 'the best system we've got'. Before they destroy capitalism, they want to know – what can they put in its place? There *is* an alternative way of running society which is worth fighting for. It is called socialism.

Socialism is built on three principles, all vital to one another.

The first is the social ownership of the means of production. Many people take this to mean the ownership of all property by some Big Brother state. They look around in their homes and see a few treasured possessions. Furniture, a television set, a washing machine, perhaps a car or some books. They do not see why they should give these things up to some bureaucratic state, or to anyone else for that matter.

Nor should they. And here is the first big misunderstanding, carefully nursed by the supporters of capitalism. They deliberately ignore the obvious difference between people's possessions and the means of producing these possessions.

If you own a washing machine, you do not get richer because you own it. On the contrary, you probably pay out large sums every month in hire purchase commitments. Even when you've finished buying it, there's no extra income to you from having that washing machine. But if you own shares in Hoover, you grow richer because other people are buying washing machines.

The means of production are the factories, the machines, the chemical plants, the printing presses, the pits, the building materials – all the things which produce wealth. It is the ownership of all these by a small handful of people – or by a state which is run on behalf of that

small handful of people – which leads to the inequalities and the chaos
of capitalist society.

If the means of production are owned by society as a whole, then it
becomes impossible for one group of people to grow rich from other
people's work.

It removes the compulsion for industries and services to compete
with one another for the general wealth. It makes it possible to *plan* the
resources of society according to their needs. The problem which dogs
all businessmen: 'who is going to buy back the goods', and the slumps
which that creates no longer arise. If, by mistake, too many goods are
made or too many services are provided, then they can be given away
or slowed down, and something else started. But there is no question
of throwing millions of people out of work, or leaving machinery idle,
or throwing food down mineshafts. These could not be possible,
because the driving force of the production plan is human need.

Under socialism there is no stock exchange, no moneylenders, no
property speculators, no landlords – no one getting rich out of
someone else's needs. All these are replaced by plans which are drawn
up to meet the means of production with people's needs.

The second principle of socialism is equality. The principle is ridiculed by rich men and their newspapers on the grounds that people are
not the same. Of course people are not the same. They have different
abilities, different likes and dislikes, different characters.

But equality is the opposite of sameness. Equality means that the *re-
wards* which people get out of society for what they do should not differ
just because their abilities differ.

Two years ago, the *Economist* magazine estimated that if all the
income in Britain were shared out evenly, every family would end up
with £80 a week. It was trying to show how *little* difference income
equality would make. Well, £80 a week per family at 1974 prices is
enough to be getting on with.

Any socialist government would fix a firm maximum income and
stop all rights of inheritance. But that is only a start. For socialism
depends on the *control* of society through the social ownership of the
means of production. And the shortest road to equality is to provide for
everyone's basic human needs free of charge. The services in today's
society which have been fought for and won by trade unionists and
Labour supporters for a hundred years, and which are now being shattered, are sometimes known as 'the social wage'. Under socialism, the

'social wage' takes on a new importance.

A free education service, founded on the principle that all children's abilities are to be encouraged; a free public transport system; the absolute guarantee that old people will live in warmth, and light and comfort; a free health service and free housing for all – with security of tenure; free meals for children at school; free basic foods for every family; free day nurseries for all children – these basic needs of society become the *top priorities of socialism.*

As we've seen already, they are all possible even with existing resources. Under a new system of production which employs everyone and does not stutter from boom to slump, they can be made more readily available. And the more available they become, the more rapidly and enthusiastically society will produce for other, less obvious and more various human needs and desires.

The third pillar of socialism is workers' democracy. Many people have a vision of socialism as a state bureaucracy, run by masses of officials, who stamp their prejudices and favouritisms on society with secret police forces and torture chambers. This caricature of socialism is played up by wealthy businessmen whose enterprises are run from top to bottom by unaccountable officials, stamping their prejudices and favouritisms on the people who do the work.

While the productive workforce declines, foremen and time study men proliferate. Every tightening of a screw, every visit to the toilet is timed and disciplined. Nor are workers safe when they leave the factory. Each corporation employs bands of security guards and experts, who not only keep guard on property but also check on the 'affiliations' of stewards and militants.

It is a central principle of socialism that the people who make decisions should be accountable to the people who are affected by them. Socialism and democracy, in other words, are indispensable to one another. You can't have socialism without democracy, and, more importantly, you can't have democracy without socialism.

When people use the word democracy, they usually mean parliamentary democracy – a democracy limited to a vote at long, often irregular intervals: the sort of democracy which exists in Britain, France, Germany, Italy and America.

But this is an extremely limited democracy. It works on geographic lines – that is, people vote according to where they live. It operates only in a small corner of society. In the areas which matter – in industry, finance, the civil service, the law courts, the police force, the army – there is no democracy at all. Power is held by people because they have wealth or are part of a class which has wealth, and parliament does not challenge that power. The 'mass of officials' therefore, whether they work for multinational companies or the civil service or the law courts, are completely unaccountable. They operate, not on behalf of society, but on behalf of one class, and there is no democratic machinery to control them.

By contrast, the fundamental unit of workers' democracy is the workers' council. Because people come together and cooperate most at work, because production of wealth takes place at work, not at home, the workplace is a far better base unit for a democratic system than the home. The workers' councils run through each part of industry and the services, but they do not operate as individual units competing with one another. They operate within the structure of an overall plan, drawn up by the government.

The government is also made up of workers' representatives, elected through the councils, grouped this time on a regional basis, to a national Congress of Councils, which then elects its executive or government.

The workers' councils form the core of socialist democracy, but they are not the only organs of democracy or of power. They cooperate and coexist with a whole number of other democratic organizations, such as tenants' and consumers' cooperatives. To be genuinely democratic their membership must be open to all working people who are not working – in particular to old workers or disabled workers or sick workers or workers who are caring for very young children.

The precise detail of these structures can't and shouldn't be laid down in advance. In all revolutions, or attempted revolutions, workers have found different patterns of workers' councils and congresses.

But the basic principle is common to all revolutions – and vital. It is the accountability of the representative to the represented. Accountability means election – far *more* elections than there are at present, and at many different levels. It means discussion and argument between different workers' parties around those elections.

Accountability means paying representatives no more and no less than the average pay of the represented. It means subjecting the representative to the instant recall by the people, or council or cooperative, which elected them. Our parliamentary democracy ignores all these principles. MPs are always asking for more money, though most Labour MPs earn twice as much as the people they represent. They are not subject to instant recall.

The principle of elected controllers extends into every area of workers' democracy. In the armed forces there are no appointed officers who are paid more than the people they order about. Instead, officers are elected and subject to control. In the law courts, there are no unelected judges interpreting and laying down the law. The jury system, a profoundly democratic method of making decisions about justice, can be extended into the area of law interpretation and of laying down punishment. In hospitals and schools, top administrators are also elected and accountable. There, as elsewhere, the 'mass of officials' in every walk of life are strictly accountable to the elected bodies.

From *Why You Should Be a Socialist*, 1977

7. Russia and Eastern Europe

A real communist*

There are those who say that the horrors of Stalin's Russia flowed naturally from the Bolshevik Revolution of 1917. They forget how much time and effort Stalin and his henchmen devoted to rooting out the Bolshevik tradition. Five-sixths of the young Communist Party of 1920, the leaders and organizers of Revolutionary Russia, had left the Party by 1939. The vast majority of these had been 'purged', many of them murdered by Stalin's secret police and terror machine. Of all the people who sat on the Politburo from 1917 to 1923, only two – Lenin and Stalin – died a natural death. All the others were either executed or died in prisons after their arrest for 'subversion'. The revolutionary communist tradition terrified Stalin and his successors far more than did their enemies without. Their unelected and totally irresponsible power was far more dangerously threatened by that tradition than by Cold War rhetoric from the West. So they reserved for the old Bolsheviks and Leninists a special brand of persecution.

Peter Grigorenko was only ten in 1917, but he was soon to come under the spell of the Revolution. In these memoirs, he describes the visit to his remote and poverty-stricken village in the Ukraine of a young communist lecturer who had come to speak about International Women's Day. He seemed an 'envoy from another world'. Grigorenko resolved at once to join the Communist Party. After some time in factories and in industrial training, he became a military officer. He served with distinction and bravery in the Second World War, and was promoted to the rank of general. Grigorenko admits that he was through all this period 'ideologically a Stalinist'. He shut his eyes to the purges of the late 1930s, preferring simply to believe that all the

*Review of *Memoirs*, by Petro G. Grigorenko.

heroes of the 1917 revolution had somehow become 'fascist dogs'. He was shaken from his Stalinism by Nikita Khrushchev's famous speech at the 1956 Party Congress, in which some of the excesses of the Stalin period were exposed. While many who felt like him basked in what they wrongly felt was a time for relaxation and liberalization, General Grigorenko was tortured by doubt. He began to ask questions based on the Leninist ideas of his youth. If such terrible things could happen under Stalin was that not a comment on the state of the Communist Party? Where was the connection between the Party and the masses on which Lenin had insisted?

These doubts came to a head in 1961 when Grigorenko was a delegate to a Communist Party conference in Moscow. He shattered the tedious calm of the conference with a stirring speech which harked on the betrayal of Bolshevik and Leninist principles. He was promptly, though not without opposition from the few rank-and-file delegates to the conference, ordered out of the hall. His life after that became a long battle with the KGB.

They singled him out for special persecution not just because he was a dissenter, but because he was a revolutionary in the Leninist tradition. The party hierarchy hated his advocacy of the removability of leaders: such a man was clearly unsafe. When the authorities discovered that Grigorenko, his son and other 'dissidents' had founded the Alliance for the Struggle for the Rebirth of Leninism – which as its first principle called for the right to recall all Party officials, and which concentrated on the strikes and demonstrations of workers against the 'workers' state' – the KGB went into action. Generals could not be dealt with like ordinary dissidents. They could not conceivably have come to such views rationally.

In 1964 Grigorenko, one of the most rational and lucid men in all Russia, spent his first spell in a Russian mental hospital, officially classified as insane. On his release, at the age of fifty-seven, he flung himself body and soul into the small, but astonishingly courageous Russian opposition. His main comrade was another Bolshevik, even older than he, who had fought in the Revolution: Alexei Kostyorin. Once again, the inspiration of the group which gathered around Kostyorin was Lenin, and revolutionary communism. 'We had faith in a "real" communism', Grigorenko explains. They were known among the dissidents as the 'communist faction'.

This faith shines through in the most moving passage in the book, which describes a meeting organized by Crimean Tatars, exiled and humiliated by Stalin. With the enthusiastic help of the Grigorenko/ Kostyorin group, the Tatars were beginning to discover their self-confidence. 'They were tired of being afraid', Grigorenko writes. His account of his speech to that meeting is full of life and hope. It was founded in the attitudes towards the nationalities which had united the Bolsheviks across Russia fifty years previously. 'In your struggle', he advised the Tatars, 'do not shut yourselves in a narrow nationalist shell. Establish contacts with all the progressive people of other nationalities in the Soviet Union. Do not consider your cause to be solely an internal Soviet matter.' The advice had its effect. In the tremendous applause which greeted the speech, one tune rose above all the nationalist chants and slogans. It was the *Internationale.*

For this insanity, Grigorenko went once again to a mental hospital – for five years and more. This time, he was force-fed and beaten up. The asylum he went to, at Chernyakhovsk, was one of the worst in Russia, where the 'patients' were consistently beaten or drugged into submission. To his credit, he does not dwell too long on the horrors. His outrage comes through much more powerfully than his pain. His quite extraordinary courage never left him: within a few months of his release – in 1974 – he was protesting and demonstrating again. Finally, the authorities got rid of him another way. They gave him a passport to America for an operation, and refused to allow him to return.

And so to the book's sad ending; to the collapse of all the grand ideas of Grigorenko's youth and of the inspiration of so many years of courageous struggle into a miserable dribble of Cold War propaganda. 'America is like a sea of light where night is turned into day. Every-thing is superbly organized', he concludes. The old Communist who had struggled so hard in his own country to make authority account-able, who had fought above all else for the equality of all people whatever their talents and abilities, is suddenly, pathetically converted to a society governed by a military–industrial complex every bit as irresponsible as in Russia, a society where inequality is raised almost to the status of religion. How the Russian secret service must rejoice that one of their most dangerous enemies has thus succumbed to Cold War partisanship, which is always just as abject and degrading on one side as it is on the other.

The sadness seeps backwards through this book, and pollutes it. It is almost as though the old man is apologizing for the ideas and inspiration which led him to such great sacrifices and triumphs. His greatest work of organization and propaganda among the working people of his country is underplayed, almost forgotten. He blurs the distinction between those dissidents who fought for the freedom of their people, and those who fought simply for one side of the Cold War against another. I don't know how much this is his own choice or that of his American publisher, but the book is badly flawed as a result. But Peter Grigorenko cannot write himself down completely. Again and again, his revolutionary past shines through his apologies. Almost in spite of himself, his story is a constant reminder that there are still indomitable revolutionaries in Russia, whose aim is to change the world, not obliterate it.

New Statesman, July 1983

The tottering thrones

All [that has happened] ... is only a beginning. The system that impedes the liberation of man in our country can only be negated by actions, not words; a revolutionary disavowal – the only authentic sort – cannot be attained by a pure and simple substitution of persons. Otherwise the tottering thrones will remain thrones from which a new oligarchic bureaucracy will exercise control over us all.
K. Bartosek, 'Open letter to the Czechoslovak workers', 1968

What was commonly known as socialism came to the countries of Eastern Europe not from any action of the working people there, but on the back of an envelope.

While discussing the spoils for the victors of the Second World War, Winston Churchill, prime minister of Britain, jotted down some suggestions for Stalin, dictator of Russia, as to what should happen in Eastern Europe. The basis of Churchill's plan was that the Russians could do what they liked in Bulgaria, Romania and Hungary provided they left Britain to 'deal with' the Communists in Greece.

Stalin was delighted with this plan, which he vigorously ticked, urging Churchill to keep the envelope as a memento of their grand diplomacy. Stalin already had control of East Germany and Poland, whose capital, Warsaw, had been almost totally destroyed by the Nazis while Russian troops stood by. He was soon to get control of Czechoslovakia too. Without further ado, he and his armies set about establishing 'socialism' in his six new satellites, whose combined population was about a hundred million. His method for bringing this 'socialism' about was exactly the same as it had been in Russia: brute force.

If there was any romantic among the Eastern European working class who imagined that the long night of Nazi occupation was now to end in a socialist dawn, he or she was soon to be disillusioned. In Bulgaria in 1944, for instance, the liberated workers set up their own councils, elected tribunals to arrest and try fascists, and disbanded the police force. All this horrified and incensed the Russian foreign secretary Molotov, who issued a declaration after meeting a Bulgarian government delegation:

> If certain Communists continue their present conduct, we will bring them to reason. Bulgaria will remain with her democratic government and her present order.... You must retain all valuable army officers from before the *coup d'état*. You should reinstate in service all officers who have been dismissed for various reasons.

The Bulgarian Army had been behaving with some jubilation in liberated areas such as Thrace and Macedonia, and had even elected workers' councils and hoisted red flags instead of their regimental emblems. This was the subject of a stern rebuke from the new minister of war, who had strong support in Moscow. His order was: 'to return at once to normal discipline, to abolish soldiers' councils and to hoist no more red flags.'

Once these initial enthusiasms had been doused, the Russian authorities set about transforming the poverty-stricken and rural countries into industrial economies. They started by setting up their stooges in coalition governments which included politicians who had supported the Nazi occupations.

In Romania for instance the minister of culture in the March 1945 government, set up with Stalin's support, was Mikhail Raila, a fervent admirer of Hitler. At least four other ministers had been supporters of the fascist Iron Guard, which had welcomed the Nazi army of occupation. The man who had commanded the Romanian troops who fought against the Russians at Stalingrad was now promoted and made assistant chief of staff.

Even before they were able to get the Eastern European governments entirely under their thumb, the Russians made sure of their control of the army and the security services. In East Germany, they inherited Hitler's intelligence service – and maintained it almost without changes. In Hungary, the Communist Party set up the State Security Authority and in the words of the hard-line Stalinist Hungarian leader Rakosi: 'We kept this organization in our hands from the first day of its establishment.'

After seizing and adopting the state machine which had persecuted the workers under the Nazis, the Stalinists set about seizing hold of the governments. There were two immediate problems.

First, the Communist parties were too small even to pretend to command mass support. The Romanian Communist Party in mid-1944 had only 1,000 members. A year and a quarter later, this had grown to a fantastic 800,000. The Polish Communist Party had 30,000 members in January 1945 and 300,000 in April. In Czechoslovakia, a party of 27,000 grew by the beginning of 1946 to a mass organization of 1,159,164 members. Were these all workers voluntarily flocking to the red flags of the revolution? They were not. The new recruits (unlike the old members) were the elite of society, the upwardly mobile minority which yearned for advancement and for privilege, and who felt that the state-capitalist programme of the Communist Party was the only way to get their country – and themselves – out of the rut.

The second problem was that in some countries there were vibrant social-democratic parties which had a far better claim to represent the workers than had the Communist parties. In Poland and in Hungary, the Socialist Party was stronger than the Communist Party. In both cases this was dealt with by a forcible merger. In Poland 82,000 members of the Socialist Party were expelled for objecting. One of them, the secretary of the Polish trade unions, Adam Kurylowicz, wrote a pamphlet accusing the Polish Communist Party of conducting a reign of terror in the factories:

> They fire and hire workers without taking into account the opinion of the workers of the plant, scorning the laws, conquests and social rights of the workers. A clique of self-seeking politicians is being formed. These new

dignitaries have discovered that a party book is more important than
technical qualifications.

Adam Kurylowicz had discovered early what the entire working class
of Eastern Europe were to find to their cost over the next forty-four
years: that the Russian government was creating in all six countries a
bureaucracy after its own image, a bureaucracy which was to play the
part of a ruling class.

Exactly the same methods which had been used by Stalin and his
henchmen in Russia were used by his satellite bureaucracies in
Eastern Europe. Every breath of democracy was squeezed out.
Workers' committees which had been set up after the war in some
countries, such as Czechoslovakia, were quickly disbanded and
replaced by one-man management. The most ruthless discipline was
imposed on the workers. At least half a million 'troublesome' East
European workers were consigned to slave labour camps.

No politician, especially if he had become a Communist under the
influence of the Russian Revolution, was safe from Stalin's periodic
purges. In the most savage of these, the general secretary of the Czech
party, Slansky, and several leading party figures were condemned to
death after confessing to anti-party crimes in exactly the same hideous
and inquisitorial ceremony laid down by the Moscow show trials of the
1930s. The Communist veterans who had fought in the underground
were effectively wiped out. By 1953, only 1.5 per cent of the members of
the Communist Party of Czechoslovakia had held party cards before
the war. It had been, per head of the population, by far the largest in
Eastern Europe.

The internationalism that had inspired the revolutionary Communists after 1917 was replaced by a wild and hysterical nationalism. All the
superstitions and vendettas which had cut swathes of blood through
Eastern Europe from the Middle Ages were revived. The Germans in
the Sudetenland, in Czechoslovakia, a peaceful and essentially social-
democratic people, were rounded up in a series of pogroms organized
by the new Communist government. The Communist minister for
education, whose party took its name from the works of Karl Marx and
Frederick Engels (both of them German), declared on 29 March 1945:
'We do not know any progressive Germans, nor are there any.'

In the same way, Czech was set against Hungarian, and Hungarian
against Romanian. No chauvinist or racist claptrap was out of bounds
for these 'communist' rulers.

All sorts of obstacles stood in the way of economic growth for the state-capitalist satellites of Russia. Russia had looted them all: 84 per cent of one year's entire production in Romania was seized in 'war reparations'. Looting by 'reparation' was followed by looting by trade. The terms of trade were fixed across the board so that the satellites sold cheap to Russia, and bought dear.

Nevertheless, roughly the same pattern of state-capitalist development in Russia was followed in its satellites. The economies, run by force and fear, grew. Backward peasant countries became industrial powers. Poland, for instance, an overwhelmingly agricultural country before the war, became by the 1970s the world's tenth industrial power (with the eighth highest military budget). In all six countries, only 14 per cent of the working population had been wage earners before the war. By 1980, this had jumped to 60 per cent. In the early years of the East European state capitalisms, growth rates were faster or as fast as anywhere in Western Europe.

As with Russia, however, after the initial burst of economic growth, state capitalism started to lose its dynamism. Wild fluctuations in the growth rates sometimes even of different industries led to a growing wrath among the workers – who now added economic discontent to their anger at disenfranchisement and bullying. Even more than in Russia, and much quicker, this resentment gave way to open revolt …

Workers' councils were to appear again and again, in different forms, in the great explosions which racked state capitalist Eastern Europe before the storm of 1989. In Poland, the authorities were in almost continual trouble with a hungry and angry people. In 1956 and 1970 there had been widespread food riots, demonstrations and strikes in protest against the price of food. It was the price of meat in particular which set off the strike, in 1980, that led to the formation of the mass trade union Solidarity.

In most developed countries of the West, trade unions had become what they were after a long, careful and cautious development. After the mass strike of the summer of 1980 in Poland, a single trade union, unfettered by craft or demarcation, was joined by ten million workers; 80 per cent of the entire Polish workforce. This was a higher level of trade union organization than in any other country in the world.

The secret of this astonishing success was the form of organization developed by the workers in their struggle. It was called, clumsily, the Inter-Enterprise Strike Committee. It was yet another manifestation of the soviet, the workers' council, the workers' committee which had been so prominent in Russia in 1917, in Hungary in 1956, in Czechoslovakia in 1968, and for that matter in Portugal in 1974 and 1975, when its fascist regime, forty years old, was finally cast aside.

The same characteristics were immediately in evidence; the courage in fighting for economic and political demands; the responsibility and discipline in their own ranks (booze was confiscated outside the gates of the striking factories and the bottles destroyed); above all the seeds of the new society blossoming in the struggle against the old one. Solidarity represented exactly what it called itself: cooperation, equality, concern for the disadvantaged, contempt for the exploiters. It created again, as part of its struggle to come into existence, the institutions which could run a quite different society – a socialist society. It too was inspired by the spirit of socialism, self-emancipation and workers' democracy.

Ranged against it was a regime which was socialist only in name, and anti-socialist in everything else. One of the two opposing forces had to smash the other – or be broken. Because Solidarity never saw itself as more than a trade union, an organization bargaining with the powers-that-be, it never struck the decisive blow. When the axe did fall, it was wielded by the Polish regime, with the full force of Moscow's support behind it. Just before Christmas 1981, in a series of carefully planned raids by the secret police, Solidarity was broken, its leaders arrested, its committees disbanded. All the hopes which it had held out for the oppressed people of Poland seemed to be drowned forever.

With the Polish revolt crushed, the regimes of Eastern Europe settled down for a brief moment into the old groove. They were still described by loyal, if weary, Communists all over the world as 'socialist countries'.

Other more sophisticated socialists sought other descriptions. They called them 'degenerated workers' states' or simply 'bureaucratic regimes' which defied any definition by class. In truth, however, the central characteristic of those at the top of these societies was that they were ruling classes, exploiting the workers and the peasants, and sliding into greater and greater chaos and corruption.

In Romania, the regime of Nicolai Ceausescu was briefly feted in the West because, allegedly, it challenged its Russian masters. Yet the Ceausescu regime had become a caricature of an exploiting tyranny.

Ceausescu bent all his energies to storing up more wealth for himself, his family and his associates out of the surplus his government and secret police wrenched from the already impoverished Romanian workers and peasants. On his command, 80,000 people were forcibly moved from their homes to make way for the most grotesque and luxurious palace in all Europe. And this was merely the dictator's second home! He selected from orphanages the cream of his secret police so that they could regard him and his wife as their Father and Mother. He sprayed them with privileges of every kind – the secret police were even better fed and clothed than the captains of industry. He published phoney statistics suggesting the economy was permanently growing and even rigged the weather reports. Workers' resistance – such as the miners' strikes in the early 1980s – was put down with the most appalling repression.

What Ceausescu did in Romania was only a more monstrous replica of what Honecker was doing in East Germany, Husak in Czechoslovakia or Zhikov in Bulgaria. Yet somehow socialists everywhere, duped by the old formulas of public ownership and 'planning', continued to pretend that these regimes were in some way 'better' or 'more working-class' than the regimes of the West.

The argument cut little ice with the oppressed people of Eastern Europe. On the contrary, as the repression and corruption grew, so the very notion of socialism, so repeatedly ascribed to the regimes themselves, became anathema.

At the top of society the ruling classes, forced more and more to trade and compete with Western capitalist countries, developed a theory of 'market socialism'. They talked about a 'socialist' society where economic decisions were made by the market. As the absurdity of a socialist system directed by the market became more and more obvious, the word 'socialism' was discreetly dropped from the formula. 'Market socialism' became 'market'. The ruling classes of the East yearned for the 'simple disciplines' of market capitalism. They longed for the day when the restrictions of state capitalism could be shuffled off, and replaced by untramelled free enterprise.

For most of the 1980s, however, the ruling classes of Eastern Europe played ball with state capitalism. Down below, however, where people were more prepared to make personal sacrifices, the revolt simmered, then boiled over.

But here too there was now an important change. In every previous uprising in Eastern Europe since the war – East Germany in 1953, Hungary in 1956, Poland in 1956, 1970 and 1980 – the intellectuals, students and workers who took part had demanded some form of socialism. No one ever suggested that they wanted to return to the capitalist society which existed in the West. As the repression and corruption dragged on, however, and as the state capitalist societies found it more and more difficult to fulfil even the most basic workers' needs, the demands and aspirations changed. People in East Germany looked across the border to West Germany and saw a more prosperous society. They envied free elections, a free press, freedom to demonstrate and challenge governments – all of which seemed to exist in the West.

Socialism fell off the agenda. Even the most committed socialists in the eastern bloc, many of them exhausted by long prison sentences, dropped their vision of a new sort of socialism and settled instead for a change from state capitalism to multinational capitalism. They were content for their detested regimes to be replaced by elected parliaments, which would preside over free-enterprise capitalism as they did in the West. All talk of revolution, and therefore of workers' councils, soviets, revolutionary committees, seemed at best out of date, at worst representative of a long and wearisome struggle against forces which seemed invincible.

When the storm broke, it broke suddenly and overwhelmingly. In a matter of months the rulers of Eastern Europe followed each other into oblivion, just as the kings, emperors and kaisers had done in the months which followed the First World War.

The collapse started in Poland, where, under pressure of more strikes and an intractable economic crisis, the same General Jaruzelski who had led the repression of Solidarity in 1981 now summoned Solidarity to join the government of Poland. Half-free elections returned a Solidarity government under the presidency of ... General Jaruzelski.

But the signal had gone out and it stirred the masses all over Eastern Europe into action. Mass demonstrations, occasionally supported by strikes, toppled the rulers one by one: Honecker in East Germany; Husak in Czechoslovakia. Kadar in Hungary and Zhikov in Bulgaria were removed more discreetly. These regimes contemplated resisting the masses by brute force, but this time there were no Russian troops on hand to prop them up. All these governments were toppled with hardly a struggle. Only in Romania did the dictator Ceausescu lash out in the only way he knew. His secret police rallied to his call to put down demonstrations and fired into crowds at Timosoara. But before long the Romanian army had sized up the balance of forces, and turned against him. Like so many dictators before him, he suddenly found that no one, not even his bodyguard, was on his side.

The governments had gone, and elections were held, often returning conservative or liberal administrations. The heads of industrial enterprises, the generals, the judges, the senior civil servants, even most of the police and intelligence chiefs remained in office. The politicians, too, who now sought votes from the people, were by and large the old bureaucrats who now declared that they had 'reformed'. One East German party leader had hastily to resign in the middle of the elections when he was exposed as a former leader of the hated Stasi – the secret police. Others, with equally delicate pasts, managed to cover up history with bold declarations of their faith in the 'new democracy'.

The actions of the people, the mass demonstrations and where necessary the strikes, had toppled the old rulers. That was the first important lesson of the astonishing events of 1989. But the demonstrators would soon have cause to remember Bartosek's prophetic warning way back in 1968: that real change could not come about just by 'the substitution of persons'. The 'tottering thrones,' he had warned, 'would remain thrones from which a new oligarchic bureaucracy will exercise control over us all.' A host of advertisers, entrepreneurs, capitalists, media proprietors and bankers flooded into Eastern Europe to vindicate this prophecy. They brought a new message from the West. State capitalism, they insisted (correctly), was a failure. Private-enterprise capitalism, good old market multinational capitalism, works.

But does it?

From *The Case for Socialism*, London 1990

8. The Labour Party and the TUC

From Marx to muddle*

The first big public meeting I spoke to was on behalf of the Liberal Party: at an eve-of-poll meeting for Derek Monsey, Liberal candidate in Westminster in the 1959 general election. When I arrived, very nervous, at the hall, everyone was very excited. 'We've got a surprise speaker,' I was told. 'Victor Gollancz.' I was very impressed, though I had never heard of Victor Gollancz.

At the end of the meeting a rather kindly old man got up and said he had supported the Labour Party all his life, but now he thought the most important issue in the world was nuclear weapons. As Derek Monsey was the only candidate in Westminster who supported unilateral nuclear disarmament, the old man declared his intention to vote Liberal.

There was loud applause from the audience, most of whom were implacably opposed to unilateral nuclear disarmament (as was the Liberal Party.)

At the end of the meeting, I was introduced to the great man. He congratulated me warmly on my speech, and then took me on one side. 'I hope you don't *believe* any of this nonsense,' he whispered. 'You should be a socialist – in fact, I think you will be one.'

I was most indignant at the time, but it wasn't long before the old man's prediction came true, and I've had a sneaking affection for him ever since.

The affection grew as I read this comprehensive and enthralling biography. Victor Gollancz never went to parliament. He never taught at university. He had nothing but contempt all his life for the right-

---

*Review of *Victor Gollancz* by Ruth Dudley-Edwards.

wing leadership of the Labour Party. Yet he had a profound effect on politics in Britain for at least two decades.

His most extraordinary achievement was the Left Book Club, which lasted from 1936 to 1948. In its first ten years, the Club published *six million books* – a quite staggering figure. At its heyday just before the Second World War, the Club had 57,000 members, each of whom was guaranteed a new book a month. There was also a wide range of old socialist classics, specialist books, scientific books, history books and pamphlets.

This enormous output of Club books was augmented, in the run-up to the 1945 election, with the 'Yellow back' pamphlets, all directed against the corruption and hopelessness of the Tory years before the war, and each selling about a quarter of a million copies. It is no exaggeration to claim, as Ruth Dudley-Edwards does, that Gollancz, with his commitment and his flair, did a great deal to shift the intellectual climate towards the Labour landslide of 1945.

After the war, when Ernie Bevin ('Britain's Greatest Foreign Secretary' as all important people always call him) was saying, 'I try to be fair to the Germans, but I 'ates 'em really'; when various Tories tried to whip up an anti-German fever such as the one which gripped the entire country after the First World War, Gollancz campaigned for an internationalist view.

He did not campaign as hard for the nationalization of German industries (the real issue) as he did for food parcels for the poor. But his campaigning on this issue did a lot to stop anti-German hysteria. Similarly, at the height of the success of Zionism in kicking out the Palestinians and setting up a new state in the Middle East, Gollancz, a Jew and at one time a member of the Jewish Board of Deputies, spoke up for the dispossessed Palestinians.

So irrepressible was Gollancz's vigour, so brilliant his intellect and so vast his conceit that it would seem that he could do anything. Indeed, Marx's famous comment about history is reversed by this biography to read, 'Gollancz made his own history and he made it just as he pleased.' But of course he did not. His life, perhaps even more than most, was circumscribed by the social forces with which he wrestled.

For instance, the Left Book Club had a membership of 57,000 in 1939, under a Tory government. Six years later, the dream of most Left Book Club members came true: a Labour government was returned with a massive majority. Everyone rejoiced, and almost at once, the influence of the Left Book Club declined. By the end of 1946 there were only 10,000 members, and in 1948 the Club was dissolved without anyone noticing.

How could it be that the thirst for socialist ideas and literature should tail off so very fast at the very moment of apparent triumph? The answer is that in social-democratic electoral politics, it is better to travel hopefully than to arrive. The expectation and hope of a victory was a far greater inspiration to socialist ideas and agitation than was the reality of Clement Attlee and Herbert Morrison.

Gollancz could sense the disillusionment all right and he never capitulated to the parliamentary cretinism of his former friends, John Strachey and Stafford Cripps. But, instead of using the Marxist method which had inspired him in the 1930s to interpret the postwar disillusionment, he turned against Marx altogether: 'The real battle is not between capitalism and more socialism, but between the liberal or Western ethic and the totalitarianism of which the Soviet Union is now the major exponent.'

Then he argued that *all* political ideas should be subordinated to higher values, liberal values, religious values. These new statements of 'value' won him praise from Tories who had denounced him in the 1930s and early 1940s.

How was it possible that such a lively and well-read socialist who did *not* simply decay as most old socialists do, should so reverse his opinions? How could a man who in 1929 described *Das Kapital* as 'the fourth most enthralling volume of the world's literature' recite so soon after the war the familiar reactionary incantations against Marx. Most of the answer, I suspect, lies in the roots of the brand of Marxism which inspired him in the 1930s, and which showed up the grim side of the Left Book Club.

In the early years of the Club, Gollancz was completely captive to the Communist Party. He conceded almost everything to them. Twelve of the first fifteen of the Left Book Club choices were vetted and approved by the Communist Party (at least ten of those, today, are quite unreadable). The amount of indigestible Stalinist trash turned out in those pink and orange covers was astonishing.

Gollancz was one of three 'choosers' of the titles. Only one of the others was Communist, and even he (Strachey) was not a party member. Yet again and again, even on the simplest issues such as the right to dissent, Gollancz capitulated.

It was not simply that Trotsky and everything Trotskyist was not tolerated in the Left Book Club. George Orwell's *Homage to Catalonia* was turned down by Gollancz. H.N. Brailsford, one of the first among British socialist writers to appreciate the horrors of the Moscow trials, was one of the authors who suffered worst – both intellectually and financially – from Victor's stubborn submersion in the Communist Party line.

As so often, the party hack or fellow-traveller, when he suddenly becomes aware of his hackery, turns to rend his former mentors, and, in the process, throws the whole ideology out with the bathwater. Gollancz was quick enough to spot the Communist Party's opportunism over the Hitler–Stalin pact but his indignation led him to reject altogether not just the Communist Party, but all Marxism which he thought they represented.

Thus, in a curious way, the Stalinism to which he was converted in the 1930s (he named Stalin as Man of the Year 1937) and the social democratic government to which he formally aspired in the 1940s were both disastrous to his political development. Disillusioned with both he turned not to new socialist ideas, but against socialist ideas altogether.

I hope I have not put anyone off this book, however. It is far, far more illuminating about the 1930s and 1940s than most of the trivial contemporary stuff on the subject. The character of the man comes through very loud if not very clear. Criticism of him is easy and obvious. But perhaps the most interesting exercise is to compare him and his times with today.

Those days of slump and 'downturn', when there was still some life and hope in social-democratic politics, threw up vast, engaging and brilliant personalities who believed they could change the world and acted accordingly. A generation of Labour governments later, there is nothing remotely as impressive as Victor Gollancz anywhere on the Labour stage.

Socialist Worker Review, October 1987

Harold, row the boat aground*

Since this is such a sad book, let us start with something cheerful. One evening in March 1966, on an assignment to cover the general election campaign in the West Midlands, I found myself at the back of the Birmingham Rag Market, surrounded by what seemed like millions of people. The thousand seats in the front had been taken up long before the start of the meeting. The huge amphitheatre was covered with people standing, jammed together, craning their heads forward so as not to miss a word.

It was, believe it or not, a Labour Party meeting, and the main speaker was the Labour leader, Harold Wilson. The 'warm up' was a brilliant speech by the MP for Stechford, Roy Jenkins, who described his leader as 'the greatest parliamentarian of his generation'. The acclamation for Wilson as he rose to speak, diminutive behind a huge lectern, was deafening. I noticed that he had few notes – perhaps one sheet of paper with a few jottings on it. He hardly glanced at it. Instead, he allowed the great gathering to control his speech for him. He preyed on his hecklers like a fisherman, goading them to interrupt on the subjects he favoured. A small gang of raucous young Tories swallowed the bait: T-S-R-2' they chanted in fatuous indignation at the cancellation of some obscure and well-forgotten fighter plane. The speaker cocked an ear and called for more. 'Did I hear TSR2?' he called sweetly. As the baying intensified, he swung into a set of devastating statistics about the waste and absurdity of the TSR2. He brought what appeared to be an ageing and respectable working-class audience to a delirium of delight. He laughed at the new technocratic Tory leader, Heath, just as he laughed at the 'ancestral voice' of Heath's predecessor, the 14th Earl of Home. The whole place resounded to his humour and his confidence.

It was the high peak of British social democracy. Wilson's government had weathered the early storms after its election in 1964. With a tiny majority, it had promulgated several substantial reforms. The old Tory hegemony seemed to have been broken. For just that brief, fleeting moment it looked as though Labour government worked: that

---

*Review of *Memoirs 1916–1964: The Making of a Prime Minister* by Harold Wilson.

it *was* possible to have full employment, a strong pound, economic growth and expanding social services at the same time, and that all could be wrapped up in the warm mantle of egalitarianism. What Wilson called 'a moral crusade' seemed to have conquered the reactionaries – and to have done so without any unpleasantness or effort. Change *was* coming about through the ballot box, and no one was being hurt in the process. The response on polling day was extraordinary. Labour were returned with a majority over all other parties of nearly a hundred seats. Thirteen million people voted Labour, more than in any other year except 1951. No one doubted that Labour with its vast new majority would improve on what they had done with a majority of five.

The descent was astonishingly fast. By the end of July, only four months after all these triumphs, the Wilson government was down on its knees, grovelling to the very bankers whom Wilson had derided in his election speeches. The old Tory medicines – wage freeze, high interest rates, increased unemployment, public spending cuts (described by one left-wing backbencher as 'ripping up the hospitals with our bare hands') – had been applied in even greater doses than in the Tory past. Labour's supporters drooped. Socialist enthusiasms vanished. Reactionary notions spread into every area of government policy. In Vietnam, where Wilson in his youth had denounced imperialist intervention, the Labour government lined up behind the American army of occupation. In Rhodesia, Labour stood back while an illegal racialist regime made hay. Tougher and tougher immigration controls – anathema to Labour's leaders in the early sixties – were introduced. Even the cherished free National Health Service – the principle on which Wilson himself resigned from the Labour government in 1951 – was breached. In the post-devaluation package of January 1968, prescription charges – abolished with such enthusiasm when Labour came to office – were reintroduced. The International Monetary Fund insisted on them as a condition for the loan. Even when the government offered to find exactly the same amount in 'savings' from cuts in other areas, the IMF stood firm. The money *must* come from health charges. Any dangerous subversive rubbish about a free health service had to be rubbed out once and for all.

The electoral consequences were inevitable. By 1970, when the next election came round, the moral crusade had turned into yet another cynical hunt for office. The Conservatives were returned for four more years. By the time Harold Wilson was back in Downing Street again, in 1974, he was sadder, more realistic, more conventional. The cheeky humour with which he denounced the 'faded antimacassars' who ruled British society had turned into deference. He was no longer the campaigner with a single sheet of notes mocking the Right and holding out a 'new vision' of a fair and prosperous Britain. Instead, he was the elder statesman, never happier than when he was chatting to the Queen. In 1976, after two more years as prime minister, he suddenly resigned. He said he was tired – and he was probably right: a million investigations to prove that his resignation was part of some weird conspiracy have run into the sand.

More than any other politician of our time, Harold Wilson is the symbol of the debacle of modern Labour. In his other two autobiographical books he reluctantly reveals some clues as to why the great dreams of the mid-sixties came to so little. In *The Labour Government: 1964–1970*, he inveighs against the 'speculators' who did not give him room for economic and political manoeuvre. In *Final Term: 1974–1976*, these have turned into 'bailiffs' who evicted him from his party's policies and aspirations. In this book, he has gone back before both governments and written about his childhood, his youth, and his political career before he became prime minister. For anyone unfortunate enough to have read all the biographies of Wilson (Leslie Smith, Dudley Smith, Gerard Noel, Ernest Kay and others even worse) there is really nothing new here. It is the same old story of the young Boy Scout, Nonconformist and Liberal. He says he joined the Oxford University Labour Party (though not the Labour Club) in time for the famous 1939 by-election, but since he gets the name of the winner (and his precedessor) wrong, his memory may be at fault.

Wilson's shift to Labour came, I would suspect, later, during the war, as he watched Labour rising high in the polls and the popular imagination. His career in parliament from 1945 to 1964 picked a careful path through the shifting fortunes of Labour's Left and Right. From 1947 to 1951, he was an extremely conventional, not to say reactionary president of the Board of Trade. In 1951, he resigned from the cabinet with Aneurin Bevan over the imposition of health charges and the armaments programme, was a Bevanite for a few years, but neatly stepped into Bevan's shoes in the shadow cabinet when his former hero resigned over Southeast Asia. He always kept on good terms with Bevan's arch-rival, Hugh Gaitskell – though he doesn't reveal whether he voted for Gaitskell against Bevan for party leader in 1956, as he probably did. He worked in close association with Gaitskell in the late fifties, but stood against him in the leadership election of 1960: only to revert to him soon afterwards.

The book trudges over all this old ground without divulging a single interesting new piece of information, and, except in occasional flashes of personal animosity (as against Herbert Morrison or Denis Healey), without much passion or enthusiasm. There is only one good joke, and it was made at Wilson's expense by Aneurin Bevan. When Wilson announced with customary Yorkshire pomposity that he was 'forged' in that county, Bevan replied: 'Forged were you? I always thought there was something counterfeit about you.'

Yet, in the dross, it *is* possible to find some clues to explain the dreadful sequel. Throughout the book, Harold Wilson revels in his distaste for political theory. He was, he insists, from first to last, a technical man, who wanted to get on with running things. He was impatient and intolerant with colleagues who tried to think about the big social movements which determined the course of politics. 'It has never been part of my political attitude,' he writes, 'to tear society up by the roots and replace it with something entirely different. I do not look at problems from that kind of perspective. I consider that the best style of government is like rowing – the ideal solution is to get the boat along as quickly as possible without turning it over.' He was like the captain of a ship who knew everything about his craft, from the attitudes of the crew to the most sophisticated computer. But he had no compass, no knowledge of the currents and tides, or of the storms which, to use one of his favourite phrases, blew him off course. His ship was at the mercy of forces much more powerful than the ones he knew or controlled. He did not recognize or understand those forces, and never wanted to.

Hoary British empiricism, in which he constantly rejoices, was his greatest enemy. This empiricism has dominated the thinking of Labour politicians ever since the party was founded. It infected the clockwork socialism which was so popular in the thirties. Men like John Strachey could see that capitalism wasn't working, and so concluded, empirically, that it could never, even for a moment, rise above its contradictions or expand. When there was a period of steady capitalist expansion for thirty years after the war, Strachey started to argue, empirically, that now capitalism was stable, it would always be so. The inflexibility of British empiricism, the inability to look or imagine further than a few feet in front, poisoned even Marxism, the most flexible and imaginative of political philosophies.

At least thinkers like John Strachey tried to grapple with political theory, however. Anthony Crosland, whose *The Future of Socialism* came out in the same year, 1956, as Strachey's *Contemporary Capitalism* and argued very much the same thing, took issue with Karl Marx. But he was quick to denounce those who wrote Marx off. 'The man was a dedicated genius,' he wrote, 'and only moral dwarfs or people devoid of imagination sneer at men like that.' Without ever even reading him, Harold Wilson sneered at Marx. He exults here in his ignorance, repeating yet again the old saw that he never got beyond page two of *Das Capital*, where he was put off by a footnote. Wilson's intellectual genesis was founded on footnotes: he spent hour after happy hour with hosts of irrelevant statistics about railways in the time of Gladstone. It was not footnotes which put him off, but ideology. He was so anxious to get on with rowing the boat that he could not, even for a moment, study the tempestuous forces which would determine its course. When his party was shipwrecked, and he himself, like so many Labour leaders before him, cast up spluttering platitudes at the House of Lords bar, he was even less able than when he started out to explain the cause of the disaster.

Can parliament bring about socialism? Marx himself, flexible as ever, changed his mind on this crucial question. In the early 1860s, perhaps to boost the flagging spirits of the defeated Chartists, he declared that universal suffrage would bring political power to the working class. His close and anxious study of the defeat of the Paris Commune in 1871 changed all that. He saw there the mighty forces which capitalism had built in its defence, and started to predict that anyone who took on those forces armed only with a majority of votes, statistical genius, an Oxford scholarship and a determination to row the boat across to the other side was doomed to catastrophic defeat.

Reading Harold Wilson's thin story in the mid-1980s, it is impossible to fight off nostalgia. For all his pragmatism, Wilson made promises which seemed to point towards a more prosperous and egalitarian society, and tried to match up to them. Labour politicians today do not even make promises, for fear that they cannot be carried out. Eighty-six years of pragmatism have plunged us back far beyond Harold Wilson's heyday. Labour's position now is more reminiscent of the late 1920s than of the 1960s or 1970s. Then the Labour leaders sought to win an election solely on the unpopularity of a Tory administration which had defeated the might of the trade unions (including the miners) in open class war. By keeping quiet, by promising next to nothing, they aimed to appease a timid electorate and creep into Whitehall. They succeeded. They lasted two years, in which unemployment tripled. Their leaders abandoned Labour for the Tories, and plunged their erstwhile supporters into fifteen years of the blackest reaction. The man in charge of Labour's economic policy at that time – the first to ditch his party for high office in a Tory 'National' government – was Philip Snowden. Harold Wilson's book opens with this sentence: 'My boyhood political hero, Philip Snowden, MP for Colne Valley, began his autobiography with the words, "I am a Yorkshireman."' Like hero, like disciple. Forged.

London Review of Books, November 1986

Late developer*

For nearly a century, Labour MPs have been going to parliament to change the world, but have ended up changing only themselves. Tony Benn is unique. He went to parliament to change himself, but has ended up determined only to change the world. This extraordinary conversion has taken place not on the backbenches, where a young socialist's revolutionary determination is often toughened by being passed over for high office, but in high office itself. Indeed, the higher the office Tony Benn occupied, the more his eyes were opened to the horror of capitalist society, and to the impotence of socialists in high office to change it.

The unique journey from right to left adds enormously to the value of Tony Benn's *Diaries*. His contemporaries Dick Crossman and

---

*Review of *Against the Tide: Diaries 1973–1976* by Tony Benn.

Barbara Castle have also published diaries. Others have written autobiographies. All are full of evidence of the impotence of office. Even
Denis Healey in his recent popular autobiography admits that the
notorious 'IMF cuts' in 1976 were probably based on a false prospectus
presented to him by international bankers who knew they were
deceiving him. But in all these cases the former Secretaries of State
have a basic belief in what they were doing. 'We tried to change the
world' is their theme. 'We had a little bit of success, and would have
done more if it hadn't been for bankers or, as Harold Wilson used to
call his hidden enemies, "speculators".' Only Tony Benn, even as he
was signing papers in the red dispatch boxes, travelling round in
chauffeur-driven limousines and dining at Lockets, began to realize
that he was playing a lead part in a grim charade whose chief effect was
to hypnotize and paralyse the people who voted Labour.

In his foreword, Benn says he has included whole passages which
embarrass him today. We have to trust him and his editors when they
say that the editing of what he read into the tape evening after evening
has not been influenced by what has happened since 1976. It does not
seem as if it has. Perhaps the most remarkable aspect of this volume is
the open and apparently unembarrassed way in which Tony Benn's
conversion – from career politician to committed socialist – lumbers
from contradiction to contradiction: here leaning backwards to his
careerist past, here leaning forwards to his campaigning future, and
here stuck in between, not knowing what to think or which way to turn.

The volume starts rather curiously with the final year of Labour in
opposition, during which Tony Benn's ideas were increasingly
winning the votes at Labour Party conferences and among the rank
and file. There runs through all the diary entries of this period a
tremendous confidence. At a CBI dinner in October 1973, he rounded
on the gloomy industrialists, telling them: 'You're licked, pessimistic.
There is more vitality on the union side than there is on the management side.... We have got to have redistribution of power and establish
a new social contract.' None of the guests, it seems, could manage a
reply. Industrialists, bankers, rich Tories of every description felt that
the day of doom was nigh. John Davies, Secretary of State for Industry
in the Tory Government and a former Director-General of the CBI,
called his children round the hearth to tell them this was the last
Christmas of its kind they would be enjoying together. Tony Benn, his
planning agreements and his Social Contract were in the ascendant.

The Tories lost the election of February 1974, and Tony Benn went straight to the Department of Industry as Secretary of State. In April, his diary glowed with confidence:

Sunday April 28. As I look at it, I can see my way through now in breaking industry's resistance to my policies. I shall win over the managers and the small businessmen, and I shall get the nationalized industries to welcome the planning agreements; I shall isolate the big Tory companies, then show how much money they have been getting from the government, and if they don't want it, they don't have to have it.

Very quickly, however, he began to find that he and his government depended on quite a different kind of confidence. At another dinner with bankers and Stock Exchange officials the same April, he was told, sternly: 'We must restore confidence.' 'What is the price of restoring confidence?' countered Benn. 'Well,' replied the Stock Exchange chieftain, 'You have got to have better dividend distribution, otherwise equities will collapse.' The confidence which mattered could be measured only by the flow of dividends. Benn replied with some heat, but as the months went on, the same argument started to be used by his own colleagues in the Labour cabinet.

He reports Denis Healey, the Chancellor of the Exchequer, saying at a meeting of top ministers which had been called to water down the already weak proposals of his Industry Bill: 'The whole of our future depends on the confidence of businessmen.' Healey's policies were bent in every particular to building up that confidence. The climax comes at the end of the book, when, at a cabinet meeting on 7 December 1976, Healey proposed yet more cuts in public spending – he had already cut savagely, in 1975 and in the 1976 Budget. Benn reports: 'Denis had a new paper to present and he was now asking for £1,199.25 million in 1977, which was nearly £200m over the billion proposed by the IMF. Crosland pointed this out but Denis said that confidence had been undermined by leaks and therefore we'd have to make more cuts in public expenditure to prevent further loss of confidence.' Hospitals, schools, social security benefits, parks, swimming pools, public transport – all the things which had been at the centre of Labour's programme – now had to be cut, not even because the IMF said it made sense (which, it later appeared, it didn't), but because there were inaccurate leaks of what the IMF might have said.

All Tony Benn's own confidence had vanished by the end of 1974 –

even though in October Labour won another general election with an overall majority. He mused, to his top civil servant, just after the election: 'I've been in the Department for seven months and I'm not aware of having done anything, made any progress at all.' The steady chip, chop at his precious Industry Bill, and the Prime Minister's continued insistence that he stop making public speeches which annoyed the City of London, drove him to reflect, as early as November 1975: 'I am afraid that somehow, without quite knowing how it happens, I will slip into the position that I occupied between 1964 and 1970 when I went along with a lot of policies which I knew to be wrong.' He could see perfectly well what was happening. His diary for the first few months of 1975 – the end of the honeymoon period between the Labour government and what Prime Minister Wilson called their 'bailiffs' – is far more perceptive than Barbara Castle's (or even Denis Healey's – though he had the advantage of hindsight): 'The Tories now think that Wilson, Healey and Callaghan are doing their work so well that they don't want a coalition government. Better to let the Labour Party do their work for them.' This analysis led him to a startling prediction. On 11 May 1975, he wrote: 'A coalition has been born without being formally declared: it is broadly the Tories and Liberals throwing their weight behind Callaghan, I think. They won't touch Wilson. They'll get rid of him just as they got rid of Heath.... I wouldn't be surprised to find a Callaghan government formed within the next couple of months.'

He was out by only eight months. Wilson resigned in mysterious circumstances in March 1976. Callaghan was elected leader of the Labour Party and formed a government. From then on, the retreat which Benn had identified continued, through the grovelling to the IMF in 1976 to the coalition with the Liberals in 1977, and the long weary stumble to defeat. Before the end of 1976, he identified what he called 'Thatcher's Private Argument':

> That the Labour government are doing to the trade union movement what the Tories could never do: that in doing it the government are getting profits up and holding prices down and therefore restoring the vitality of the capitalist mechanism; and that by doing so they will disillusion their own supporters and make it possible for the Tories to return.

He could see what was happening all right, but what was he doing about it? From early on, he started to think about resigning from the government in protest. All his most reliable political friends – Dennis

Skinner, Audrey Wise, Ken Coates, most of the activists in his Bristol constituency, even his son Stephen – advised him to do so. Benn's own belief, often expressed here, that the power and influence that mattered came from below, from the shop stewards and socialist trade unionists, led logically to a resignation and a return to the rank and file. But he did not resign. In the summer of 1975, as the Labour government collapsed under the biggest run on sterling ever, he humbly accepted his demotion to Secretary of State for Energy. He sat through the cuts of 1976, opposing them in cabinet, but necessarily keeping his mouth shut outside it. His reasons for this – chiefly that resignation would be seen as disloyal to the government – are unconvincing, even apologetic. Doubt, hesitation and pain replaced the glad confident morning. On one page, for instance, he reveals his ambition: 'If I want to do anything other than frolic around on the margins of politics, I must be leader and prime minister.' On the very next page, he is not so sure: 'If you set yourself that target, it is bound to begin the process of corruption.' As the book goes on, the balance seems to tip against his ambition, but he still remains in office, and there is another volume to come which must somehow explain how he stuck it out right until the bitter end – until the Tory victory over a punch-drunk Labour movement which he had so accurately predicted. But even in 1975 his clinging to office was disturbing his sleep.

> Friday, 10 October: I had a dream that Harold called me in and said: 'I want you to be Vice-Chamberlain of the Royal Household with a seat in the House of Lords in charge of boxing under the Minister of Sport.' He told me this in the great Cabinet room, which was full of people. 'I'm afraid this doesn't mean a place in the Cabinet for you,' he said. I replied, 'Harold, I must think about it,' and Sir John Hunt said: 'Boxing is very important. We must preserve the quality and excellence of the Lonsdale Belt.'

The book is full of political treasures. There is a host of stories, for instance, to prove what is now established fact: that MI5 or sections of it were using their vast and secret powers against the government they were meant to be serving. Benn was constantly at the sharp end of this. He proved on more than one occasion that his home telephone was tapped – but he, a senior secretary of state in the cabinet, could do nothing about it. When he complained to the general secretary of the telephone engineers' union, Brian Stanley, Stanley said he thought his

own phone was tapped too – by his own members. Jack Jones and
Hugh Scanlon, the 'terrible twins' of the trade unions in the period
which toppled the Heath government, became the leading spokesmen
for wage restraint and cuts during the Labour government, and were
rewarded by being blacklisted by MI5. Benn confirms that he wanted
Jones on the National Enterprise Board but Jones was banned after
hostile MI5 reports, which also, initially, knocked Hugh Scanlon off
the Gas Council.

Tony Benn's household was the subject of repeated press inquiries,
mostly at the dead of night, about his son Joshua being in hospital. At
least five times in two years, the Benn family was shattered by this
dreadful news, conveyed usually by a concerned reporter from the
Daily Mail. Each time, the information was entirely false. Joshua was
not in hospital. When, after one specially unnerving inquiry, Benn rang
David English, *Daily Mail* editor and Thatcher knight, to protest, he
was told that the editor was at home, and could not be disturbed. Such
double standards are the stuff of national newspaper editors. But
where did the rumour originate? Perhaps from the same intelligence
source which replied to Tony Benn when he complained about the
sacking of a chiropodist in the civil service. The woman, said the reply,
'may be a fairly regular reader of the *Morning Star*, the newspaper of the
Communist Party'. Of course, she may not have been, but even if not,
'she is known to have been interested in holidays arranged by the
Young Communist League and in a sea trip to the Soviet Union'. To
compound this scandal, 'there was a reliable report in 1974 that her
father also reads the *Morning Star*'. The intelligence officer's report
explained that 'we would prefer to err on the side of caution in this
case.' The chiropodist remained sacked and there was nothing a secretary of state could do to reinstate her.

Benn has a sense of mischief which keeps his story rolling along.
His sharp comments on his colleagues have stood the test of time. Of
Tony Crosland: 'For him informality is a sort of substitute for radi-
calism.' Of Shirley Williams: 'the most reactionary politician I know'.
Of Neil Kinnock: 'not a substantial person. He is a media figure really.'

The central fascination of these diaries is the gradual transformation
of the bright young dynamic dinner-party careerist of the early sixties
into the powerful and committed campaigner of the eighties. It emerges
in fits and starts, but its progress is persistent, almost dogged. It shines
most clearly on the rare occasions when Benn discusses what he has

read. One of the insidious ways in which reformers are broken when they become ministers is by the denial of time to read. Reading anything outside red boxes or blue books is frowned on by literary civil servants, who encourage their minister to concentrate on the job in hand. Benn's *Diaries* suggest that he started to read real books for the first time when he was a minister in the 1974–79 Labour government. As he declares his childlike zeal, say, for the Levellers or the Diggers in the English revolution, he gives the strong impression that he had never heard of any of these people before he met and quarrelled with Sir Anthony Part at the Department of Industry. The civil service mandarins seem to have driven him back to a glorious time when the King had his head chopped off and all his civil service supporters fled for their lives. Even more remarkable is his sudden discovery at the age of fifty of the socialist theory which inspired the movement which put him in parliament in the first place. The whole book bears warm testimony to the closeness and affection of the Benn family, and it is, apparently, to Caroline Benn that we owe the most gratitude for her husband's conversion. At Christmas 1976, the Secretary of State hung out his Christmas stocking (as he had done for the previous fifty years or so). In it the next morning he found a copy of the *Communist Manifesto*. He read it on Christmas Day, and it led him to this remarkable, and moving confession – the real key, I suspect, to his extraordinary political development:

> There is no doubt that in the years up to 1968 I was just a career politician and in 1968 I began thinking about technology and participation and all that; it wasn't particularly socialist and my Fabian tract of 1970 was almost anti-socialist, corporatist in character. Up to 1973 I shifted to the left and analysed the Left. Then in 1974, at the Department of Industry I learned it all again by struggle and by seeing it and thinking about it, and I have been driven further and further towards a real socialist position.... I record this now while I am reading all the basic texts in order to try to understand what is going on.

I don't really care whether it is Sir Anthony Part or Caroline Benn or Marx that we have to thank for that, but British politics of the last ten years has been the richer for it.

London Review of Books, February 1990

Norman the nothing

Spitting Image a couple of Sundays ago had a panel game in which three famous people guessed at the price of a peerage.

Two millionaires guessed (one right, one wrong). Then Lord (Len) Murray put his bid in: 'Doing nothing,' he suggested. The price was right! He got his peerage.

I hope Len Murray's successor, Norman Willis, was watching. Like Len, Norman is a career trade union official. He has never worked anywhere else except in a trade union office.

When he came out of Oxford in 1959, he went straight to the head office of the Transport and General Workers' Union (TGWU), where he was personal assistant to the general secretary, Frank Cousins. Eleven years later he became head of research and education in the TGWU, and in 1974 he was moved across to the Trade Union Congress as the TGWU's golden boy, waiting to inherit the general secretaryship.

Norman's role is and has always been *representing* trade unionists, *talking for* them in high places, *putting their point of view*. His education, pleasant manners and wit won him a place as a workers' leader without his ever having been a worker.

As a representative, of course, his job has always been secure, his position as a leader unchallenged.

As a leader, Norman Willis has to deal with realities, not dreams. When he formulated policy for Britain's biggest union in the early 1970s, he was all against incomes policies and wage controls. He also drafted some very powerful union documents against cuts in public services and the welfare state.

But when the Labour government asked for a voluntary incomes policy and wage control in 1975, Norman Willis was the first to advise his former general secretary, Jack Jones, to agree to it.

When in 1976 the Labour government demanded cuts in welfare and public spending, the TGWU conceded.

That was a Labour government, of course. What about the Tories?

When the Tories came in, no one was more hostile to their anti-union laws than Norman Willis. No one more enthusiastically supported a policy of active defiance of the laws.

But when the laws were defied by the NGA, the TUC, with Norman Willis now its deputy general secretary, completely reversed its policy and sold the union out.

Now, as general secretary, Norman Willis supposedly supports the miners in their struggle for jobs. So he tries to negotiate with the government and Coal Board on their behalf.

When the Coal Board don't concede an inch, Norman Willis agrees to become the messenger for them. He raises the miners' hopes of a good settlement, only to reveal that the message he brings is the same old stale recipe for unemployment in the coalfields.

Again and again in the dispute the wretched Willis has been rebuffed and humiliated in this way. Each time he goes cap in hand to the Coal Board, they send him packing with a kick up the pants. His *only reaction* is to pick himself up and wheedle and whimper for another hearing.

Surely he must have some sense of dignity? Surely now, after this last hammering, he will stir himself and his movement to just a tiny little bit of solidarity action? I doubt it.

For the key to Mr Willis's actions is his *position*. His position as trade union leader for life is not seriously threatened by Tory rebuffs, however long he has to put up with them.

In the 1930s people like Willis went through a whole decade without putting in a single wage claim, and still held on to their positions, their prestige and their peerages.

On the other hand, if Willis were to stir the embers of revolt among his own members, his position could be threatened. He could not be sure that he could contain mass sympathy action as he can control policy-making at Congress House or speechifying on the television.

So he sticks to what he knows – negotiation and discussion in the corridors of power. If the Tories refuse to negotiate, then you can be quite sure that Norman Willis will go on trying until they don't next time.

For Norman, there's a lot to be said for doing nothing. After all, look what it did for Len.

Socialist Worker, May 1985

Labour's MI5 connections

For once the newspapers (the half sane ones, that is) are quite exciting to read as the MI5/Wilson saga slowly unfolds.

The most interesting revelation this week is that leading Labour right-wingers in the 1960s called in MI5 to trap left-wingers with information about their connection with the KGB.

The operation wasn't a great success, apparently. There was only one genuine prosecution, of Will Owen, Labour MP. Another MP, Bernard Floud, committed suicide when some rather irrelevant facts about his KGB contacts were likely to be disclosed.

The really interesting part of the story is the close contact established between Labour's right wing and the intelligence establishment. This coincides rather nastily with some other facts about Labour right-wingers at that time.

There was, for instance, a rather shadowy organization called the Ariel Foundation, whose main purpose seemed to be to provide Labour right-wingers with funds for trips to Africa. Its stated intention was to 'further relations' between progressive people in Britain, and the newly independent governments of Africa.

You didn't have to be a Labour MP to be associated with it. Indeed, one of the founding fathers of the Foundation was Charles Long-bottom, a Tory MP. (In those days of Butskellism there were lots of Tory Party members like Mr Longbottom who could just as well have been right-wing Labour; and vice versa.) What you certainly couldn't be was left-wing.

In the late 1960s the American magazine *Ramparts* exposed a host of front organizations funded by the CIA. The true founders of the Ariel Foundation, it revealed, were the security services on both sides of the Atlantic. Other bodies dominated by Labour right-wingers such as the Fund for International Student Cooperation (FISC) were also exposed as CIA fronts.

The chief British figure in FISC was Gwyn Morgan, who worked at Transport House. He was a candidate for the general secretaryship of the Labour Party (he lost by one vote), and then went on to staff the formidable Labour right-wing hierarchy in Brussels.

This hierarchy was crowned in 1977 when Roy Jenkins left the

Labour cabinet to become European Commissioner. Jenkins, of course, was the first leader of the Social Democratic Party when it was formed in 1981.

The main mystery about the formation of the SDP, which has never been fully explained, is the extent to which it was backed by American influence and, in particular, the intelligence services on both sides of the Atlantic.

Certainly, no greater blow could possibly have been struck at the danger of left-wingers winning power in the Labour Party than the creaming off of a substantial sector of Labour voters. The prognosis was triumphantly vindicated in 1983, when the Alliance vote was nearly as big as Labour's.

It now appears that MI5 (backed by the CIA) was party to the attempted replacement of a Labour government in 1968 by Cecil King, Lord Robens and others in a 'national government'.

It further appears that they tried to subvert the elected Labour government (and even the Liberal Party) in the mid-1970s.

So is it not reasonable to assume that they might have (to say the least) enthusiastically welcomed the foundation of a new right-wing Labour Party, freed forever from the cloying attentions of the organized working class?

Socialist Worker, May 1987

Less peasants, more Poplars

It would be a relief at poll tax protest meetings if we heard less about Wat Tyler and more about George Lansbury.

What we don't need at these meetings is rhetoric and martyrdom. Every time I hear a Labour councillor say he won't pay the poll tax and they can haul him away to prison if they like, I mark him down as the first man to pay.

Similarly, every time I hear an important Labour dignitary refer to

Wat Tyler, ('the last time they had a poll tax – when they had a peasants' revolt) I sigh a little and conclude that the speaker is not terribly
interested in history, and certainly not interested in doing anything
about the poll tax.

As long as people's attention can be cast back 600 years, then it's a
fairly safe bet that any genuine movement against the poll tax can be
wrapped up in the mists of time.

George Lansbury is a different matter. Labour Party people may
have heard of him, for he is after all a former leader of their party. It is
not his time as leader which pushes him into the history books,
however, but his time in prison. He went to prison more than once, but
the time which matters most is when he led almost his entire council
there.

What was the issue in the London borough of Poplar in 1921? It
sounds very familiar.

Put simply, it was that the system of financing local government
meant that the poorer areas had to levy rates from people who could not
afford them, to look after the poor. The rich areas, which could afford
much money, did not have to levy the same kind of rates, because there
were so few poor people in them.

The population of Westminster was 141,317. The rateable value of
the borough was £7,913,538. The rateable value of Poplar, which had
162,618 people, was £947,109. Yet Poplar from this very low rateable
value had to find the money for *seven times* more people on poor relief
than lived in Westminster, which was much richer.

By early 1921 the situation in Poplar, where unemployment was
specially high, was quite desperate. The councillors were faced with
either raising the already high rates (they had doubled since 1917) or
refusing to pay the dole to the people on poor relief.

This is exactly the situation which will be faced by the poorer
Labour councils when the poll tax comes in. They will be forced to
raise more and more tax, which will hit the working class in their area
even harder than it did in 1921 (when the local taxes were based on
property, not people).

Nowadays when the poll tax is discussed among Labour councillors,
the prevailing view is that there is nothing for it but to collect the tax,
and go on running the councils, even if it means cutting services to the
most desperate of the poor.

The problem for them will be either to charge more tax, which will hit the poor, or to cut the services, which will hit the poor. They will be trapped by the system which finances their councils in just the same Catch 22 situation which infuriated George Lansbury and his colleagues in 1921.

Lansbury took an entirely different view to the fashionable notions of Labour councillors today. In *Labour Monthly* in 1921 he wrote:

> The workers must be given tangible proof that Labour administration means something different from capitalist administration, and in a nutshell this means diverting wealth from wealthy ratepayers to the poor.

When the system stopped him doing that, Lansbury concluded, 'I prefer contempt of court to contempt for the poor.' Poplar council voted not to pay the police and mental hospital precepts to the LCC, but to spend the money on the poor instead.

In the end they went to prison. But so huge was the support for them in their area that the government backed down and equalized the rates, boosting poor Poplar by a huge half million pounds, more than half the borough's entire rateable value.

Most poll tax protest meetings today are addressed by Labour councillors, honest men and women who make decent speeches against the dreadful monster which will inflict itself on the people some time next year.

When pressed, they say they will not, as a council, lead a campaign not to pay the tax. 'That sort of thing', they say, 'never does any good.'

Precisely that advice came to George Lansbury and his mates from all sides. Jimmy Thomas, the railwaymen's leader, called the Poplar councillors 'wasters'. Everyone told them that their stand would not succeed, that the system would win out in the end, and it was better to cling to office in the town hall, even if you were stopping poor relief (or cutting the vital services of the poor).

George and Edgar Lansbury, Key, Sumner, Cooper, Susan Lawrence – these were Labour councillors at the time in Poplar. They bucked the system and they won.

Socialist Worker, March 1989

Naughtie and Neil

A funny thing happened to Neil Kinnock the other day. He was at a loss for words.

At his own request, he went into the radio studio at Westminster for an interview on the Tory government's economic policy. His interviewer was James Naughtie, one of the very few radio commentators who is known as a Labour Party supporter (quite a strong NUJ militant he was in his time, this Naughtie, but that is another story).

During the interview, which by all accounts was going very well for the Labour leader, Jim Naughtie turned to the subject of interest rates. He interrupted a tirade from Neil Kinnock to ask what a Labour government would do to bring interest rates down.

There was silence. James Naughtie repeated the question. Again there was silence.

He thought the Labour leader had been cut off, and broke off his interviewing voice to call out 'hello, hello, hello'.

At last the Labour leader replied. He did not answer the question. Instead he rebuked Jim Naughtie for asking it.

On and on he railed about how the Tories were ruining the country, how he had come on the radio to say how they were ruining the country, not to be regaled with what he called 'a bloody WEA lecture on what the Labour alternatives might be in three years time'.

In a flash of the moderate language which has made Neil Kinnock what he is today, he bawled: 'I'm not going to be bloody kebabed talking about what the alternatives are.'

The interview was not broadcast but the Tory press quickly got a copy of it and published it in full, with great glee. Unanimously, they criticized Kinnock for swearing on the radio. Their point was that a man who swears in such a manner is not fit to be prime minister.

As usual, the Tory press got the wrong end of the kebab stick. Kinnock's rugby club language doesn't do him an ounce of electoral damage. When he got involved in a brawl in a restaurant not long ago, his poll ratings moved up a couple of points.

The point the Tory press seems to have missed is that Kinnock cannot give an answer to a question about the 'alternative' to high interest rates *because he does not have one.*

I hope I am not breaking the official secrets act, or a family confidence, if I disclose here an anecdote told to me by uncle Michael (Foot) after he had attended a shadow cabinet meeting in 1973.

Labour was in opposition at the time and doing well in the polls. At the meeting the shadow cabinet had discussed inflation. After drawing together some woolly clichés, the meeting was rather shocked by a remark from Anthony Crosland.

Crosland was a right-winger, who understood rather more about capitalist economics than most of his contemporaries. He was also given to a disconcerting habit of making caustic comments which upset the Labour leadership.

At this stage, he commented dryly, 'I hope no one asks us too closely about this because none of us has the slightest idea how to cure inflation.'

The Crosland comment, unspoken and until now – as far as I know – unrevealed, hung like a cloud over the Labour administration which was elected the following year.

No one knew how on earth Labour policies could be put into effect without a steep rise in inflation. Within a year of Labour's election inflation had risen to fantastic heights. At one stage it was 25 per cent.

At that stage, Labour *did* find an 'answer' to inflation. James Callaghan, who became prime minister in 1976, described it as 'squeezing inflation out of the system'. This meant cuts in public spending and rises in interest rates, exactly the same policies pursued by the Tories.

When it comes to inflation and interest rates, the Crosland formula applies even more to Labour's predicament today than it did in 1973. No one in the National Executive has the slightest idea what will happen to interest rates, or to inflation, if and when Labour is in office. The only remedy they have for the one is to put up the other – the Tory remedy.

When Neil Kinnock and his advisers talk openly about 'managing capitalism' when next they are in office, they forget a simple fact. Capitalism, has its own dynamic. It is not 'manageable' in the sense that Neil Kinnock means.

Indeed Labour governments, whatever they have wanted to do, have never managed capitalism at all. Capitalism has managed them.

They start off as keen and confident cooks. They end up as kebabs.

Socialist Worker, June 1989

'Almost a revolution'

Slogging wearily through the reports of the TUC last week, I came upon a surprising suggestion from Alan Tuffin, the postal workers' general secretary.

Speaking in the 'green debate', Alan said that the business of defending the environment from pollution was a very serious and difficult one. 'It will', he concluded, 'need almost a revolution to do it.'

The concept of 'almost a revolution' has excited socialists for many decades. Indeed, it has divided the socialists who consider themselves left-wing from those who consider themselves right-wing. Right-wingers will have nothing to do with revolution. They would rather not hear the word spoken.

Left-wing socialists are more ambitious. They would like a revolution – well, *almost*. They would like things to get better for the dispossessed under the existing order of things.

They would like electorates to vote in progressive governments, laws to be passed redistributing wealth and power, and the wealthy and powerful to surrender their wealth and power in the common interest. There would be *almost* a revolution, a change of social conditions, but not a change in social order.

All through this century in almost every country influential people have wanted to achieve almost a revolution.

The USPD, the Independent Socialists in Germany after the First World War, broke away from the mainstream Social Democratic Party because they wanted every change on earth, provided the means of changing things was not changed.

Fifty years later in Chile, Salvador Allende was twice elected at the head of a social-democratic party which wanted lower prices, more public ownership, better housing and welfare for the poor, and less power for the rich. He achieved almost a revolution.

In the end, though, the USPD held back the workers' struggle, diverted it into a parliamentary cul de sac and helped pave the way for the most frightful reaction the world has ever known.

If we had to think of a reaction in our generation which was as bad as Adolf Hitler's, we would plump at once for the tyranny which toppled Salvador Allende's social-democratic government, and which turned almost a revolution into the slaughter of the entire membership of Allende's party, including Allende himself.

The British example of almost a revolution which is constantly held in front of us as the pinnacle of political achievement is the Labour government of 1945 to 1951. National health, national coal, national railways, national utilities, relative equality, strong trade unions – all these replaced the dreadful upper-class reaction of the 1930s.

It was almost a revolution, except that the Tories won an election after it, and the British upper class was far more confident and aggressive *after* the almost revolution than before it.

Many socialists were greatly disappointed that the almost revolution of that time did not go further. A classic book on the weaknesses and failures of that Labour government to pursue its own objectives was written by an American academic called Arnold Rogow. It starts with a poem by Robert Frost:

I advocate a semi-revolution.
The trouble with a total revolution
Is that it brings the same class out on top.
Executives of skilful execution
Will therefore plan to go halfway then stop.
Yes, revolutions are the only salves,
But they're one thing that should be done by halves.

To this classic statement of the almost revolution, Rogow attached another poem by someone called Oscar Williams.

I advocate a total revolution.
The trouble with a semi-revolution,
It's likely to be as slow as evolution.
Who wants to spend the ages in collusion
With Compromise, Complacence and Confusion?
As for the same class coming out on top
That's wholecloth from the propaganda shop;
The old saw says there's loads of room on top.
That's where the poor should really plan to stop.
And speaking of those people called the 'haves'
Who own the whole cow and must have the calves
(And plant the wounds so they can sell the salves)
They won't be stopped by doing things by halves.

I say that for a permanent solution
There's nothing like a total revolution!

I have no idea who Oscar Williams was. He certainly wasn't as famous as Robert Frost. But I reckon he had the edge in the argument.

Socialist Worker, September 1989

9. Workers in Action

Steelworkers on strike

'Before the strike, when you came in here, you felt you were coming to see God. Now the place belongs to all of us.'

Bob Bartholomew, crane driver at the Templeborough Steel plant, Rotherham, was talking at the Rotherham headquarters of the Iron and Steel Trades Confederation, the steelworkers' union. You could hardly hear him above the hubbub of voices. Voices organizing, voices arguing, voices telling the story of yesterday's picket.

This prim building with its thick carpets was built for tidy and genteel officials with tidy and genteel routines. It has suddenly become the central powerhouse of the steel strike.

As with the miners' strike exactly eight years ago, the motivating power behind the action has shifted to South Yorkshire.

John Ratcliffe, a branch secretary and strike committee member, spelt out the details. There are fifty 'cells' each of fifty steelworkers, each of them based on a steel plant or a stockholder in the Rotherham area. These cells mount pickets twenty-four hours a day. They also provide volunteers for the flying pickets. John says that the strike organizers have the names of 7,000 workers, all of whom can be mobilized at very short notice indeed.

The very energy of the strike activity from the Rotherham centre has brought workers into the action.

'We forgot about the women workers,' says John. 'We hadn't allocated them for any action. But yesterday they were in here demanding to know why *they* weren't in cells, and flooding out on to the pickets with the others.'

As the plants and stockholders shut down in Rotherham and the surrounding towns, so the pickets began to move further afield. News came in of possible steel movements into the ports.

Pickets visited Hull where the dockers, without even asking their union leaders, have stopped moving anything which could even remotely be used by the steel industry. The same has happened at Grimsby, Immingham and Boston.

Last week the steelworkers started to move off for long stays in places they had hardly ever heard of: the smaller ports of East Anglia and Kent.

John Ratcliffe says: 'We get news and offers from contacts in these places: often it's the local Socialist Workers Party or Labour Party Young Socialists. We send advance parties to scout out the possibilities of accommodation and assistance for the pickets. Then we send the pickets on.'

John said that by last weekend there were South Yorkshire steel pickets guarding every port in Kent.

The money and accommodation for that huge operation had been supplied without a moment's hesitation by the Kent miners. The miners have contacted dockers and other transport workers. The information is accurate and it moves fast. And the steel, or most of it anyway, is stopped.

Most of the steelworkers who have moved out on these pickets are men and women without much experience of travel or of being away from home for long.

The Yorkshire steel industry is insular. Workers stay in the same plants and in the same environment. But already these Rotherham pickets have acquired a nationwide reputation for militancy.

Stephen Banks, a mighty melting shop worker, announces with pride that he has had 'two days off since day one of the strike'. He has been everywhere, even to Birmingham.

At one Birmingham firm, he says, the steel pickets from the area had been pushed aside each day by offensive cowboy lorry drivers. 'When we drove up,' says Stephen, 'the pickets gave a great cheer, turned round to the firm's gates and shouted at the lorry drivers who weren't very keen to drive out: *Come out, you bastards. The Rotherham lads are here.* The invitation was not accepted.'

Before their very eyes, the workers feel themselves changing.

'What do we talk about in the plant?' asks Bob Bartholomew. 'Every day it's the same: sex, booze and sport. On the picket line, and in the cars and vans, it's all different. People start talking about the government, about the Labour Party, about the union; about how we're going to change the world.

'You see blokes on the picket line you'd never have dreamed would be there. And often they are the ones who have the best ideas about what to do next.

'I've got four kids all under ten. We get just enough to feed them. After that, we just don't pay any bills, because we can't. And I feel we can go on for ever.

'I suppose most of the blokes still feel that this is just part of ordinary life, but I must admit for me its like living history. I feel that one day I'll be telling those children's children what it was like being in the Great Steel Strike of 1980.'

The mood and spirit of the South Yorkshire steelworkers has frightened the government and terrified the ISTC leadership. It has surprised even the most enthusiastic and optimistic socialist.

It has invigorated those officials like Keith Jones, organizer of the strike committee, whose natural militancy has been held back for years.

And by activating almost the whole rank and file in the area, by holding regular weekly mass branch meetings to report on and supplement all the picketing activity, the organizers have taken away from the Tories their one hope for outright victory over the steelworkers – an apathetic and uninformed rank and file.

If only it were so all through the industry! The South Yorkshire men and women know that it is not. They can see how in other areas, even in Scunthorpe which is only a few miles away, the strike is still held firmly by the old leadership, with picketing limited and the rank and file told to stay at home and watch the telly until they are told to go back to work.

A great tussle is already joined between the powerhouses at places like Rotherham and Stocksbridge, and the slow-witted pessimism in many other steel areas.

The Yorkshiremen find that they are now obliged to send envoys into Wales and Scotland to enthuse the workers there with their own energy and confidence.

Socialist Worker, February 1980

Remembering the miners' strike

On 1 March 1984 Margaret Thatcher and her ministers embarked on a class battle. It was to be as tough and crude a class battle as had ever been attempted – even by Margaret Thatcher's beloved Victorians. The Tories were taking on their most formidable and feared enemy: the National Union of Mineworkers.

Coal stocks had been built high. The police force had been reorganized and retrained to break strikes. Oil-fired power stations were taken out of mothballs, and oil ordered far ahead. Secret public opinion polls reassured them that a ballot among all the mineworkers for a national strike would almost certainly be lost (as had ballots three times in the last three years).

Ian MacGregor, a grisly class warrior whose life had been devoted to breaking unions all over the world, had taken up office as Chairman of the National Coal Board. After three years spent halving the workforce of the British Steel Corporation and reducing its unions to quivering servitude, he was ready for his most ambitious mission, to bring the miners to heel. This was to be the final victory over a trade union movement already cowed by the horror of four million unemployed.

The closure of Cortonwood, in Yorkshire, was the gauntlet flung down by the government. It was the first pit with coal in it to be closed since the signing of 'A Plan for Coal' in 1974; the first of twenty pits to be closed in direct contravention of the agreement; 20,000 jobs were on the line, four million tons of coal capacity was to be taken out.

Reaction was swift. Flying pickets from Cortonwood brought the rest of the huge Yorkshire coalfield to a standstill. Kent followed. Before long the traditionally militant coalfields of South Wales and Scotland were silent. But in the big Nottingham coalfield, and in most of the smaller, weaker areas where ballots were held, the vote went against. The strike was deprived from the very first day of the unity and solidarity which won the day in the seventies.

Some 30,000 miners had decided to work. At least 165,000 miners were out on strike, and were clearly determined to stay out for far longer than the most pessimistic Tory had ever imagined.

In the early days, the pickets set out as confidently as they had in 1972 and 1974. They found a different police force, controlled from one 'reporting centre', using powers which even they did not believe they had, to stop pickets' cars and turn them back, to cordon off whole villages and areas, to arrest at will and finally to break the pickets by weight of numbers and by force. Press and television joined enthusiastically in the fray. Their tactic was based on the old demonology. They turned the miners' president, Arthur Scargill, into a devil incarnate. Even A.J. Cook, the miners' leader in the lock-out of 1926, had not had to endure the violence and malevolence of the attacks on Arthur Scargill.

The strikers soon discovered that they were much poorer than they had been in 1972 and 1974. The Tories had deducted £15 per week from the already desperately low benefits that their wives and children were entitled to. It seemed as though they must soon break under this pressure. But they didn't. Indeed, as the miners fell back from the battles on the picket lines of Nottinghamshire and Orgreave to protect their own heartlands, the strike seemed to gain a new spirit, a new strength.

Walking down a road in Upton, Yorks, in September I stopped to talk to a large miner whose battered car had stopped beside me. I had heard, I said, of the sadness and the wretchedness of the mining areas, so why was he beaming from ear to ear? 'I've enjoyed it, me,' he declared, and started to explain. Of course he and his family had very little money, of course they were worried by the cold, of course, of course. But life was different. The daily grind had been removed. Decisions, about picketing, about welfare, about the political ebbs and flows of the strike which were on television every day had to be taken not by someone else, some high-up somewhere, but by themselves. He did not put it quite like this, but he was in charge of his own destiny, and he enjoyed it.

There was *change* all about. People were changing. In the strength of their collective action they felt a new confidence in themselves and the people around them. Ideas and prejudices which had been grafted into them like barnacles were suddenly blasted away. The change in themselves was quickly translated into changes in the way they behaved towards one another.

In tradition and in fact, the miner had been the master in his home. The role of the miner's wife was to feed her man, bring up her children, and keep her mouth shut. Suddenly, in the most unlikely area, the ideas of women's liberation became reality. Whole communities were suddenly run by women. The strongest, most energetic and most forceful of the support groups were made up, almost exclusively, of women. This led to new relationships in the community and in the home – to new uncertainties, perhaps, but also to new respect. In the same way, the socialist ideas which inspired people's brains were suddenly resurrected in physical reality. An injury to one was an injury to all. The strong *did* help the weak, the able-bodied *did* help the disabled. The seeds of a new society founded on co-operation, common interest and human effort bent to human need were sown in the struggle against the old one.

These changes burst out of the mining areas. Through the summer and autumn of 1984 they started to infect and inspire hundreds of thousands of people who had called themselves socialists but had begun to give up hope.

Into every crack and crevice of the Labour movement came the black-and-yellow slogan COAL NOT DOLE, waking and inspiring all but the most somnolent and sectarian fossils.

At the start of the strike, all donations were collected by the union officials and sent off to the areas or to the national solidarity fund. By the late autumn, the vast mass of individual donations went to individual pits, through the 'twinning' of union branches, Labour Parties, even street committees with pits and villages. The miners and their families moved out of their areas, while supporters from outside moved in. New friendships sprouted, spawning new solidarity.

In August, September and October, the strike held; utterly and incredibly solid.

For a time, the government wavered, only to realize that another defeat by the miners, when all the odds were for the government, might threaten 'civilization as we know it'. New pressure was brought on the stumbling MacGregor to stand his ground.

Tim Bell, personal adviser to the Prime Minister and managing director of Saatchi and Saatchi, the advertising agency which had spurred the Tories to office in 1979, joined a new advertising agency which was promptly granted the entire anti-strike account of the National Coal Board. David Hart, an imbecile property tycoon and right-wing fanatic, was authorized by MacGregor to start up and fund a 'Working Miners Committee' from the dregs of the strike-breakers. In four days of advertising in Tory papers, Hart's 'Committee' raised more than £100,000. Newpapers, television, police, even Special Branch joined the growing campaign to push the miners back to work. As miners started to go back in big numbers, in November, Coal Board executives predicted an end to the strike by Christmas.

The ratchet slipped a notch; then held again. The support groups mobilized a huge effort over Christmas. Every miner's child enjoyed their Christmas – some say more than ever before. As the New Year started after nine months of strike there were still 130,000 miners out.

Still the miners held out. The bitter cold of January did not bring the power cuts. The oil-fired power stations, at full blast, could light, heat and power the homes and industries of Britain as long as the crucial 50,000 tons of coal a week came in from Nottingham. Instead the cold was just another new misery to add to poverty and hunger.

The Coal Board and the government had been certain that the strike would peter out in January. But it went on and on. Each week cost the government another forty or fifty million pounds in unbudgeted spending. When, in the first week of March 1985, the flow back to work had become too strong to resist, and the miners were finally starved back to work, together, without formally conceding surrender, their heads held high, they had been on strike for a full year, the longest mass strike in all British, European or American history.

One of the most remarkable pictures in this book shows the faces of the miners in the cage on the first day back. It shows how quickly the change which had worked such wonders in the strike worked the other way as soon as the strike was over. The men are, once again, caged. Their expressions are depressed and bored. The miners were subject once again to the Coal Board's commands and its instructions. The cage was bad enough, but worse would probably follow. There was only one thing worse than having a job; not having one.

Outside the pits, the mood shifted in the same sudden way. The end of the strike led to a collapse of aspirations and morale among its supporters. Neil Kinnock, who had been attacked in almost every Labour Party in the country for his weasel words about the strike, suddenly became 'the only hope'. Labour and Communist Party members returned to their party organizations and their enervating or ideological priorities. People who had supported the strike to the hilt, including even some miners' leaders, started to say that the strike had been a mistake, that it would have been better if it had never happened, that it was all the fault of Scargill and Benn, that it would have been better to have had a ballot and lost than to have gone through a 'year's hell' for nothing.

These arguments were enthusiastically rehearsed by the trade union leaders who had spouted great rhetoric at the TUC but had organized nothing to campaign for the miners in the places it mattered most: the power stations, the haulage depots and the docks; by local miners' leaders, who showed such lack of confidence in their own rank and file, and hugged the strike close to their short-sighted strategy, never once unleashing the potential for leadership which was there in the newly awakened rank and file; and by the Labour politicians who never missed a chance to fasten on the weakness of the miners' case, rather than its strength, for rotten long-term electoral advantage. Such people were delighted to greet so many converts from direct action to the pillars in the cloud in the shape of a possible Labour government at least three years away.

As the ranks of the doubters grow, as their arguments become more and more fashionable, the real friends of the miners must fight all the harder for the memory of the strike. *We must remember* that it was a hundred million times better to have fought, even if the strike's aims had not been achieved, than not to have fought at all.

For the first time in five years, Thatcher's government was stopped in its tracks for a full year. It was forced to fall back on the crudest class bludgeons in its 'objective' state machinery. *We must remember* the potential for change which the great strike represented. *We must remember* that the strike fell short of its aims not because it happened nor because it was led by extremists nor because a ballot wasn't held but because the other side was better organized and better prepared than ours was; and that therefore next time we must be better prepared.

Introduction to *Blood, Sweat and Tears*, photographs of the miners' strike,
London 1985

The battle of Trafalgar

The *Times* was very angry with the demonstration in Trafalgar Square. It called for 'the sternness of the Americans in repressing offences against law and order'. American police, the *Times* reminded its readers, 'carry revolvers and use them without mercy when they see signs of resistance'.

The conclusion was obvious. 'If the people of the United States do not hesitate when order is persistently disturbed to restore it with a strong hand, why should we be afraid to give effect to the general will?'

This was published in the *Times* not this week but 102 years ago, on 12 November 1887.

The *Times* and all the other papers, whether they supported the Liberal Party or the Conservative Party, were extremely worried about what they saw as insurrectionary demonstrations in and around Trafalgar Square.

For weeks groups of unemployed, inspired by a large black banner which symbolized the dark prospects of the dole, mingled with the masses of the city's homeless in the square. They made it their base, and held meetings there.

Most of the meetings were called and addressed by unemployed people who were members of nothing. The Marxist Social Democratic Federation had called a few demonstrations, while the Socialist League felt it was too pure to associate itself with the great unwashed.

The most regular visitations to these meetings were from the police, who took special pleasure in 'mopping up' the meetings with the combined use of the horse and the baton.

In three successive days – 17, 18 and 19 October – Trafalgar Square was completely cleared by police raids of the utmost brutality.

It was plain to everyone who observed the events that the Metropolitan Commissioner of the time, Sir Charles Warren, firmly backed by the Tory government, was determined to wipe out forever the old fashioned notion that 'anyone in England can say what they like in Trafalgar Square'.

Every day in the first week of November the police arrived with their batons to disperse the spontaneous meetings.

On 4 November, the red flag, which had momentarily replaced its black predecessor, was seized. Sir Charles Warren announced a complete ban on all meetings in the square from 8 November.

This frontal assault on the citadel of free speech stirred some political organizations into action. The radicals under the campaigning journalist W.T. Stead; the Irish, in protest at the imprisonment of the Irish MP William O'Brien; and assorted socialists from Bernard Shaw of the Fabian Society to William Morris of the Socialist League joined together to call a demonstration for Sunday 13 November.

The cry went up, 'To the square!' There were effectively only three days to organize. There was no television, no radio and no mass circulation newspapers. Yet the combination of radicals, Irish and socialists produced an enormous crowd on that Sunday morning.

The aim was simple, to take possession of Trafalgar Square by sheer weight of numbers. William Morris, speaking to one of the feeder marches before it set off from Clerkenwell Green, gave some crucial words of advice to the cheerful crowd.

'When the procession passes through the streets, those behind must not fall back, whatever happens to those in front. This is only passive resistance and passive resistance is not enough. I hope that you will shove the policemen, rather than hit them, for the police are armed and we are not....'

The crowd laughed. The people were in a carnival mood. The police, some scoffed, could knock out a handful of unorganized unemployed meetings. How could they deal with a massive throng converging from all sides on Trafalgar Square?

The answer came soon enough. The armed might of the British ruling class, which had shown its strength in far-flung outposts of the British Empire, was now deployed in deadly earnest against its most feared enemy, the British working people in revolt.

The whole of the sunken section of Trafalgar Square was packed with policemen clutching their batons, and with soldiers, each armed with twenty rounds of ammunition. Rows of mounted police covered the roads round the square. Each entrance was blocked with shouting rampaging mobs of armed police.

Despite extraordinary courage from the unarmed and unprepared marchers, they were quickly dispersed. Bernard Shaw, never the most courageous of leaders in times of trouble, took off at once. In his own word, he 'skedaddled'.

The radical leader Cunninghame Graham was arrested. As he stood by his arresting officer, another two policemen came up from behind and struck him mighty blows on the head. He fell and was dragged by the hair out of the square. Even so, as he regained his feet, he noticed: 'A poor woman asked a police inspector ... if he had seen a child she had lost. His answer was to tell her she was a "damned whore" and to knock her down.' Cunninghame Graham, together with John Burns, later to be one of the first Labour MPs, was sent to prison for six weeks.

Three demonstrators were killed that day, 'Bloody Sunday'. The police took control of the square for the next few weeks, riding rough-shod up and down.

A few days later they added to their kill. A law writer, Alfred Linnell, who had gone down to the square to see what was going on, was run down by a police horse.

The press unanimously blamed the unarmed demonstrators for their own dead. Familiar phrases appeared on front pages and in leader columns. The *Times* led the pack.

> The active portion of yesterday's mob was composed of all that is weakest, most worthless and most vicious in the slums of a great city. No honest purpose animated these howling roughs. It was simple love of disorder, hope of plunder, and the revolt of dull brutality against the rule of law.

The *Times* was joined by parliamentary politicians from both sides of the House. The Gladstonian Liberals, out of office because they insisted on some rights for people in Ireland, seemed not at all concerned about rights for unemployed, homeless or, for that matter, Irish people about 200 yards away from the Mother of Parliaments.

Some demonstrators that day (though they did not join in the chorus) concluded that the political activity of the streets could now reasonably be abandoned. Men like Bernard Shaw turned away to the more peaceable paths of Fabian reform.

But others learnt a different lesson. They maintained the dignity and unity of Bloody Sunday in the vast demonstrations which accompanied the funerals of the three dead and Alfred Linnell, and in the even bigger meetings which welcomed Burns and Cunninghame Graham out of prison.

Many victims and losers on Bloody Sunday resolved that the ruling class could and would be beaten. Annie Besant, one of the most militant demonstrators on Bloody Sunday, started to organize the match girls of the East End of London soon afterwards. Their successful strike lit the fuse for the Great Dock Strike of 1889.

There was a new toughness and sense of class purpose about the tactics of many socialist demonstrators that November Sunday.

When William Morris came to write *News From Nowhere*, he put in the mouth of old Hammond a grand description of a bloody massacre in Trafalgar Square.

The narrator listened, horrified. He was appalled. 'And I suppose,' he asked mournfully, 'that this massacre put an end to the whole revolution for that time?'

'No, no!' cried old Hammond. 'It began it!'

Socialist Worker, April 1990

10. Tributes

Blair Peach

From Manchester to Tolpuddle, the martyrs of our movement have been humble people. They neither sought the limelight nor found it. They were unknown except to a close circle of friends and family. They became famous not because of their ambitions nor their vanity, but because of their deaths.

Such was a man called Alfred Linnell. No one knows very much about him. He earned a pittance by copying out legal documents. On 21 November 1887 he went down to Trafalgar Square to join the fighters for free speech in the week after 'Bloody Sunday', when a great demonstration had been broken up by police truncheons.

While he was standing unarmed and unsuspecting, by the side of the crowd, a posse of police, who had orders to keep Trafalgar Square free of demonstrators 'by whatever force was necessary', charged straight into him, breaking his neck with the horses' hooves. The police openly despised the people they were charging. They saw them, as the *Times* leader put it on the day after Bloody Sunday, as 'all that is weakest, most worthless and most vicious in the slums of a great city'. These were the 'sweepings', which deserved only to be swept.

But the poor of London flocked to commemorate Alfred Linnell. Tens of thousands of socialists, Irish Republicans, radicals, feminists and working people of no party and no persuasion joined in what Edward Thompson described as 'the greatest united demonstration which London had seen'. The streets were lined all the way to Bow Cemetery with crowds of sympathetic onlookers. The few rather shamefaced policemen who dared to appear were greeted with cries of: 'That's your work!' Very, very few of that mighty crowd knew Alfred Linnell. Yet they hailed him, in the words of William Morris at

Linnell's funeral, as 'our brother and our friend'. He was a representative of all the tens of thousands who had nothing, and when they took
to the streets to demand something were ridden down and battered by
the forces of law and order.

That was nearly a hundred years ago and can easily be dismissed as
'the sort of thing which happened in the bad old days'. The killing of
Blair Peach proves that the same things are still going on today. He
was attacked at a demonstration by policemen who, as at Bloody
Sunday and its aftermath, were licensed to clear the streets by brutality
and violence.

In Southall, as in Trafalgar Square a hundred years ago, the police
were driven on by a contempt for the demonstrators – 'black scum', as
one mounted officer so politely put it. No doubt the savagery of the
blow which ended Blair Peach's life was prompted at least in part by
the fact that his skin was dusky. And Blair Peach, like Alfred Linnell,
has been hailed as brother and friend by thousands of working men
and women who did not know him.

On 28 April fifteen thousand of the Asian people of Southall
marched in his memory. They stood with clenched fists over the place
where he was murdered. And they chanted a single triumphant slogan:
'BLAIR PEACH SINDABAD' – 'LONG LIVE BLAIR PEACH.' It was perhaps the
greatest demonstration of solidarity between people of different
colours but with similar interests and similar purpose that the town
had ever seen.

Why? Because Blair Peach, like Alfred Linnell, is a representative of
all the people all over Britain who see in the strutting perverts of the
National Front the broken bodies of black people battered in the
street; who can detect further off but no less horrible the awful spectre
of Fascism looming over all society, and who stand up and say NO.

To me, and all members and supporters of the Socialist Workers
Party, Blair Peach means even more than that. I never knew him
personally. But I knew him as one of the party members who kept
socialist organization alive and well during the worst times. These are
not the great speechmakers; they organize meetings and demonstrations, but are not to be seen on the platforms; they enjoy the big party
occasions, but do not take the credit for them; the meetings they speak
in are the vital ones, the little groups of twos and threes who meet to
organize this or argue about that, and from whose arguments and
ceaseless activity the very existence of socialist organization depends.

They're not very good, these people, at the quick quip or noble turn of phrase. But they know how to sustain the Anti Nazi League in an area where two or three delegates turn up to a meeting to which twenty had promised to come.

They have endless patience and endurance and they try to excite others into political activity without straining too hard at their patience and endurance. They seem to be at all the meetings and all the demonstrations. They are not in the front line when the press cameras are clicking, but they are in the front line when the SPG wade in with their coshes. In the last three years – the period, by the way, in which Blair Peach joined the Socialist Workers Party – these people have been strained to breaking point as more and more of the burden of the organization of the Left has fallen upon them. Blair Peach was killed in the process, and that above all is why we honour him.

We march at his funeral not just in sympathy with the people who loved him, nor just out of respect for all he did for us, but in anger.

Socialist Worker, June 1979

Ruth First

I imagine there are few socialists in London (or who have recently travelled to London) who have not by now seen *A World Apart*, the story of Ruth First, as seen through the eyes of her daughter.

I fear the film is so very, very good, and its message so powerful, that it may not last long on the screen. So if there is anyone who hasn't see it – just get down there as soon as possible.

There may be some people who are a little puzzled by the final titles which announce that Ruth First was assassinated in Mozambique in 1983. So she was, but the film ends some twenty years earlier, and admirers of Ruth (and there could hardly be any non-admirers after the film) might be puzzled as to what happened in the interim.

During the film Ruth First's life is all in South Africa, and she died not far away, so you might think that she spent all her life there. She didn't. Soon after the period covered by the film, she escaped from house arrest and fled to Britain. She was here all through the rest of the 1960s and, I think, all the 1970s. She joined a huge army of South African exiles who made a profound impact on the British Left in those years.

Ruth wrote some marvellous books. Her book *117 Days* is the finest account I have ever read of the disorientation of the rebel prisoner in a torturer's prison. Anyone who enjoyed the film should get hold of that book.

Unlike many of her friends and contemporaries, Ruth First believed that no progress would ever come to South Africa without armed struggle. I met her often at meetings, which she arranged, of South African guerrillas, trained in armed struggle, who came to London to build support for it. All these people, like Ruth, were members or supporters of the Communist Party. I was always both delighted to be invited, and rather ashamed to find myself (*every* time) arguing with them. I couldn't understand why the discussion kept turning back to the *governments* of the new African states.

I remember one furious argument with Ruth about the deposing of Ben Bella in Algeria and his replacement by Boumedienne. She, and the others, regarded this as a great sign of progress. They had the facts to prove it: Boumedienne's record in struggle, in commitment and in guns.

Over the years the same basic argument rocked back and forth. I was told that the Rhodesian armed struggle depended on 'the friendliness of the front line states' for its existence. These states, perhaps against their will, behave like bosses towards the people, and as agents for the great companies that carve up Africa. I could not understand the argument that placed these governments above the guerrillas' own commitment and their own strength.

In the end, Ruth First and these brave young men and women wanted a society precisely *a world apart* from the world run by Kaunda, Nyerere, Boumedienne, Nasser and the rest.

Since they wanted something different, since they represented something different, since they were fighting literally to the death for something different, why did they pretend and speak so eloquently for people who represented more of the same?

I never got an answer to these questions. On the other hand, to be fair, I never stopped getting the invitations.

Ruth First had a sort of grudging respect for the International Socialists (the Socialist Workers Party's forerunners). She thought that underneath it all we were 'Trotskyist splitters', but she did notice that whenever there was a demo or a clash of any kind with apartheid, we were always in the front line.

On 14 September 1973 she spoke at a demonstration organized by the IS in Hyde Park. It was to protest against a mine disaster which had killed, I think, twelve African miners as a result of the most appalling employers' negligence.

I remember the date exactly because the disaster happened on the 11th, the same day as the Chilean coup.

The Communist Party organized a huge demo on Chile. We guessed wrong and organized one on South Africa. About 600 came to ours, about 20,000 to the other (which we joined rather abjectly, after our meeting was over).

In spite of the clash of party loyalties, Ruth First agreed at once to speak on our platform. Before the meeting, we watched the masses forming elsewhere in the park. 'You made a mistake coming here,' I laughed at her. 'No', she grinned back. 'I'll speak at any meeting against racist South Africa. You made the mistake, not I.'

For once, I thought, she won the argument.

Socialist Worker, January 1988

T. Cliff and Zionism

Pondering the critical comments of the representatives of American Jewry on the Christmas upheavals in Gaza and on the West Bank, I go to Central Books to buy myself a Christmas present.

I know there is one there for me because Dave, who runs the shop and is a crafty fellow, has informed me that for £10 I can get a copy of

Red Russia. This is a marvellous pamphlet by John Reed, published in this country in 1919.

Dave has something else up his sleeve, however, which brings me back to Gaza. This is another pamphlet, completed on 12 November 1945, called *Middle East at the Cross Roads.* It was written in Jerusalem by someone called T. Cliff.

I rush through the pamphlet and find one or two clues in it which help a lot in understanding the Christmas crisis in the occupied territories. For instance:

> Zionism occupies a special place in imperialist fortifications. It plays a double role, firstly, directly as an important pillar of imperialism, giving it active support and opposing the liberatory struggle of the Arab nation, and second as a passive servant behind which imperialism can hide and towards which it can direct the ire of the Arab masses.

The same point is made in a rather different way a couple of pages later, under the heading: 'Can Zionism be Anti-Imperialist?'

> Zionism and imperialism have both common and antagonistic interests. Zionism wants to build a strong Jewish capitalist state. Imperialism is indeed interested in the existence of a capitalist Jewish society enveloped by the hatred of colonial masses, but not that Zionism should become too strong a factor. As far as this is concerned, it is ready to prove its fairness to the Arabs.

This 'double role' and these 'common and antagonistic interests' are likely to lie fallow for many years of unchallenged exploitation, but when the volcano erupts, the contradiction is stretched to breaking point.

On the one hand the instinct of the American State Department and its business backers is to support the brutality of the Israeli army; on the other they know they must somehow keep up the fiction of their 'fairness to the Arabs' to maintain their robbers' conspiracy with the reactionary regimes in Egypt, Saudi Arabia and Iraq.

The dilemma solves itself for the moment in the cautious criticism by American Jewish organizations and in the US abstention in the United Nations Security Council.

Such matters are seized on by all those people who call themselves socialists and supporters of Labour, but who line up with the Israeli state. They point to the criticisms of the American Jews, and to the UN abstention as examples of the 'moderate approach' to Zionism. 'How much better', they exclaim, 'is this kind of fraternal criticism to the nasty hostility to Zionism which so often spills over into anti-semitism!'

Of all the many prevarications of what is known as the 'soft left' I find this line on Zionism the most distasteful. Otherwise humane and intelligent socialists seem able to discuss these matters without even for a moment considering the unimaginable horrors inflicted on the Palestinian people by Zionist aggression and imperialism.

This is an old and quite appalling story of lands seized, a people expelled, starved, brutalized and robbed of their own country by naked military force. Whatever the double role which Zionism performs for imperialism, the fact is that Zionism from first to last has never wavered in its support for imperialism and capitalism in the Middle East.

If it once unleashed terrorist forces against the British mandate, it did so solely to embarrass British imperialism in the eyes of American imperialism and to shift its allegiance from one to the other.

The explanation of the 'softness' stems from the feeling that the Jews are a persecuted race, and suffered horribly at the hands of Hitler. Yet how on earth can one set of concentration camps justify another? Concentration camps are precisely what are being built in Gaza and the West Bank this very moment.

The pamphlet puts it well:

It is a tragedy that the sons of the very people which has been persecuted and massacred in such a bestial fashion ... should itself be driven into a chauvinistic militaristic fervour and become the blind tool of imperialism in subjugating the Arab masses.

That sounds pretty good today. To write it in 1945 took the most extraordinary courage and clarity of Marxist thought.

Who was this chap T. Cliff anyway?

Socialist Worker, January 1988

Harry McShane

The commonest jibe of reactionaries against revolution is that it is an infatuation of youth. When people get old, we are constantly told, they drop the silly idealisms of their youth. They become 'old realists'.

I contemplated this jibe last Saturday as I stood (it was standing room only) in Craigton Crematorium with some 300 other people, many of them elderly Glasgow workers. We were paying our last respects to Harry McShane.

Harry died last week. He was ninety-six. He became a revolutionary Marxist in 1908, and he died a revolutionary Marxist in 1988. Can anyone show me one other person in the whole history of the world who was a revolutionary Marxist for eighty years?

It would be wonderful enough if it were just that Harry managed to sustain these ideas all that time. But ideas like his are not 'just' sustained. They can *only* be sustained in the heat of the struggle between the classes.

All his life Harry was an agitator in that struggle, a fighter. He made up his mind very early on (somewhere round 1910) that the socialist society he wanted was not going to be made by anyone *for* the workers; it was going to be made *by* the workers or not at all – and therefore their battles against employers and government were central to the whole process of political change.

The workers needed to use their muscle ('We never realize how strong we are,' he used to say again and again) but their muscle alone was not enough without politics.

Ever since he broke with the church at the age of sixteen and became a lifelong incurable atheist, Harry read books – books about British imperialism in Ireland and in Africa; about women's liberation; about the Russian Revolution; about religion. He read these books, and encouraged others to read them, not in the interests of some arid scholarship but in order to improve his understanding of the world – so that it could more speedily be changed.

Harry was an engineering worker. He was a close ally of the Scottish Marxist John Maclean, and campaigned with him on Clydeside against the imperialist war of 1914–18. He joined the Communist Party almost as soon as it was founded and was a member for thirty years.

He was the Scottish correspondent of the *Daily Worker* and Scottish organizer of the National Unemployed Workers Movement. Like pretty well all other Communists of the time, he was unwilling to accept the collapse of the workers' state in Russia. He once told me of his excitement when he visited Russia in 1931. 'It was so easy to believe the workers *were* in charge,' he said.

After the war though, his doubts grew. They sprang from his faith in the rank and file of the working class. What was happening to that rank and file in Czechoslovakia in 1948, or East Berlin in 1953?

In Britain the rank and file of the Communist Party were treated increasingly as a stage army, always expected to agree with the leadership. When he was disciplined for *not* taking part in a standing ovation for a party official, Harry had had enough – if he'd been disciplined because he *had* given a standing ovation, perhaps he would have understood.

There is a picture in the Glasgow *Daily Record* sometime in 1953 of Harry walking across Queens Park with his hat in his hand. It was the day he left the Communist Party. 'I couldn't stop them taking the picture,' he explained.

But when the same paper (and the *Daily Express*) offered him £500 – more than a year's salary – to 'tell all' about the Communist Party, he swore at both of them (he seldom swore, but he did on that occasion). Instead, he went back (at the age of sixty-two) to the yards as a labourer, and worked until he was sixty-nine to pay the stamps to qualify for a pension.

When I met him first in 1961, he was supported politically only by two outstanding socialist workers, Hugh Savage and Les Foster, who had broken from the Communist Party with him. He was seventy – but full of the joys of life, and of the hopes of a better world. He was still a revolutionary socialist through and through. He was quite determined that a socialist world could and should be won.

He was scarred from his bitter experience with the Communist Party, and wary of joining another political organization. But when, in 1963, we set up the first fledgling organization of the International Socialists (forerunner of the Socialist Workers Party) in the Horseshoe Bar near Glasgow's Central Station, Harry never missed a meeting. When in the same year the TUC called for a demonstration against unemployment, Harry helped to organize the buses.

In the great debates which took place in the Glasgow trades council at that time (and they *were* great debates; greater by far than anything you hear in parliament) Harry relentlessly attacked his former Communist Party colleagues for selling out simple class solidarity in exchange for a ship order from Russia, or to send another cosy delegation to Warsaw or Budapest.

He identified Russia as state-capitalist, and the Communists as unwitting stooges of another imperial power. Yet when he was approached by the organizer for Catholic Action in the trades council, and asked to form a loose anti-Communist alliance, he swore again.

'At least these people believe they are socialists – you don't believe in anything except your god,' he spat at the frightened delegate, who (literally) ran away.

The Right to Work marches of the late 1970s were meat and drink to Harry. He sent off the first march from Manchester with a truly magnificent speech, bettered only when he spoke to 6,000 people at the final rally in the Albert Hall.

His theme in these speeches was a simple one. With his sly humour he would outline the government's 'plans for unemployment'. 'Plans for this, plans for that, they've always got plans,' he would say. Then he would show how no government ever had the slightest effect on unemployment. The ebb and flow of the capitalist tide swept over all governments and all plans. Only the workers in action could do anything to roll it back.

We all know that great men and women don't make history, but we also know that working-class history would be a mean thing if it were not enriched by great men and women.

Great revolutionaries cast aside the temptations and pressures of the capitalist world in a single-minded commitment to change it. Harry McShane did all that with a cheerfulness and comradeship which charmed and enthused any socialist (or any potential socialist) who ever met him.

He died in an old people's home. He left a few books to his friends. He had survived on his pension, almost without supplement, for the last twenty-eight years of his life. He never had any property, yet he was perhaps the most contented man I have ever met; utterly happy as long as he was fighting for his class.

He kept up that fight with undiminished enthusiasm through good times and through bad. Because his politics were based on the working class, he had a sharp instinct for the shifts in the class mood.

One afternoon as he sat in the back of an old van which was carrying a party of us to speak on disarmament at the Mound in Edinburgh he remarked, just as a matter of interest: 'Last time I was here there were 20,000 people at the meeting.' That day he spoke to twenty.

These desperate turns in the mood of his class never deflected him from his purpose, or even from his speaking skills. On the days when he spoke to very few people (I once held the platform when he spoke outside John Browns shipyard in Clydebank to *no one at all!*) he was as persuasive and passionate as ever I heard.

'Things will come up again, Paul,' he reassured me as we trooped home that day. 'When they are not listening, then it's even more important that we keep the ideas alive.'

Anyone who knew Harry knows their good fortune. Anyone who didn't know him can reflect on his extraordinary life whenever they feel worn down by the old realism or the new. He was, is and will be an inspiration and example to us all.

Socialist Worker, April 1988

PROFESSIONS
AND
CONFESSIONS

11. Ireland

The elephant's path*

Hypocrisy, the most persistent of parliamentary virtues, has been much in evidence during all the House of Commons debates on Northern Ireland. Most British MPs have agreed on most subjects, but on one in particular there has been deafening unanimity. All of them have wanted to condemn the violence. What seems to have escaped the MPs is that the history of Ireland is a history of violence, almost all of it commissioned and sanctioned by the British parliament for use against the Irish people. The plantation of Ulster for the benefit of the court favourites of the first Queen Elizabeth was carried out with a savagery unbeknown in any other British colony, or in any other colony for that matter. The Governor of Carrickfergus in 1599 was Sir Arthur Chichester. His job was to kill Catholics and he set about it with a will. Of his first expedition he boasted:

> I burned all along the Lough within four miles of Dungannon and killed one hundred people, sparing none of what quality, age or sex soever, besydes many burned to death. We kill man, woman and child; horse, beast and whatsoever we find.

Sir Arthur's civilizing mission was continued by Oliver Cromwell, who thanked God for presiding over the mass slaughter of Catholic women and children in Drogheda and Wexford. British violence, robbery and destruction continued through the eighteenth and nineteenth centuries. Sir Arthur Chichester had warned in 1600: 'It is famine and not the sword that must reduce this country to what is

---

*Review of *Ireland Since the Famine* by F.S.L. Lyons; *Governing Without Consensus* by Richard Rose; *Ireland's English Question* by Patrick O'Farrell.

expected', and the British government made full use of both. At least one and a half million people died in the potato famine of the mid-nineteenth century. Many more emigrated. As the British violence met, inevitably, with violent Irish resistance, the racist fury of British ruling-class thinking knew no bounds. 'Ireland,' wrote the former Radical, Thomas Carlyle, 'is like a half-starved rat that crosses the path of an elephant. What must the elephant do? Squelch it – by heavens – squelch it!'

Such thoughts, no doubt in cruder form, spurred on the hordes of British barbarians who ravaged Ireland – from General Lake in 1798 ('nothing but terror will keep them in order') to the Black and Tans after the First World War. Anti-Irish racism and anti-Catholic sectarianism was planted by Britain with the settlers, and fostered by continuing British violence. The doctrine of racial and religious superiority was rooted deep in the Protestant settlers, who were always ready to believe what they were told by British Tories and Christians – that their destiny was different and superior to that of the Papist natives. Sectarianism was used by the British government and by the local gentry and industrialists as and when it was needed. Subsidies, aristocratic messages of support and even arms were forthcoming for Orangemen when industry and property had to be protected from 'native' rebellion.

In his huge and powerful history, *Ireland Since the Famine*, Professor Lyons quarrels with the view that religious sectarianism in the North is the result of class and property divisions: 'Sectarianism has been there all the time, and can only be explained in terms that go deeper and further into Irish history than latter-day Marxists seem prepared to penetrate.' Further, too, apparently, than Professor Lyons seems prepared to penetrate, for in the course of 730 textual pages he does not tell us how and why this sectarianism took root, nor how it flourishes long after religious frenzy elsewhere in Europe has died away.

Yet some of the facts about the concurrence of class interest and Protestant fanaticism are right there in Mr Lyons's book. Industry, he tells us, grew fastest in Protestant Belfast. By the time Home Rule was on the British political agenda, the big landlords had safeguarded their property with the necessary legislation, but

> amongst the industrialists of the North East, membership of the great
> British free-trade area was vital. For them, the nationalist emphasis on

tariff autonomy under Home Rule spelt ruin, since it would condemn them, so they believed, to a protectionist regime that would expose them to retaliatory discrimination in the world outside, offering them as recompense only the impoverished Irish hinterland.

This led, the professor tells us, to a 'new burst of activity' among Unionists and 'a revival of the Orange Order' which had been dormant for several decades. Orangeism once more became respectable in Northern Ireland and in Britain. When the British Liberal government, backed by a large parliamentary majority, published their Home Rule Bill, the Tory Opposition roundly rejected the right of parliament so to 'imperil the rights' of Protestants in Ireland and of British businessmen to make profits out of Belfast industry. Tory lawyers and businessmen openly defied parliamentary decisions, until a permanently Protestant and reactionary junta was established in Northeast Ulster.

Sixty repressive years later, the Tories are still defending their junta in Northern Ireland with violence. But the bias of their economic class interest has shifted south. The Irish Republic is third in the list of countries receiving British exports – higher even than France, which has a population twenty times Ireland's. Civil strife in Ireland has to be avoided now to protect property in the South rather than in the North, and this calls for a policy of 'gradual de-escalation' from the theory and practice of Protestant Ascendancy. Both Labour and Tory governments in recent years have found this more difficult than they imagined, and the Tories in desperation have slipped back into their traditional Irish posture of military coercion and political procrastination.

One crucial question, therefore, about the North of Ireland today is: how strong would the Protestant Ascendancy in the North be without the support of the British Conservative Party which spawned and nourished it? Unhappily, there is no adequate answer to this in Professor Richard Rose's book, *Governing Without Consensus*. The book conjures up the picture of the professor sitting happily in his study contemplating piles of answered and codified questionnaires from one of the most successful social studies ever conducted. Suddenly, the window bursts open letting in a hurricane which scatters the papers into irretrievable chaos.

The 'Loyalty Survey' – the answers to the survey came from 757 Protestants and 534 Catholics in Northern Ireland and form the basis of Mr Rose's book – was conducted in the spring and summer of 1968. Two months after it was completed, the top of the pot of 'the Northern Ireland problem' was finally blown off by the banned Derry demonstration of 5 October. Events have since moved so fast that much of the survey is worse than useless. Professor Rose has tried feverishly to 'update' his material by writing a rather hasty account of events in 1969 and 1970 in the front of his book, but it doesn't work. His survey found that 45 per cent of the Protestants questioned 'disapprove of any measures to remain Protestant' and that almost half of these 'dislike the use of force'. I doubt whether such statistics have the slightest significance in 1971.

Mr Rose's last chapter is devoted to comparisons between the political situation in Northern Ireland and those of other regimes. The important comparisons are with those 'enclave' states, like Israel or Pakistan, set up on exclusively religious lines in the wake of direct imperial rule. Mr Rose mentions Israel once, in passing, and Pakistan not at all. After proving, according to his own formula, that the Northern Ireland regime is 'not legitimate', Mr Rose cannot suggest any policy for dealing with the situation there. 'To do nothing is to make a contribution to discord,' he writes, 'yet action is full of uncertainty.' Trapped by this dilemma, the professor seeks asylum in a few banalities from Abraham Lincoln and leaves us to work it out for ourselves.

It is a relief to turn from those dry pages to the lively account of Professor O'Farrell, from Sydney, who gets things the right way round with his title: *Ireland's English Question*. 'This book,' explains Mr O'Farrell, 'is given to the argument that religion was the fundamental barrier to Anglo-Irish relations.' He argues, first, that the various attempts by liberal landowners and civil servants to make concessions to Irish demands were doomed because of religious differences. In fact, the failure of reformers like Plunkett was rooted in their insistence on continuing British political rule.

Mr O'Farrell argues too that any opposition to British rule depended for success on the support of the Catholic Church. In 'proving' this, he grossly underestimates the influence within the Irish nationalist movement of men and women who saw beyond national freedom to economic and social emancipation. The tradition spreads from Wolfe Tone (whose role is monstrously underplayed in this book) through James Finton Lalor and John Mitchel of the Young Ireland movement, through James Larkin and James Connolly down to Bernadette Devlin, Michael Farrell, Eamonn McCann and the growing group of socialists in the official IRA. Their views were never predominant in the nationalist movement, but neither were they, as Mr O'Farrell tends to suggest, entirely without influence.

He is right to point out that calls for social and economic freedom in Ireland are hollow unless accompanied by the demand for an end to British rule. James Connolly understood very well, and died proving, that no socialist will be taken seriously in Ireland unless he or she is also a Republican. With Connolly in the Dublin Post Office at Easter, 1916, were men who openly reviled his socialist opinions. Connolly fought with them unconditionally. He also predicted, more powerfully than many 'pure' nationalists, that if Ireland was partitioned and 'Black Ulster' hived off in a separate statelet, political and economic development on both sides of the border would be held up, and in the North there would be a 'carnival of reaction' until the connection was cut.

But Connolly also pointed out that a nationalist movement which looked no further than Home Rule, and which submitted itself to the reactionary hierarchy of the Church, was doomed at best to disillusionment, at worst to sectarian civil war. Connolly knew that 'there are more poor Protestants in the North of Ireland than poor Catholics', and he spent the latter part of his life seeking to inject into the nationalist movement a socialist consciousness. He called for an Irish workers' republic which would guarantee political and social as well as religious freedom.

John Mitchel of Young Ireland had it right 123 years ago when he wrote:

> In fact, religious hatred has been kept alive in Ireland longer than anywhere else in Christendom, just for the simple reason that Irish landlords and British statesmen found their own account in it; and so soon as Irish landlordism and British dominion are finally rooted out of the country, it will be heard of no longer in Ireland.

None of these three professors can improve on that.

New Statesman, December 1971

Enniskillen, Ken Livingstone, and the media

Ken Livingstone attacked the Enniskillen bombing last week. He did so clearly and unequivocally. He made the point in two radio broadcasts and a television programme, and at a speech for the Troops Out Movement, that the planting of bombs among the civilian population is indefensible *and* counterproductive. It kills and maims innocent people, and sets back the cause, however commendable, of the bombers. When the Troops Out Movement meeting opened with a minute's silence in respect for the dead at Enniskillen, Ken Livingstone stood with the rest.

I report this, I think, exclusively.

This is not because I was the only person listening to the broadcasts. The speech was widely reported in all the newspapers on 17 November but the attack on the bombing was pretty well ignored.

Instead, the *Star* led its front page with an enormous headline: THE WIDOW MAKER. The gist of the article which followed, and continued on pages 4 and 5, was that Ken Livingstone was directly responsible for the widows and orphans of murdered men in Northern Ireland. The *Mail* and the *Sun* published long articles which drew on past quotations from Ken Livingstone to show that he was in some way responsible for IRA bombings in Britain and in Ireland. *Today*, under a heading 'Madness of Livingstone', concluded: 'If madmen weren't banned from becoming MPs we'd have to say Ken Livingstone was insane. Criminally insane.'

This fever spread right through the press. The *Times* and the *Independent* both carried hysterical leaders – 'Whipping Mr Livingstone' and 'The IRA's savage cheerleader'.

How could all this have been written about someone who had quite plainly condemned the Enniskillen bombings? The answer is that Ken Livingstone, unlike pretty well all other politicians, did not stop at horrified reaction. He went on to give his view about the situation in Ireland, which has, as far as I know, been quite consistent ever since he came into politics. It is founded on the following two propositions:

1. That the Northern Ireland state is a fag-end of a colony, which is founded on domination by Protestants (60 per cent), over the Catholics

(40 per cent); that as long as this state goes on it will engender violence from both sides; that the state is underpinned by the presence of British troops; and that the withdrawal of British troops is a necessary condition for the ending of the Northern Ireland state and for some hope of eventual peace.

2. That the IRA and its political wing Sinn Fein represent a substantial section of the beleaguered Northern Ireland minority; and that any settlement of the problem will have to involve them.

The first of these propositions is not unique to Ken Livingstone. Indeed, as far as it is possible to judge, it is shared by the majority of the British people.

British public opinion on these rather important matters is tested very rarely. Gallup last asked a question about British troops' withdrawal from Northern Ireland *in 1981*. Thirty-seven per cent wanted troops out at once, 17 per cent in five years; and 33 per cent wanted them to remain until a settlement was reached. A clear majority, therefore, wanted the troops out whether there was a political settlement or not.

NOP last asked about this in November 1984, immediately after the Brighton bombings. The question was very loaded: 'Should Britain withdraw its troops and leave the island to sort itself out between Catholic and Protestant politicians of Ulster and the Republic.' Even so, however, and despite the very strong feelings about the Brighton bombings, 45 per cent answered yes, and 44 per cent wanted the troops to remain.

MORI asked about troops in Ireland in January this year. Twenty-two per cent wanted troops out immediately; 39 per cent after a pre-set period, and 34 per cent thought they should remain as long as the violence continued. This poll showed a marked shift (from 53 per cent to 61 per cent) in favour of withdrawing troops unilaterally now or at some set time in the future.

MORI also asked about the political position of Northern Ireland. Only 29 per cent thought it should remain part of the United Kingdom (compared to 56 per cent who thought it should become part of the Republic or an independent statelet). This matches a Gallup poll in May 1986 which found 26 per cent for Northern Ireland staying in the UK; 24 per cent for unity with the Republic and 35 per cent for independence.

Sorry about all the figures, but they tend to show, don't they, that the majority of the British people support the political aims of Sinn Fein. As for recognizing the IRA and talking to them, that was done in the 1970s by the Tory government (the talks were organized by William Whitelaw, now deputy prime minister) and by the Labour leadership (Harold Wilson himself met IRA leaders in Dublin).

Perhaps all these people are widow-makers or criminally insane. But if, as I suspect, they are not, if Ken Livingstone is voicing the view of most people that there must be some political initiative on Ireland, and that the only credible initiative is withdrawal of British troops, and the end of British support for the Northern Ireland state, why the fantastic hysteria in the press? Ken Livingstone himself believes the answer is political. He suspects a desperate conspiracy to keep the real issue – withdrawal of troops – off the political agenda. I tend rather to the view that the press needs a scapegoat for public anger and dismay after the Enniskillen horror. The truth may lie between the two. Either way, it is, for journalists, another miserable example of the current fashion for replacing news and rational comment with abuse and prejudice.

Finally, by the way, does the *Star* really believe Ken Livingstone is a widow-maker? If so, why did they offer him a weekly column only a few weeks ago? Ken Livingstone tells me he was approached by Michael Gabbert, then editor of the *Star*, and offered the column vacated by Labour MP Joe Ashton.

'The *Star*?' Ken replied, surprised. 'Isn't that all tits and bums?' 'Not at all,' replied Gabbert. 'We really need a lively left-wing columnist.'

Ken Livingstone says he went to look at the *Star*, found it was all tits and bums, and turned the offer down.

UK Press Gazette, November 1987

Britain out

My proposal is very simple: the British government should declare that it intends to withdraw its troops from Ireland forever; and that it will no longer sustain a separate state in the North of Ireland. It should set an irrevocable date for that withdrawal and make it clear that the decision is irrevocable. To this proposal there are four familiar objections.

1. 'We owe the people of Northern Ireland a duty. They have been promised again and again by consecutive British governments that their state will be sustained by Britain. How can we break these pledges to them without their agreement?'

It is quite true that successive British governments have made these promises. They are enshrined in the legislation which governs the North of Ireland, and in the recent Anglo-Irish agreement.

However, no promise made by a past government can bind a present or future government. If a government decides that the state which it set up and promised to sustain is no more than a breeding ground for religious prejudice and discrimination, it can and should break the promise to sustain it.

If there is a 'duty' to the majority in the North of Ireland, there is also a 'duty' to the minority. Even the original constitution of Northern Ireland demanded of the new state's government that it should not discriminate against the Catholics on religious grounds. This pledge has been consistently broken.

2. 'The Protestants are a majority, who have voted again and again to uphold the Northern Irish state. How can any democrat flout the will of the majority?'

The Unionists or Protestants of Northern Ireland have *not* always been the majority. The last elections held in all Ireland (in 1918) returned seventy-three Sinn Fein, six Nationalists, and twenty-two Unionists. The Unionists were then a minority. They had *always* been, in all Ireland, a minority. They were created into a majority by Lloyd George and his henchmen, who divided Ireland, precisely so that a majority could be made out of a minority.

Any minority which loses an election can always claim that, if the boundaries were changed, the election results could be made to look different. If a separate state had been created out of the city of Manchester after the British general election of 1987, then Labour would have won the election there. The majority in the North of Ireland is not a true majority at all, but a cosseted minority which persuaded the British government, by defying the declared will of an elected parliament, to shift the goal-posts, and make it into a majority.

3. 'Well, if the Protestants of the North of Ireland are not a majority, they are certainly a large minority which fears, in a united Ireland, that its rights to worship and its individual freedoms will be trodden underfoot by a Catholic majority.'

There is certainly a deep fear of such persecution against Protestants in a united Ireland. This fear has hardly been allayed by the arrogant and offensive way in which the Catholic Church, almost without opposition, has interfered in politics in the South. When James Connolly predicted that there would be a 'carnival of reaction' North and South if Ireland were divided, he was dreading not just black Ulster, a sectarian Protestant state in the North, but the untrammelled influence of the Catholic Church in the South. (Connolly was a Roman Catholic, though a bitter opponent of that church's interference in politics and individual freedom.)

His prediction has been fulfilled in the South as it has been in the North. Again and again the Catholic hierarchy has intervened to roll back progress in the South. The attitude of the Church to divorce, to abortion, to homosexuality and to a whole host of issues which affect individual choices is as backward in the South of Ireland as it is anywhere else in the world. Similarly, the progress towards a national health service and to a non-sectarian education policy has consistently been obstructed by a church which believes that health and education are matters not for human choice but of the ineluctable (and undebatable) law of God.

Protestant fears, therefore, have some force. But how best are minority rights protected in any society? Are they best protected by partition, by isolation of the minority in a separate state of their own? Throughout the world, where these problems of racial and religious minorities are repeated over and over again in a thousand different forms, separation and partition of communities on racial or religious lines merely inflames the differences, institutionalizes them in politics and in government, and turns one former minority, fearful of persecution, into a persecuting majority, seeking others to discriminate against, to mock, bully and suppress.

Guarantees of religious and individual freedoms are what they say they are: *guarantees*, which every society owes to its minorities. The way to ensure that the Jewish or black minorities in Britain are safe from persecution is to hold out to them the rights of free citizenship which are available to everyone else; to ensure that there is no privilege afforded anyone because of their race or religion; and to persecute racial and religious persecutors.

Wherever such guarantees are upheld, they ensure freedom for religious and racial minorities a thousand times more effectively than do separate states which shore up the political power of gods or skin colour over human beings, and create and persecute other minorities.

4. 'If Britain pulls out of Ireland, there will be a bloodbath. The Protestants, all of them, will fight to the death rather than be part of a united Ireland.'

This is by far the most powerful of the arguments against British withdrawal from Northern Ireland. In support of it are called up the Ulster Covenant of 1912, and the undoubted determination in those days of almost all the Protestant people in the North to fight for their new state; the extraordinary solidarity of the Protestant people now against even the most minor move towards a united Ireland, such as the Anglo-Irish agreement; and the continued success of extremist Protestant ranters like the Reverend Ian Paisley. These are all signs, it is said, that the Protestants would fight with far more determination, unity and military skill than the Catholic minority has ever done. The violence of the IRA, it is said, would be as nothing compared to the violence which would be unleashed on the Protestant side if the British decided to withdraw.

It is a strong argument, which is often won because it is not answered. But there are many flaws in it.

The first is that the situation is very different to what it was in 1912 and 1922. Then, as we have seen, there were many wealthy and powerful British supporters of the Protestant cause. Northeast Ulster was one of the richest places on earth, and there was a lot of money to be made by a lot of rich people if it stayed in the Imperial Free Trade Area. None of these arguments applies now. Northern Ireland is one of the poorest places in Europe. It suffers hugely from its isolation and its divisions. There is no reason, economic or otherwise, why anyone in the world should support a Protestant rebellion in favour of a sectarian and discriminatory state.

In 1912 and 1913 there was profound support and sympathy among the British people for the Protestant cause. A deep imperial solidarity was tapped by the Tory Party in monster meetings and demonstrations. Today, there is very little such support. Outside the coteries of MI5 fanatics and military seminars, no one feels very strong sympathy for the Ulster Protestants. For every act of terror carried out by the IRA, there is another by a Protestant extremist organization, and there is little sign that people in Britain distinguish very carefully between the two.

The bedrock of British and international support, upon which the Protestant people could rest their case and from which they could draw money and arms in 1912, is no longer available to them.

What about their Protestant solidarity? Would they stand and fight together?

The existence of the Northern Irish state, and the support it gets from the British government and armed forces, is the central prop of Protestant solidarity.

One of the most significant developments of recent times in the North of Ireland is the fragmentation of the old Unionist monolith. This has shown itself, first, in the splits which have riven the Unionist Party – the splits to the right, which led to the Democratic Unionist Party under Ian Paisley, and to the left, which led to the formation of the small Alliance Party. Even more remarkable than the formal splits between the Unionist parties are the different views which emerge from every corner of Ulster Unionism about the best way forward for Northern Ireland Protestants. Some argue for the old order, the 'connection' with Britain; others for complete integration with Britain – another county of Scotland, perhaps; others for 'devolution' – a separate government like the old Stormont parliament; others for outright independence from Britain. Fifty years ago, it was hard to find an Ulster Unionist who would speak ill of the British government, especially if it was a Tory government. Today in the North of Ireland there is among the Protestant people a profound opposition, rising in many places to hatred, to Mrs Thatcher's government. For all the froth and indignation which pours from the mouth of the Reverend Ian

Paisley and his supporters, for all the huge crowds he still draws, the old Unionist monolith is split all ends up. A sudden shock, like the withdrawal of British troops, would open those splits up wide, and lead, among the Protestants, more to dissension than to unity.

The unity of the Protestant monolith in the past has depended on one factor above all others: the presence of British troops and the support of the British government. As long as the troops and the government from Britain are there to protect them, there is every reason for the Protestants to appear united. Their unity and their solidarity has been sustained for seventy years by the armed might of Britain.

Kick away that prop, remove British support for the Northern Ireland state and withdraw the troops – whom then will the Protestants be fighting? Against whom will they be called upon to display their solidarity and their unity?

Separatist Protestants will be left suddenly high and dry without any armed protection for their state save what they themselves, without international support or sympathy, can provide. For the first time in history they will have to fight on their own.

It would be foolish to dispute that there may be numbers of Protestants who will be prepared to fight, and to unleash all the fury of four centuries on the neighbouring Catholic population, and on anyone else who comes to their defence. But the degree of involvement in such violence, the commitment to it, how widespread that commitment would be – all these are matters which are impossible to predict with any certainty. What must be likely is that the Protestant community would be far more divided and anxious as to their future than ever they have been in the past. Some would argue for an all-out war, which would almost certainly end in all-out defeat. Others would be unhappy about laying down their families' lives in such an uneven contest. Very few people sign up to die for their country if they know their country is going to lose. Even less do so if their country no longer exists.

The degree of violence, then, would depend very much on the way in which the withdrawal was accomplished. If there was any uncertainty or dithering in the withdrawal, this would fire the Protestant enthusiasm for a battle. Moreover, any British troop withdrawal would have to be accompanied by a ruthless disarming of the sectarian elements which are currently armed by the British state. The UDR – the Protestant militia – would have to be disarmed. So would the Royal

Ulster Constabulary. The slightest sign that the British government was still supporting the Protestant supremacy would have to be removed once and for all.

The chief answer to the 'bloodbath' argument, however, does not depend on speculating on the likely balance of forces after a withdrawal. It rests on the *positive potential* on both sides of the border if the British troops are withdrawn. If carried out with a mixture of determination and compassion, there is every chance that such a withdrawal could break the log-jam of sectarian hatreds and suspicions which have plagued so much of Irish history; and could hold out a genuine alternative of free choice and free worship. There is a chance, after withdrawal, that Irish labour, so long truncated by religious feuds between workers, might come together to demand the new Ireland of which Connolly dreamed. In the shock of the sudden collapse of the old order, the positive sides of the people of Ireland of both religions could well prevail over the narrow superstitions which have kept them at each other's throats for so long.

Connolly warned of the vampires at the feast of the dismemberment of the corpse of Ireland. If the British connection is finally cut, if the two halves of the dismembered body are put together again, there is at least a hope that the carnival of reaction might be ended; and the vampires shooed away forever.

Is it really the case, after all, that Protestants and Catholics in Northern Ireland are doomed forever to hatred and strife? Do they disagree about everything, fight about everything? For all the gloomy history of that part of the world, there is plenty of evidence that when social issues become so large that they obscure religion, Protestant and Catholic people can unite. Whenever that happens, the people of Northern Ireland can suddenly become as strong and confident as any other people in the world.

The rebellion of 1798, as we have seen, was led by Protestants. In the 1907 Belfast dock strike, in the campaigns against unemployment in the 1930s, even in the battle to save the National Health Service in 1988, religious differences have been shrugged aside, and the people of Belfast have forged themselves into a fighting force which seemed, momentarily, as if it could change their world.

It is on these occasions that the Orange and Green Drums have been banged most fervently, have shattered the fragile unity, and driven the two communities back into their laagers. The existence of the Orange state has made that relatively easy. The most powerful of all the arguments for ending the British state and for the withdrawal of British troops is that the impact of the change would remove the sanctuary of the Protestant laager, and encourage the more positive, optimistic and confident of the Protestant people to forge unity across the religious divide; to demand – and create – a carnival of peace, prosperity and progress, North and South.

Why, therefore, when it costs much more than it earns for Britain, when it leads all the time to the death of British troops and to the insecurity of British ministers – *why* does the British government hang on limpet-like to the excrescence of the Orange state?

Some say it is for strategic reasons: that NATO bases in Ireland are crucial. This argument has little force. Britain left Cyprus nearly thirty years ago, and British bases have been sustained on that island all that time, in spite of the island's invasion by Turkey, and its enforced partition.

Some say that Northern Ireland is now an indispensable training ground for the security services; where the SAS can practise shooting people in the streets; where telephone-tappers, surveillance freaks, spooks and spies can carry out their sinister trade without check or accountability.

There is no doubt that the security services *are* free to roam at will in Northern Ireland, and many and fearful have been the results. Powerful though they are in the corridors of power, however, their operations are not reason enough on their own for Britain to stay in Northern Ireland.

The real reason can probably be found in the old rhyme of Hilaire Belloc:

Always keep a-hold of nurse
For fear of meeting something worse.

This 'something worse' might be the 'bloodbath' which so many people fear after withdrawal. In the past, British governments, after deciding to withdraw from colonies, have not been overly squeamish about bloodbaths. When Britain left India there was a bloodbath. When Britain left the Central African Federation there was a bloodbath. Yet no one but the most oddball reactionaries argued then (or argue now) that Britain should not have left these places.

The 'something worse', therefore, is probably not so much a possible bloodbath as the fear of a 'defeat'.

After each IRA bombing (on the whole Protestant bombings are not reported with the same indignation), the cry goes up: 'we must not give in to terrorism'. The argument is that the withdrawal of troops from Northern Ireland would be seen as a defeat for the British government by the IRA. Such an argument can survive in perpetuity. *Forever*, it can be argued, Britain must keep troops in Ireland for fear of appearing to be beaten by the IRA.

The best way, however, to end the violence is to root out the cause of it. The cause of IRA violence is not the moral degeneracy or otherwise of IRA members. It is the permanent persecution of a substantial minority who live in a state over which they can never have the slightest influence. As long as that persecution – and that state – remain, violence, and the sectarianism which breeds it, are certain to continue.

The fear of 'defeat' therefore, is nothing more nor less than political paralysis. It prolongs violence. It sustains sectarianism. It holds out no prospect of any solution – just another decade of hatred and slaughter; and another, and another.

It is time the British people shook their government out of its paralysis, by demanding that the troops come home. British governments and troops in Ireland have caused nothing but wretchedness and disorder for six centuries. Nothing would become them like the leaving it.

From Counterblasts 8: *Ireland: Why Britain Must Get Out,* 1988

12. Injustices

An eye for an eye or a taste for blood?

Eldon Griffiths, a Tory MP who is paid by the Police Federation, is very worried about murder. So he asks us all to commit it.

He is upset by increasing violence against human beings. So he asks us all to join him in even more violence against human beings.

He yearns for the good old days when murderers were kept in condemned cells, looked after by special warders, given a special meal on the night before their execution, and then, one early morning, frog-marched by four strong men, stood on a trap door, blindfolded while a priest or parson muttered some last duties, and plummeted through the floor with a noose around their necks.

The technology of hanging is, as the old hangman Pierrepoint reported to a Royal Commission in 1950, very awkward. He had known of cases where the rope was fractionally long, and the victim's head came off, making a nasty mess all over Mr Pierrepoint's equipment. Then there was a time when the rope was too short and the wretched prisoner choked to death.

Another unpleasant thing which happens, according to Mr Pierrepoint, on every single occasion is that the hanged person's stomach splits and his bowels spill out beneath him.

None of this worries Mr Griffiths and his friends in the very least. For them, the bowel-spilling is a sort of inferior substitute for the hanging, drawing and quartering with which law and order enthusiasts enforced their will in the old days.

During the parliamentary debate on hanging this week, Griffiths and Co. will have resorted to 'argument' in an attempt to persuade us why we should all join in these prison murders. He will have said that the death penalty *deters* other people from committing murders; and that however unpleasant hanging one person may be, it saves other people from being murdered in the streets.

As proof of this theory, he will show that the numbers of murders have gone up since capital punishment was abolished in 1965. That is true. It is also true that more crimes of every description have been committed since that time.

Manslaughters, for instance (unintended killings), malicious woundings, and rapes have increased by a far higher percentage than have murders, although none of these was a capital offence.

Murder is very rare. Only 376 people were indicted for murder in 1977, which is a tiny percentage of the number of people at risk (compare it to the thousands of people every year who are killed on the roads). It is also very largely a domestic crime. As Louis Blom-Cooper and Professor Terence Morris point out in their recent pamphlet, *Murder in England and Wales since 1957*:

'More than half the persons indicted for murder each year have a familiar relationship, and up to two-thirds have had a personal relationship of some duration and intensity with the victim.'

As a result the number of murders fluctuates violently from year to year. There is very little overall pattern, because most murders are explained by upset personal relationships.

The types of murders committed show perfectly clearly that murder is not a crime from which people are deterred. That's why all the evidence shows that capital punishment makes no difference to the murder rate at all. In America, some states have abolished capital punishment. Some haven't. The murder rates are the same in both. The Royal Commission on Capital Punishment which sat for four years concluded: 'The general conclusion which we have reached is that there is no clear evidence that the abolition of capital punishment has led to an increase in the homicide rate or that its reintroduction has led to a fall.'

There is *no proof at all* that murdering murderers stops murders. Why then do Mr Griffiths and his friends seek to increase the murder rate by hanging people?

The answer goes all the way back to the most primitive barbarism. It is summed up in the old Mosaic law: 'An eye for an eye; a tooth for a tooth.'

Griffiths' campaign comes up from the dark ages through all the years when people were hanged for stealing rabbits or even for making love to people to whom they were not married. It is the product of a divided society where the only remedies available to people who offend against that society's laws are the most awful retribution and violence.

Socialist Worker, July 1979

Left to rot

I am sending out thirteen Christmas cards today to people in prison for life. All were convicted of murder.

Is this soppy philanthropy? Not at all. It is because I firmly believe that all thirteen have spent a total of 144 years in prison for crimes someone else committed.

The first cards go to Paddy Hill and Hugh Callaghan (Gartree Prison), Billy Power and Richard McIlkenny (Wormwood Scrubs), Gerry Hunter (Wakefield), and Johnny Walker (Long Lartin).

These six were convicted in 1975 of the Birmingham bombings – in which twenty-seven innocent people were done to death in pubs. For twelve years, they have been insisting that they had nothing to do with it.

They confessed to the crime after signs of nitroglycerine were allegedly found on a hand of two of them soon after the bombings.

In court all six denied their confessions, which they said had been beaten out of them by systematic torture.

The 'Griess test' which proved positive on the two men's hands was carried out by Dr Frank Skuse who has now retired, early, from the Home Office forensic laboratory at Chorley, Lancs.

In 1985, Granada's *World in Action* commissioned two independent scientists to do the same test.

The then head of the Chorley laboratory, Mr George Walker, wrote to one of them, Mr David Baldock, giving details of the 'recipe' used in the test.

Using exactly the same recipe, Mr Baldock showed that a positive result could have been got from lots of other things apart from nitro-glycerine – like playing cards which the men had been using just before their arrest.

The Home Office did their own tests, which confirmed this.

Then the Home Office swiftly moved the goalposts. They now claim that the recipe used by Dr Frank Skuse was *not* the same as the head of their own (Home Office) laboratory had stated! Now they say Dr Skuse used 0.1 per cent of caustic soda – not 1.0 per cent, as Mr Walker had written.

But in another programme a few weeks ago, *World in Action* produced Dr Hugh Black, a former Home Office explosives expert, who appeared for the defence of the six men.

He said Dr Skuse told him at the time that he used 1.0 per cent caustic soda. He has notes to prove it. He told me: 'I am absolutely certain about this.'

Dr Skuse will not talk to me. Neither will Mr Walker.

The Home Office say they have a 'guide paper' distributed early in 1975 by Dr Skuse which says he used 0.1 per cent. I asked the Home Office if I could see the guide paper. 'No,' came the reply. Could I quote from it. 'No,' came the reply.

How could they refer to a document as proof, and not even produce it?

'It forms part of the evidence for the Home Secretary to consider referring this case to the courts,' was the spokesman's reply.

Six men's freedom hangs on this decimal point.

Sixteen months ago the Home Office set up an 'urgent' inquiry into the case. There will be no decision before Christmas.

The second batch of cards go to Paul Hill (Wormwood Scrubs), Paddy Armstrong (Gartree), Carole Richardson (Styal) and Gerard Conlon (Wormwood Scrubs). They were convicted in 1975 of pub bombings at Guildford, which killed five people.

The only evidence against them were their confessions in police custody, which they all insisted had been beaten out of them.

Soon after their conviction, an active IRA unit was arrested after a siege at Balcombe Street, London.

One of the men arrested said that he had taken part in the Guildford bombings. The people convicted, he said, had nothing to do with it.

Scientific evidence about explosives linked the Guildford bombings to others committed by the IRA after the four were in custody.

This evidence was struck out of the forensic scientists' reports in the Balcombe Street trial – by the order of the police and the Director of Public Prosecutions.

After a book and a television programme about the case this year, the Home Office set up an 'urgent' inquiry. It has been going on four months. There will be no decision before Christmas.

My other cards go to Michael Hickey (Park Lane), Vincent Hickey (Long Lartin) and Jimmy Robinson (Gartree). These three men were convicted in 1979 of the murder of newspaper boy Carl Bridgewater.

They were named in a confession statement, made in police custody by a 52-year-old Irishman Pat Molloy.

Molloy, who has since died in prison, denied his confession from the moment he could see his lawyer.

He claimed it was beaten out of him by the police.

This year another prosecution witness came forward to say he lied in court.

The Home Office set up an urgent inquiry.

Three months later the investigating officers have not got round to interviewing the two main prosecution witnesses who retracted their evidence.

There will be no decision before Christmas.

I am sending no cards to the Home Office, whose officials will, no doubt, enjoy a sumptuous Christmas, quite oblivious to the distress caused by their interminable and ridiculous delays.

I leave them with this seasonal message:

God Rot Ye Merry Gentlemen,
Does Nothing You Dismay?

Daily Mirror, December 1986

An innocent confesses

A young black lad, who gave police a fifty-page confession to his part in the Tottenham riots, walked free from a court last week.

Howard Kerr, seventeen, was dragged from his bed early one morning last October by twenty policemen.

Barefoot and half-naked he was hauled off to Barnet police station.

Howard has a reading age of seven and a half. A recent report from teachers at his special school stresses that he finds conversation with adults very difficult.

At the police station, he wasn't allowed to see a lawyer or a friend or any member of his family.

Alone and unrepresented, he was interviewed for nine hours over two and a half days. Detective Constables Brian Faulkner and Paul Biggerstaff asked him where he was on 6 October, the night of the riots at Broadwater Farm, Tottenham.

He said he was in Windsor with his girlfriend. The officers said they didn't believe him. They said they were sure he was taking part in the riots.

Then Howard Kerr changed his story. He gave them a long, rambling and detailed description of his part in the riots.

- He told them he threw stones at the police.
- He said he threw petrol bombs.
- He described a petrol bomb 'factory' where the bombs were stacked in milk crates.
- He named at least twenty other rioters.
- He admitted watching while other black youths hacked at a body on the ground where PC Keith Blakelock died.

Howard's confession filled fifty pages – he was charged with affray. But even before his confession was over, the police had strong evidence that Howard *was* in Windsor on the night of the riots.

Claire Speakman, Howard's girlfriend, said he had been in Windsor and Slough until 11.20 on the night of 6 October. Claire's mother, Mrs Margaret Speakman, said she drove Howard and his friend to Slough station at 11.20 that night.

Seven people backed up Claire's story that she was with Howard and his friend in a Windsor pub all evening.

Then Howard's solicitor found a bus conductress who confirmed Howard's story that he and a friend got the last bus to Tottenham, arriving there shortly before two in the morning – when the riots were over.

The alibi was cast-iron. The confession was completely false. Still the charges were not dropped.

Last Thursday, more than *three months* after Howard was first charged, the prosecution offered no evidence against him. Howard's lawyers asked for costs against the police.

Susannah Johnston for the police said the confession was 'full of detail' and had been signed. The prosecution has 'no choice but to proceed to this stage,' she said.

Howard Kerr's barrister, Stephen Irwin, said that detail in a signed confession was common to many cases of suspect confessions in the past.

'The detail is there because suggestions are made in interviews which are then taken up,' he said.

Tottenham magistrates awarded costs out of public funds. Howard Kerr was discharged.

Outside the court, he said: 'I was frightened, so I just told them what I thought they wanted to know. I'm glad it's all over now. Why did it last so long?'

Daily Mirror, March 1986

Stalker

In the autumn of 1982 three policemen in Northern Ireland were killed by a landmine planted by the IRA. At once, the Royal Ulster Constabulary plotted their revenge. Acting on information provided by one of their informers in the IRA – who has been paid many, many thousands of pounds – they identified five Republicans who were said to have been responsible for the landmine, and a hay shed which was, according to the informer, used by the IRA to hoard weapons. There is a lot of evidence that the informer's information was incorrect, and that he himself 'set up' the shed as a possible arms store by planting in it two old rifles, without ammunition.

The Special Branch of the RUC organized the assassinations of the five men – three of them were gunned down in one car, the other two in another. Two young men, one of whom had no connection whatsoever with the IRA or the Republican movement, were then shot in the shed. One of them was killed instantly, and the other was terribly wounded. Cover stories based on a completely fictional sequence of events pretending that the murdered men had defied the police were prepared by Special Branch before the shootings and issued to the press immediately afterwards. The official pathologists stayed away. Much of the evidence of what really happened was destroyed. For instance, the cartridge cases from the police guns in one of the murders were collected up and taken away by the police. A story circulated suggesting that they had been swept up in a priest's cassock as he administered the last rites.

So crude were the murders and so bungled the cover-up that there was an outcry among the Catholic community in Northern Ireland. This led, eventually, to the prosecution of certain junior police officers involved in the shooting (though not of the Special Branch men who organized it). When the cases came to court, several policemen lied, on instructions from the Special Branch and the security services. The defendants were found not guilty of murder. Some were congratulated by the judge for bringing the IRA men to the 'final court of justice'.

Not surprisingly, this ugly charade did not satisfy the spokesmen for the Catholic community. They demanded an independent inquiry. The British government of the day was struggling with yet another of its 'initiatives' to 'bring the two communities in Northern Ireland together', and a sop was needed to pacify the 'moderate' wing of the Catholic community – the Social and Democratic Labour Party, which had been losing ground at the ballot box to Sinn Fein. An inquiry was conjured up. It had to be an inquiry which appeared to be thorough and fair, but whose conclusions did nothing to disturb the forces of law and order: the Royal Ulster Constabulary, their Special Branch and, crucially, MI5.

There was a well-tried method for just such an inquiry: a call to senior officers of an 'outside' police force to conduct a secret investigation and issue a secret report. This has been the traditional manner by which police malpractice in Britain has been covered up for generations. In comes the 'outside police force'. It sets up a long, thorough and fair inquiry. It interviews all possible witnesses, thoroughly and fairly. Then it reports that although there were one or two procedures that went a bit wrong, and perhaps even one or two junior police officers who acted in an over-enthusiastic manner, there was nothing fundamentally wrong about the way the police conducted themselves.

For this case, which involved murder, deceit and perjury on a grand scale, the police inquiry had to be on a grand scale too. No less a VIP than the Deputy Chief Constable of the biggest provincial police force in Britain – Greater Manchester – was called in to command it. John Stalker was an excellent choice. Nothing in his life had distinguished him as a subversive. It is true that his father had been a Labour man, and an admirer of the *Daily Herald*, but he himself had not shown any such dangerous symptoms. He was a highly competent detective, tough as nails when it came to dealing with race riots in Moss Side or even demonstrators against the Home Secretary. There was nothing 'soft' about his attitude to organizations like the National Council of Civil Liberties. He had nothing but contempt for the 'hard left' Manchester Council and their representatives on the Police Committee. He had been vetted (twice) by MI5, and drilled in the top school of police officers.

What was required of Mr Stalker and his team was summed up by a Belfast community leader, whom he quotes in the book he has published: 'Get in and get out as quickly as you can. Tell the government what they want to hear: that the RUC are a fine brave force.' Very quickly, however, almost as soon as he got to Belfast, John Stalker started to ignore this advice. He interviewed hundreds of police officers, including some very senior ones, under caution. He found out exactly what had happened to the six dead men. He was shocked, not just by what he calls 'the methods of a Central American assassination squad', but by the immediate and consistent efforts of the Chief Constable of the RUC and his colleagues in the Special Branch to obstruct his inquiry. His central complaint, which he pursued for eighteen months, was that a tape-recording of what had happened before, during and after the murder in the hay shed was in the hands of the

RUC, but was not made available to him.

He wrote an interim report and submitted it in September 1985. The report recommended the prosecution of a number of officers for conspiracy to murder and to obstruct the course of justice. Whether or not very much more senior officers should be prosecuted for these and other offences, he made clear, depended on whether or not he could get hold of the tape.

The report caused such a sensation in the RUC offices, where it was delivered, that the Chief Constable hung on to it for five months before he handed it over to the Director of Public Prosecutions. During those five months, the authorities (I am sorry to use that vague phrase, but the authorities *are* vague) did everything in their power to solve what had become for them 'the Stalker problem'. On the one hand (the carrot), Stalker was advised by his Inspector of Constabulary, Sir Philip Myers, and his Chief Constable, James Anderton, to apply for a couple of chief constable's jobs which happened to be vacant. They offered themselves as referees if he chose to do so. On the other (the stick), secret police inquiries started into a Manchester Conservative businessman, Kevin Taylor, who had been John Stalker's friend. Inquiries were discreet at first, but they were what Mr Stalker calls 'a trawling operation' to see whether there was any dirt on the Deputy Chief Constable which could be flung at him at a later date if he persisted in his obstinacy.

He made it absolutely plain that he intended to get his hands on the tape, once and for all. He cleared the matter with the Inspector of Constabulary, with MI5, with the Chief Constable of the RUC, and most importantly with the Director of Public Prosecutions. He arranged to go to Belfast to get the tape. The visit was postponed at the request of the Inspector of Constabulary. Then it was postponed again. Finally, three days before his visit, Stalker was told to take extra leave because certain allegations (unspecified) had been made about certain associations (unspecified) with certain people (unnamed) of dubious repute in the Manchester area.

He was promptly removed from the Belfast inquiry, and replaced by the Chief Constable of West Yorkshire, Mr Colin Sampson, who was also instructed to carry out a full investigation into Mr Stalker. Stalker's association with Taylor, who had no criminal convictions, started as the main plank in Mr Sampson's platform. Mr Sampson discovered that at one of Mr Taylor's parties attended by Mr Stalker there had been some people with criminal convictions. One of them, whom Mr Stalker admitted knowing, had been convicted during the war, while a juvenile, of stealing two bags of potatoes; another of stealing a roll of sellotape valued at two pounds.

As this part of his inquiry ran rapidly into the dust, Mr Sampson turned in desperation to the use of police cars. He found that Mr Stalker used police cars rather less than most officers of his rank, but he did manage one or two unlikely journeys in police cars. The total amount of petrol used on these was worth slightly less than six pounds. The more Mr Sampson (who for this purpose had postponed his investigations into murder, lying and perjury in the RUC) 'looked into' Mr Stalker, the more the awful and extraordinary truth became clear: he really didn't have anything to hide. Nevertheless, Mr Sampson recommended that Stalker be suspended while the serious allegations about the bag of potatoes in 1944 and the six pounds' worth of dubious petrol were more thoroughly investigated. All this piffle was enthusiastically endorsed by the Chairman of the Police Complaints Authority, a brilliant lawyer called Clothier, and his deputy, a former Labour minister, Roland Moyle.

At the same time, a smear campaign was organized against Mr Stalker. Despite Stalker's furious (and accurate) denials, the *Daily Mail* published a story saying that he was suspected of involvement with criminals. *Panorama*, which had originally questioned Stalker's treatment, weighed in with another programme (by the same reporter, Peter Taylor) which had a very definite anti-Stalker bias. A prisoner called William McPhee gave a statement to the *Guardian* saying he had been approached in prison by two police officers (one with strong RUC connections) and offered lenient treatment if he would deliver a sinister package to Stalker's home. He refused. His statement was passed to the Police Complaints Authority, and nothing has been heard of it since.

But the smear campaign was not a success. Much of the media, including the *Manchester Evening News*, rallied to the Deputy Chief Constable. When the Manchester Police Committee, which, unlike the police force, has some elected people in it, saw the Sampson report, they gave a groan of disgust and disbelief, chucked it into the rubbish bin and ordered Stalker's immediate reinstatement.

Back in his office, however, he was snubbed by his boss, Chief Constable Anderton, sanctimonious, unstable, petulant and fanatical, who worked closer and closer with his new appointees to the top posts in the Manchester CID – in particular, Peter Topping, a freemason who once admitted to Stalker that, other things being equal, he preferred to work with colleagues who were masons. The final blow fell when Topping, who had never conducted a murder investigation in his life, announced that, in the dead of winter, he was taking Myra Hindley to Saddleworth Moor in an attempt to find the bodies of children murdered and buried there more than twenty years previously. Of this grotesque and, in winter, utterly futile exercise, Stalker was not even informed. Yet he had been involved in the original Moors Murders inquiry, and, in Anderton's absence, was theoretically in charge of the police force which undertook the search.

Even curiouser was the fact that John Stalker was kept off the Northern Ireland inquiry. He had been found guilty of nothing – he had been shown after ruthless investigation to be entirely clean. His inquiry in Northern Ireland was above reproach. Yet now, without any explanation, he was removed.

It seems to me that if Chief Constable Anderton or Chief Constable Hermon or Chief Constable Sampson want to hang onto a single shred of their reputation, they must sue – or resign. Police inspectors-general Sir Philip Myers and Sir Lawrence Byford must surely explain how they came to supervise this shambles. If the Chief Executive of Legal Services of MI5, Bernard Sheldon, wants to preserve the independence of the MI5, he must sue or resign. If Sir Cecil Clothier or Roland Moyle are concerned for the impartiality of the Police Complaints Authority, they must sue or resign. If Tom King can explain why he, three times, misled the House of Commons about the Stalker affair, he should do so, or sue, or resign. If Chief Superintendent Topping does not prefer masons as colleagues, he should sue.

If I guess right, however, there will be no writs and no resignations. All the murders, perjuries, lies, perversions of justice, disingenuousnesses, rudeness, callousness and plain filth which is unearthed here has had the desired result. As in Byron's 'Vision of Judgment', the people in charge float once more to the top and stay there:

> For all corrupted things are buoyed, like corks,
> By their own rottenness.

The card-players*

For several weeks after 21 November 1974 most Irish people in Birmingham took cover. Even the most respected and entrenched felt unsafe. Outrage and grief overwhelmed the city and spread far beyond its boundaries. Twenty-one people had been done to death. Another 162 had been injured, many of them maimed for life. Most were young and working-class. Many were of Irish origin. Not a single one of them could by any stretch of the imagination be held responsible for or even sympathetic to British government policy in Northern Ireland.

The universal horror at this, the biggest killing of civilians in British postwar history, was to some extent assuaged when the police announced on 24 November, three days after the bombing, that they were satisfied they had caught the 'men primarily responsible'. Next day, six Irishmen were charged. They all had some connection with the Republican movement in Birmingham. Five of them had been arrested as they tried to get on a ferry to Belfast to attend the funeral of James McDade, a prominent IRA member who had blown himself to pieces planting a bomb in Coventry. They had left Birmingham by train less than half an hour before the bombs went off, and the bombs were planted within a few hundred yards of Birmingham's New Street Station. Before long, it leaked out that at least three of the five men had recently handled nitroglycerine: a well-tried Home Office explosives test had proved positive on their hands. Within a day or two of the arrests, four of the men confessed to planting the bombs in one or other of the pubs. When the case finally came to trial at Lancaster in June 1975, it seemed open and shut. There were six Irish Republicans. There was proof that five of them set off to Belfast on the night of the bombings, and that the sixth saw them off. Then there were the positive results of the Griess explosives test. And there were the confessions. Mr Justice (now Lord Justice) Bridge, one of the country's most austere judges, declared that the evidence against the defendants was 'the clearest and most overwhelming I have ever heard'.

He weighed in heartily for the police whenever there appeared to be some discrepancy in the prosecution case. In fact, there were quite a

---

*Review of *Error of Judgement: The Truth about the Birmingham Bombings* by Chris Mullin.

few discrepancies. None of the 'positive' results in those early Griess tests stood up when they were subjected to much more sensitive tests in the laboratory. The confessions looked a bit odd when compared with some of the evidence about the bombs which blew up the pubs: everyone agreed, for instance, that the bombs in the pubs had been placed in a hold-all and a briefcase or a small case with a lock – but three of the four confessions said the bombs were planted in plastic bags. The unchallenged forensic evidence was that the bomb in the Mulberry pub had exploded from inside the pub – while the confessions said it had been left outside. Then there was an awkward doctor from Winson Green who kept insisting that the six defendants had sustained serious injuries before they were admitted to prison. He was sharply put down by Mr Justice Bridge. The injuries, the judge concluded, had probably been 'self-inflicted'. 'It is quite apparent,' he explained, 'that some scratching type of discolouration upon the chest is a very easy mark for a man to produce on his own body.' There were also the consistent and passionate denials of all six defendants that they had anything to do with the bombings, or had been members of the IRA.

All this was trivial compared to the case against the six men, which seemed impregnable. Were not the contradictions in the men's confessions to be expected in the circumstances – indeed, might they not have been deliberately devised to throw their interrogators off the scent? Didn't people who gave confessions always pretend that they had been beaten up? And who was to say no to the Home Office forensic scientist, Dr Frank Skuse, who told the court he was '99 per cent certain' that the three men whose hands turned positive in the Griess test had been handling nitroglycerine? When the unanimous guilty verdict came, it was fully expected, and greeted with widespread relief. The bombers were behind bars for life. Their families had suffered the humiliation due to people responsible for an atrocity of this kind. The West Midlands police had a jolly party and basked in the congratulations of the judge. It seemed plain that those responsible for a vile crime had been promptly and properly punished.

There appears to be a link between the enormity of a crime and the ignominy which attaches to any journalist or investigator who publicly questions the guilt of those convicted for it. This has been especially true in the case of Irish people convicted of bombings in Britain. Anyone who questions the verdict against an Irish bomber is assumed to be a bomber himself. As a result of this extraordinary logic, the authorities have been able to get away with mistakes, inconsistencies and far worse. No praise is too high, then, for Chris Mullin and the way he has pursued the Birmingham bombings case over the past eight years. He has tried to influence other journalists with access to larger circulations than he had when he was editor of *Tribune*. From most of them (including me) he got every encouragement short of help. Most of us felt that there was so much injustice in the world that to concentrate on the Birmingham bombings case was eccentric to the point of perversity. There was one exception. Granada Television's *World in Action* gave Chris Mullin the resources he needed. They furnished him with forensic experts who alone could tackle the complicated evidence about nitroglycerine. With the help of *World in Action* and Chatto and Windus, Mullin has destroyed the case against the six men which seemed so powerful in 1974 and 1975.

What has happened to the Griess tests for explosives on three of the men which was so important to the prosecution case at Lancaster? Dr Skuse told the court that a positive Griess test had only one meaning: contact with nitroglycerine. Since the trial, Mr David Baldock, former head of the Home Office forensic laboratories at Nottingham, carried out exactly the same test on a series of quite different substances – on nitrocellulose lacquer, for instance, on nitrocellulose chips and nitro-cellulose aerosol spray. Tests on all three proved positive. Dr Brian Caddy, head of the Forensic Science Unit at Strathclyde University, carried out exactly the same tests and found positive readings on a varnished wooden surface, a cigarette packet, a picture postcard, and two packs of old playing-cards. The convicted Irishmen had been playing cards in the train just before their arrest. Mr Caddy gave the cards to a *World in Action* producer, who shuffled them for a few minutes. Then Mr Caddy did the Griess test on the producer's hands. The test proved positive. If the *World in Action* producer had been at Lancaster Crown Court, a Home Office scientist would have said it was 99 per cent certain he had been handling nitroglycerine.

Every single one of the positive tests which played such a crucial part in the trial has been utterly discredited by subsequent research; and there is now no evidence whatever that any of the men had ever handled an explosive. 'I've never touched a bomb in my life,' one of them, Paddy Hill, has said. There is now nothing to contradict him. There are signs that the authorities have since recognized the weakness of the Griess tests. Poor Dr Skuse, the Home Office scientist who carried out the tests, was retired early, at the age of fifty, only three weeks after the *World in Action* programme discredited his efforts. No one in authority, certainly not Dr Skuse himself, has explained why. At the Court of Appeal, the Lord Chief Justice – Widgery – made light of the forensic evidence, asserting that 'this was not a point of great importance'. It was, of course, as the trial judge put it, 'absolutely critical' to the prosecution case. If the Griess tests had not proved positive, the five men would, almost certainly, have been allowed to continue their journey to Belfast. Before the Griess tests, they were treated courteously by their arresting officers. After the tests the whole atmosphere changed.

What happened to the five men at Morecambe police station on the morning the tests proved positive – the morning after the bombings – and at Queen's Road police station, Birmingham, where they were taken the next day and joined by their mate Hughie Callaghan? That is the most important question in this important book. The men have alleged throughout that they were savagely beaten. Billy Power says he was led into a darkened room where he reckons about half a dozen policemen waited for him. They systematically beat his body – his testicles, especially – until he agreed to sign a confession. His screams were heard by the others, who were then taken in turn for their beatings. Special savagery was reserved for Paddy Hill, who refused, then or ever, to make a statement implicating himself in the bombings. Johnny Walker said he had a lighted cigarette pushed into a blister in his foot; Richard McIlkenny said that he was suffocated under a blanket. The brutality, the men alleged, continued as they were driven, barefoot and terrified, to Birmingham on the day after the bombings. At Queen's Road station, they all said, the violence continued. The men were kept awake all that night, and given next to nothing to eat and drink. All except Power, who had already confessed, were beaten up again and again. More sophisticated methods were brought into play. The men were threatened with guns. A gun was fired at Richard McIlkenny, and he thought he was dead. When he opened his eyes he saw threads of black material coming out of the barrel and floating down to the floor. Again and again the men were told that they would be killed if they did not confess: they had 'gelly on their hands' and no one could care less if they were found dead. McIlkenny, Walker and Callaghan signed confessions though Hill and Hunter did not.

There is a word for all this: torture. The allegations of each of the six men, though they were made quite separately when the men were not in contact with one another, read like a training manual in deep interrogation techniques for use in time of war. The systematic 'breaking down' of a suspect depends, above all, on terror, and fear of pain. A common myth is that 'beating up' is old-fashioned and counter-productive. It is not. Violence and pain are crucial to such techniques. It is only when the violence fails, as it did in the first instance with four of the five men at Morecambe, that more 'subtle' methods, such as shooting with wax bullets, taking suspects to open windows and starting to throw them out, threats to the suspects' families, enforced sleeplessness and so on are introduced. When Gerry Hunter admitted that he did not like dogs, he said, a snarling Alsatian was brought into the room and told to 'get him, get him'. They let it come within six inches of Hunter, and then took it away. This was the torture immortalized in George Orwell's *1984*, after Winston Smith admitted he didn't like rats. Indeed, there is nothing in the allegations which could not have fitted neatly into the two great British novels about torture in a totalitarian state – Orwell's *1984* and Koestler's *Darkness at Noon*, both of which have been used ever since they were written as justifications for the 'Western way of life'.

Did all this happen? The police vigorously denied that there was any violence at all, either in Morecambe, or in the journey to Birmingham or at Queen's Road. Their denials were at once accepted by judge and jury at the Lancaster trial. Since then, not one policeman has told a different story, though Chris Mullin and Charles Tremayne of *World in Action* appear to have tracked down every policeman who was involved, even those who have since retired. It would indeed be comforting if we could dismiss the allegations of violence as the fantasies of desperate men who had committed foul murders, confessed to them, and had somehow to explain their confessions in court.

What has happened since the trial, however, suggests that this isn't possible. There can now be no doubt that all six men were savagely beaten in the week after their arrest. The evidence of their bodies proved that incontestably. The West Midlands police have an explanation for it. They say that the men were beaten up at Winson Green prison on their arrival there. Accordingly, in 1976, fourteen prison officers from Winson Green were charged with assaulting the Irish prisoners. They did not give evidence at their trial. Their defence relied on attacking the prosecution witnesses, who were, in the main, the six convicted men. The jury found all the officers not guilty. The result is that although everyone agrees the men were beaten up, no one has yet been punished.

In the course of the case, the accused prison officers were persuaded to make secret statements to their solicitors about what happened in the prison. Chris Mullin has had access to them, and the result is the two most chilling chapters in his book. The statements describe the most awful assaults on the men in the prison corridors and bathrooms. On occasion the accounts read like records from the torture chambers of the secret police in Russia or in Chile. But the statements also allege that the men were beaten before they got to Winson Green. Prison Officer Brian Sharpe declared, for instance: 'I saw bruises on many parts of Walker's body. His torso was more or less covered. They were all colours: black, blue, yellow, purple, and most of them looked oldish.' There was only one credible source for such injuries: the inter-rogating police officers.

There is other recent evidence that some of the men's stories might not be as farfetched as had been assumed at the trial. There is, for instance, a firing range at Queen's Road police station where guns are used with wax bullets: bullets which leave precisely the residue which Richard McIlkenny describes. He could not possibly ever have seen a wax bullet fired elsewhere. This evidence enabled the six men to get legal aid to sue the West Midlands police for assaulting them at More-cambe and at Queen's Road. The police applied for the action to be struck out. Mr Justice Cantley turned them down. The police appealed, and the Court of Appeal obligingly struck the action out. The judgement of Lord Denning in that hearing needs to be read care-fully by anyone who still believes that the judiciary is 'independent'. He spoke as follows:

> If the six men win, it will mean that the police were guilty of perjury, that they were guilty of violence and threats, that the confessions were involuntary and were improperly admitted in evidence and that the convictions were erroneous. That would mean the Home Secretary would either have to recommend they be pardoned or he would have to remit the case to the Court of Appeal. This is such an appalling vista that every sensible person in the land would say: 'It cannot be right that these actions should go any further.'

If the six men won, in other words, it would be clear that the fantasy world of *1984* and *Darkness at Noon* had emerged in the real world, at Morecambe and at Queen's Road police stations. In a free society, such a possibility could best be avoided by not allowing the legal action to proceed.

There is a lot to criticize in Chris Mullin's book. His story is a complicated one. He has to introduce six defendants, their families and their movements on the day of the bombings. Much of this introduction is hard to follow, and the division of the story into forty untitled chapters without explanations or subheads does not help. Chris Mullin reports at the end that he has met the men who organized the bombings, including one man who planted the bombs and is now living in Dublin. I believe this, because I know Chris Mullin is a diligent and honest journalist. But it is no use at all to assert who the guilty people are without proving it, and Mullin cannot do that because he has agreed to his suspects' anonymity.

Radical and challenging journalism requires a higher burden of proof than allegations which run in tandem with received opinion. Chris Mullin claims too much for his anonymous bombers. He would have been better advised to claim less, and to fasten on the fact that one of his informers told him the codeword used by the bombers when, too late, they phoned in a warning. No one except the police and the man who took the call know this codeword. Will the police, after all these years, confirm or deny that the codeword was Double X? If it was, then there is proof that Chris Mullin's informers are substantial ones.

These criticisms are minor ones, however. Some right-wing newspapers started a witch-hunt on Chris Mullin when the book was published, claiming that he knew who the bombers were and should be prosecuted for withholding information. This silly campaign soon stopped. Its implications no doubt became obvious to the dumbest editor. For if Chris Mullin *does* know the bombers, then the six men who have now been in prison for nearly twelve years are not the bombers and the most terrible crimes have been committed against them, in the names of all of us. We should not have to wait until Chris Mullin becomes MP for Sunderland South before a campaign is launched to discover the truth, and if the truth is half as bad as he suggests, to punish those responsible.

London Review of Books, September 1986

Tell the truth – and be maligned

Mrs Joyce Lynass, a young mother who works part-time for the local church, was watching a television programme with her husband one weekend last November. The subject was bullying in the army, and the programme ended with an appeal to all those who knew of or who had suffered from such bullying to come forward and tell the authorities. The programme urged its audience against the easy course – keeping quiet. It was important for the army and for society that the truth should come out. Above all, those who did so could rely upon the sympathy and protection of the authorities.

The programme greatly disturbed Mrs Lynass. Late into the night, she and her husband discussed her predicament. The previous day – a Friday – she had given evidence at the Court of Appeal in the case of the six men convicted in 1975 of blowing up two Birmingham pubs, killing twenty-one and injuring 160. New evidence in the case, and independent public doubt about the convictions, had persuaded the Home Secretary to refer the case back to the Court of Appeal.

Mrs Lynass had not given evidence at the original trial. She was called to the appeal because she had given a statement to the Devon and Cornwall police, who had carried out a secret inquiry into the police treatment of the six men after their arrests. She had, she said, been a police cadet in 1974, and was on duty at Queen's Road police station, Birmingham, on the weekend the six prisoners were brought there.

She had told the Devon and Cornwall police of the unsteadiness of the men when they had been moved from the police station after a night in the cells. She repeated this at the Court of Appeal. She was asked specifically whether she had seen any assault or ill-treatment of the men by the police, and answered that she had not.

Her problem, she told her husband, was that the evidence was false. Partly because she had been put off by a sinister comment from a Birmingham police officer ('remember, we all have families'), partly because she did not want to get involved in public controversy, she had not revealed that she *had* seen a brutal assault by an investigating police officer on one of the six men.

The television appeal about army bullying disturbed her. Should she have told the whole truth? Was it too late to make amends? The easy course was to do nothing. That way, nothing would ever be heard of the Lynasses again. That is the course which the vast majority of people in Mrs Lynass's position would have taken. Anyone with the remotest experience of trying to overturn a suspect jury verdict knows that most witnesses, even if they are confronted with proof that they have something new and important to say for the defendants, are reluctant to 'get involved'. To her considerable credit, Joyce Lynass decided to set the record straight.

The following morning, entirely on her own initiative and without discussing the matter with anyone else, Mrs Lynass contacted the appellant's lawyers. On the Sunday she was in London, making a statement. On the Monday, she was in the witness box.

Nervous, but determined, she said she had gone into one of the interviewing rooms at Queen's Road police station on the weekend after the men were brought in. As the door opened, she said, she saw one of her police colleagues knee the prisoner in the groin, remarking: 'That's what we do to fucking murderous bastards.'

Most observers in court that day were impressed by Joyce Lynass's courage and credibility. She had perjured herself, it was true, but here she was, in the interests of justice and for no other conceivable reason, putting that right.

Moreover, her testimony fitted the statements at the trial of all six men who said they had been systematically attacked at Queen's Road – and that beating, kneeing or grabbing their testicles was the form of assault most favoured by the police officers.

What protection and encouragement has she had from Britain's most senior judges? In their judgement last week, they announced that they didn't believe a word she said. If they had to believe any version of her story, they believed the first one which did not specify any violence. But they did not believe her at all. They offered no explanation for her change of heart save the darkest hint: 'We shall never know what happened that weekend.' Joyce Lynass, a woman without a blemish on her record, was blackened for life.

Joyce Lynass gave fresh evidence on the first of the two crucial issues before the court: the allegation, made by all six men at their trial, that they had been beaten and tortured after their arrest, and that the beatings and torture had extracted confessions from four of them.

As a result of the inquiry by Devon and Cornwall police, the defence was able to produce a number of other new witnesses all of whom testified (as no independent witness had testified at the men's trial) to injuries the men sustained before they were taken to Winson Green prison where they were beaten up again.

Former Constable Tom Clarke, who was on duty at Queen's Road, said he had seen injuries on the men's faces and bodies. He said that police had aimed guns at the prisoners in the cells. He said that a dog had been used in the cells. These last two points fitted closely (though not in exact detail – Mr Clarke was remembering events thirteen years ago) with the men's allegations that they had been threatened with guns; and that one of them, as soon as he admitted his phobia for dogs, was confronted in his cell with a snarling, snapping Alsatian. Former Sergeant Garrington remembered seeing the men lined up as though for punishment – scared and injured. PC Paul Berry, a serving police officer, remembered seeing one of the men with a cut lip and black eye. Former prison officer Peter Bourne gave evidence about the documents which committed the men to prison. They had not been properly filled out, he said, and did not disclose, as they should have done, the physical condition of the prisoners. Another officer, Brian Sharp, said he was the first to see the six men naked in the prison. He saw fresh injuries on their faces and old injuries on their bodies.

All this new evidence was coolly dismissed by the judges. Clarke was, they said, 'an unconvincing witness'. He had been found guilty of stealing £5 from a prisoner and sacked from the police. He was therefore 'embittered' and had made up his evidence out of revenge. Berry's evidence, said the judges, 'doesn't help the appeal' – apparently because there was no other evidence that the man he saw had a cut lip. Of former Sergeant Garrington, the judges said: 'The kindest explanation is that his memory was playing him tricks.' Of Peter Bourne: 'His evidence was characterized by a refusal to admit that the men had been subjected to a violent attack in the prison.' The same allegation was made against Brian Sharp. 'We are not surprised that Sharp was not called at the trial,' said the judgement. 'We did not believe him.'

The conclusion was plain. There had been no violence. The police had behaved impeccably. The confessions were all voluntary.

How did the six men come to be suspected of the bombings in the first place? They were arrested as they sought to leave Britain for Ireland on the night the bombs went off. They were held in Morecambe police station, where their hands were tested for explosives.

The chemical test used was the 'Griess test'. The man who tested them was Dr Frank Skuse, a forensic scientist at the Home Office laboratory at Chorley, Lancs.

Skuse got positive results for nitroglycerine on two of the hands of the men he tested at Morecambe police station. Neither of these two 'positives' was confirmed by more sophisticated tests he carried out later in his laboratory. All his samples produced 'negatives' on 'thin layer chromatography' tests. Only one test on the ultra-sensitive Gas Chromatography/Mass Spectrometry (GCMS) showed any reaction at all – and that so small that it was described by another Home Office scientist as only 'possibly' positive.

In 1985, Granada's *World in Action* commissioned two scientists to carry out Griess tests with exactly the same ingredients which, the Home Office assured them, had been used by Skuse at Morecambe. The tests showed 'positives' on a wide range of substances, including playing-cards (the men had been playing cards in the train), lacquer such as that on a train table, cigarette packets and cigarettes (the men had been smoking). It seemed that the main evidence had been smashed – until Dr Skuse announced that he had used a *different* concentration of caustic soda in his tests – different, that is, from the concentration which his own Home Office chief had said he had used.

The cross-examination of Dr Skuse over four days by Michael Mansfield QC was an astonishing experience for anyone lucky enough to be in court. Skuse started by admitting he had left his Home Office post a few days after the Granada programme – though he did not agree that he had been threatened with the sack for incompetence.

He could produce no notes of the ingredients of his tests at More-cambe. Again and again he contradicted what he had said at the trial; seemed vague about figures he had been specific about previously; and at one point admitted being wrong *by a factor of 100*. For Dr Skuse, however, the three judges had nothing but understanding and patience. Dr Skuse, they were sure, was sincere. He couldn't be expected to remember details after such a long period of time.

On the main point, however, they were obliged to disagree with him. In perhaps the most remarkable sentence in the whole judgement, Lord Lane said: 'The Griess test is not specific for nitroglycerine.'

If indeed it is not, the six men should never have been considered suspects in the first place. The tests should not have been made on the men at Morecambe, and there would have been nothing else to connect them to the crime. Lord Lane concluded, however: 'Nothing from the mass of new scientific evidence which the appeal has heard has caused us to doubt that one or more of the appellants had explosives on their hands.'

How could he reach that conclusion? The Griess test, he said, could be excluded. So could the tests which were made with ammonium nitrate. These were demonstrably not specific for nitroglycerine, but could have proved positive from a wide variety of different substances, including urine.

There remained the single 'possibly' positive test on the ultra-sensitive GCMS machine at Aldermaston. To testify to this, another new witness was produced by the Crown – Dr Jane Drayton. She agreed that she had written that the test on one of the men's hands was 'possibly' positive for nitroglycerine. Why? Because the line on the print-out from the machine had shown a 'peak' at the right time.

Where was the proof of this? How big was the alleged 'peak'? Dr Drayton could not say – the print-out had been 'mislaid'. She could only assert, without documentary evidence, that the time was right. Dr Skuse had said in evidence that while he and Dr Drayton were doing the test, she had used a large stopwatch. Dr Drayton said emphatically that she had not used a watch. From this single shred of uncorroborated evidence, the judges were able to conclude: 'Nothing has caused us to doubt one or more of the appellants had explosives on their hands.'

Lastly, Lord Lane addressed the awkward question: *why* had none of the positive Griess tests been confirmed on the GCMS test, which is at least a hundred times more sensitive? 'Nitroglycerine is volatile,' he said, 'and it could have evaporated or deteriorated.' Yet an independent scientist, Dr David Baldock, had carried out extensive tests leaving quantities of nitroglycerine of the order it was suggested had been found on the men's hands in bowls above a radiator for days on end. In none of them had the nitroglycerine evaporated or deteriorated to anything like the extent necessary for a 'negative' finding on GCMS.

The three judges made great play of the circumstantial evidence against the men: their Republican sympathies, their journey to the funeral of an IRA bomber, their association with IRA sympathizers in the Midlands. Mr Justice Bridge in the original trial said of all this: 'These matters fall a long way short of anything that anyone could possibly regard as proof.'

The appeal judges improved greatly on that. 'There was a wealth of evidence,' they said, 'as to the surrounding circumstances – which strengthened the case.' Once again, if you believe what you want to believe, and disbelieve anything which contradicts it, you can come to the conclusion you first thought of.

Few of the many visitors to the Appeal Court hearing in the Birmingham case could fail to notice all three judges' open and obvious irritation with the defendants and their lawyers. Their distaste for Michael Mansfield could not be contained. 'We are not a jury,' snapped Lord Lane at Mansfield as he complained yet again about the barrister's 'histrionics'. The message was clear: juries are swayed by histrionics; judges only by cool, clear reason.

On the contrary, however, juries introduce into judging an element of popular democracy. They come to the court to hide nothing and to protect nothing – but simply to assess the evidence and the witnesses. Judges on the other hand have a great deal to protect. For the Court of Appeal, every bit as much as the Crown Court at Lancaster, was responsible for the imprisonment of the Birmingham Six, because it turned down their appeal at the time. Any mistake in the case against the men would reflect badly on the Court of Appeal, which is why the judges in that court are the very worst people to try their cases again. Indeed, their irritation even with the cautious Home Secretary, Douglas Hurd, burst into their judgement. 'As with so many cases referred to us by the Home Secretary,' said Lord Lane, the original verdict seemed more safe the longer the appeal went on. What else could that possibly mean except that the Home Secretary would do better to keep his faintly democratic fingers off the due process of law; and that the business of deciding whether or not the courts have made fools of themselves should be left exclusively to the courts?

Unlike juries, judges inhabit a narrow, introverted and reactionary world: a world where deeper, perhaps simpler considerations are often more relevant than the facts of a particular case. The logic of this world was brilliantly outlined by that hero of the modern legal system, Lord Denning, who explained an earlier decision by the Court of Appeal to refuse to allow the six men to sue the police for assault with his now famous dictum. To let the six men win, he said, would mean that the police were guilty of perjury and more. 'That is such an appalling vista that every sensible person would say: "It cannot be right that these actions should go any further".'

So it is that to save society and its judiciary from Lord Denning's 'appalling vista' Patrick Hill, Johnny Walker, Billy Power, Hugh McIlkenny, Gerry Hunter and Hughie Callaghan have been sent back to prison to serve out sentences for murders they quite plainly did not commit.

New Statesman, February 1988

They are rotting *

'The evidence, or should I say lack of it, is still the same. All that's changed is the people telling it.' Carole Richardson, then twenty-nine, was writing to a friend from Styal prison in 1986. She had been in prison for twelve years, ever since she had been arrested for questioning over the bombing of pubs in Guildford in 1974. In her letter she reflected on the renewed interest in her case after so long a time.

Her point was that the basic facts about the Guildford bombings, for which she and three young men had been convicted in 1975, had been known for at least ten years. The 'Guildford Four' had been convicted solely on confessions which they had made to the Surrey police. There was no independent evidence against them – no fingerprints, no identification, though Carole herself, for instance, had stood on several identity parades in front of witnesses who had a clear sight of suspicious characters in the Guildford pubs before they were blown up.

The confessions, however, had been detailed and explicit. Of course there were contradictions between them, but it was, then as now, difficult for any rational jury to imagine that entirely innocent people could say they had committed such monstrous offences if they had not done so. The four, of course, had an explanation. They all said they had

---

*Review of *Time Bomb: Irish Bombs, English Justice and the Guildford Four* by Grant McKee and Ros Franey.

been intimidated, often by most savage violence, into saying exactly what the police wanted them to say. Gerry Conlon, for instance, gave a shocking account of being beaten and abused by senior Surrey detectives. When he finally, in terror, agreed to confess, he didn't know what to write. So the police helpfully brought him another confession signed by Paul Hill. This in turn (according to Hill) had been beaten out of him. Conlon obligingly and in some relief wrote down what Hill had written and forever afterwards, through the long ritual of trial and appeal, police, prosecuting counsel and judges marvelled at the way the statements corroborated one another.

The police denied all violence. In court they appeared as smart, decent, humane gentlefolk who would never harm a fly. How on earth could the jury believe such fantastic allegations from such intrinsically unreliable young people?

Even at the trial there *was* one way of testing the point through an independent witness. Frank Johnson had been to a concert with Carole Richardson on the night of the Guildford bombings. The concert had started in south London at eight o'clock. Frank and Carole, together with her friend Lisa Astin, had arrived at the south London hall at about 7.45pm. There was no dispute about this. In the end, the prosecution brought a witness to say he saw Carole, Lisa and Frank at about a quarter to eight. Police drivers, upholding the speed limit, proved that it was *just* possible to get to the concert after planting bombs in Guildford an hour earlier. But Frank recalled very clearly that he had met Carole and Lisa at a pub for a drink at least half an hour before the concert. Frank's story, supported throughout by Lisa Astin, provided for Carole Richardson a complete alibi for the Guildford bombings.

Frank Johnson did not realize this until several weeks after Carole was arrested. He was then living in Newcastle, and it was on a trip to London that he heard that Carole was being held for the bombings. He thought hard about the concert, checked the date with the band which was playing that evening, and constructed a careful account of what had happened.

He then started to search for Carole's solicitor. The search was fruitless. A solicitor in Newcastle referred him to the court at Guildford; but the court would not release the solicitor's name. Frank tried the National Council of Civil Liberties, but the line was constantly engaged. Eventually, against his better judgement, he went alone to a police station in Newcastle and said he wanted to stand alibi for Carole

Richardson. Before long, three police officers from Guildford arrived to interview him. They told him he must be mistaken about the time. He insisted he was not. He went on telling them they had made a terrible mistake.

When he finished, he was *arrested*, and placed in a cell without even a blanket for the night, and (with a blanket) for most of the following day. A few days later he was *arrested again* outside his workplace and flown to Guildford. After some hours' interrogation by the Guildford police, who told him they suspected him of being part of an IRA plot to concoct a false alibi, he made a completely different statement, saying the times were much later than he had previously argued, and that he had 'made the whole thing up'.

In court, Frank Johnson was adamant. What he first said to the police in Newcastle was absolutely correct. He had changed his statement at Guildford because he had been abused and beaten for two and a half days, threatened with being thrown off the roof and asked if he would like to see his mother go up in flames in her wheelchair. He was, he said, terrified.

It is hard to discover a credible explanation for Frank Johnson's change of tune, unless it is the one he gave the court. If he was indeed concocting an alibi to assist an old friend, why was he not charged with perversion of the course of justice, of which he would certainly have been guilty? Was he not further running the risk of such a prosecution by going back to his original story – a very unpopular one with the police – when he appeared in court? On his own initiative he decided that he had met Carole and Lisa at a time when she could not have planted the Guildford bombs. Later, in evidence under oath, he said the same. Only in police custody did he say something entirely different. When he was a free man, he stuck to the alibi.

The vehement denials of the police that they had been guilty of any impropriety cannot explain the contradiction in Johnson's statements. Nor could any policeman explain why Johnson's alibi evidence, once it had been submitted to the police, was not immediately made available to the defence so that Carole's lawyers could interview Frank and take a statement from him; and at least be present when he was seen by the police. All these things were considered by the jury who came to unanimous guilty verdicts.

No jury, however, ever heard the evidence of the IRA squad which admitted some months later that it had carried out the bombings at

Guildford and at Woolwich; and were able to give chapter and verse about the strength of the bombs, when and where they were placed, which cars were used, and even who was in the Guildford pubs. One of the IRA men, Eric Butler, could describe two elderly men who were indeed at the pub before the bombings and whose presence there had not been mentioned by anyone in public.

No jury heard about this because the awkward confessions of the IRA squad, three of whom had been arrested at the famous Balcombe Street siege, were taken as part of the Guildford Four's Appeal. The Court of Appeal sat without a jury. Blithely accepting that the IRA men *had* attacked Woolwich and Guildford (they had no option since the evidence was so strong), the Appeal judges equally blithely concluded that the Guildford Four must have been there as well. In spite of the failure to associate a single one of the Guildford Four with any of the numerous identical bombings carried out by the IRA team in other parts of London and the Home Counties in 1974 and 1975, the Court of Appeal concluded that they had in fact been accomplices of the four IRA men at Guildford.

When the IRA team came up for trial, every single one of the bombings they said they committed before December 1974 – including the two which were by far the most destructive, Guildford and Woolwich – were left out of the indictment. The expert forensic officer Douglas Higgs had referred in his early statements to the similarities in the bombs used at Guildford and Woolwich and those used in other IRA attacks. On the orders of very senior Scotland Yard officers, Higgs obligingly left out all references to these similarities in his later statements. He admitted in court that he had altered his scientific findings *simply because the police has asked him to.*

This marvellous book extends the case for the Guildford Four far beyond Robert Kee's comparatively thin account, *Trial and Error*, published in 1986. It starts with a report of how the bombings took place – a contentious way to begin the argument; but it never departs for a moment from the facts. The 'new evidence' it reveals, though important, is, as Carole Richardson noted in her letter, not really the point. There is a new witness who was with Paul Hill at the time of the bombings; Carole Richardson was injected with pethidine shortly before confessing. This is shocking enough, it is true, but not half so shocking as the entire story of deceit, corruption and conspiracy which led to the imprisonment of four innocent people for fourteen years, and perhaps more. It is impossible for any reasonable person to read this book and to continue to believe that any one of these four people had anything to do with the bombings at Guildford or at Woolwich.

How to express, then, the enormity of what has been done here? It is true that none of the victims here has been killed, though poor Giuseppe Conlon (Gerry's Father), an utterly law-abiding and innocent man, arrested with the McGuire family as part of the police hunt after the Guildford bombings, and then accused (when their innocence at Guildford was undeniable) on random charges connected with handling explosives on perhaps the flimsiest forensic evidence ever put before a court – poor Mr Conlon died in prison from his illnesses which were greatly exacerbated by bullying and plain bad treatment.

None of the Guildford Four is dead, but the crimes against them have been committed by individuals and organizations which purport to protect the public, to be accountable to the public, to act *in our name*. For the harassment, intimidation, false imprisonment of these people and for the robbery of their youth, we must all accept some responsibility.

Those of us who write on public affairs have perhaps a special responsibility. For us the most dreadful aspect of the story is that none of us noticed while it was happening. In a dramatic moment, expertly conveyed in this book, the solicitors for the four accused, grouped together in a Wimpy Bar during the committal hearings, suddenly confessed to each other that they thought their clients were innocent. This instinct, so abruptly and surreptitiously shared, grew, in Alastair Logan's case, into a certainty. But he and his clients fumed and delayed while no one came to their assistance.

Grant McKee, Ros Franey, Yorkshire Television and Robert Kee have started to pay back this fearful debt. They have been joined in recent weeks by important people. The Archbishop of Canterbury now says he is dissatisfied with the verdicts. The test of whether that dissatisfaction turns into action depends on how much every single citizen joins in the clamour for an instant reopening of the case. 'They are rotting', this book concludes of the four tragic victims, 'and with every day that passes English justice is rotting with them.'

Spectator, December 1988

13. Idiosyncrasies

Memories of public school*

The main characteristic of the school I went to was barbarism. It was a 'top flight' public school – Shrewsbury – and it was run on the standard lines of British public schools throughout the ages.

It cost a lot of money to go to Shrewsbury, and what the parents got in return was children well equipped to be rulers.

'You are the leaders of the future,' a general bellowed at us every year as we dressed up in uniform and paraded around like toy soldiers. 'See that you live up to it!'

To be leaders of the future it was necessary to know what it was like to be bullied in order to turn out a good bully yourself. Almost every relationship at school was founded on discipline, violence and hierarchy.

Looking back on all this now, I wonder how it was that, at least in the last two years of my schooldays, I enjoyed them so much. The answer lies in the character and style of two teachers whose very presence at the school seemed to flout its essence.

One of these men was small, bald, and on first acquaintance, almost certainly off his rocker. He taught English to boys who were learning other subjects for exams, and was therefore not expected to help anyone pass anything. On my first appearance in his classroom he made one of my friends stand on a chair and recite two lines which he had written on the blackboard. I recall them exactly

anyone lived in a pretty how town
with up so floating many bells down.

---

*Review of *Dead Poets Society*, a film by Peter Weir.

The teacher – we called him Kek – told us that these lines were by a man called ee cummings (who spelt his name like that without capital letters, and the whole of the rest of the poem was like those first two lines – gibberish, and badly punctuated gibberish at that).

We learnt his 'spells', as he called his gobbets of prose and poetry in endless different languages, were hypnotized by them, learnt the bits around them and became quite literally spellbound. All the guff learnt for exams has long since been forgotten but Kek's spells still roll around in my head today.

They are still part of a new world, something completely different to the world I can see and feel day to day.

The only other teacher I remember at Shrewsbury was also an eccentric. I think he was a Liberal, or even perhaps a 'moderate' Tory, but he was constantly provoking dissent.

He introduced us – in 1956 – to the *New Statesman,* which was quite shockingly subversive of everything the school seemed to be telling us. He pushed us to write in the school magazine all kinds of subversive and satirical material.

So far did he push me down the road to radical ideas that I even started (just before I left) wondering what he, and Kek for that matter, were doing at Shrewsbury at all. Were they not contradicting everything the school stood for? Were they not subverting the very values which inspired people to go out and form an empire?

The answer was, in part, yes. The Kek spells and the *New Statesman* did open up closed minds.

Nevertheless, there was even at Shrewsbury in the 1950s, as in every public school, the eccentric oddball teacher. It was perhaps important for boys to learn to think for themselves, if only to come to the correct conclusion about their role in life as rulers. The question which dogged the authorities was: how far can we let these eccentrics go?

I do realize that not everybody who goes to see *Dead Poets Society* was likely to have been at Shrewsbury (or any public school) in the 1950s.

Some may have gone to the film simply because they read a disgustingly philistine and reactionary review in *City Limits.*

But as the film went on, I felt it could hardly be a coincidence that so many experiences of mine at a British public school in the 1950s should be reproduced in a film about an American school founded on all that's worst in the British school tradition in 1959.

The hero of the film is a teacher who wants to break the walls of convention which hem his pupils in. He wants them to see things differently, which is one reason he makes them stand on their desks to recite poetry.

Just as Kek was hooked on Auden and Eliot and ee cummings because they used words which sounded like what they should mean, so Mr Keating in the film is turned on by the great idealists of the American tradition: Thoreau, who was forever writing of utopias where people behaved decently to one another; Robert Frost and Walt Whitman, who spent their lives urging people to take the unlikely and unusual paths of life rather than perish in conformity.

The question for Keating is the same as it was for Kek. How would the authorities react? Would they patronize him? Or would he stray too far beyond the bounds of orthodoxy?

As always in such matters, the dividing line is crossed when talk turns to action; when cosy theory about an ideal society turns into practice which changes the very lifestyles and aspirations of the leaders of the future.

Many who see the film and did not go to a school of this kind will find it incredible if not a little contemptible, that a man of Keating's idealism and visions could find himself in a barbaric place like that in the first place.

They underestimate the ability of the public school system to patronize eccentricity and, where possible, to make a virtue out of it. When one of his pupils revolts against the headmaster in a quite wonderful prank, Keating himself quite genuinely intervenes on the side of authority.

He is happy to flout the authority of the world outside, provided he does not flout the authority of the school. In the end the logic of revolt takes its course, and he is seen, wrongly as it turns out, to go too far.

Socialist Worker Review, November 1989

No ordinary flogger

A letter in the *Spectator* mourns the death of Mr Anthony Chenevix-Trench, 'a great headmaster', and yearns for the return of the *Times* obituary column to pay proper tribute. This diary is no substitute for a *Times* obituary of course but I would hate to miss the opportunity of paying my respects to Mr Trench who was my housemaster at Shrewsbury School twenty-five years ago.

Trench made his name as a great innovator, especially in corporal punishment. He would select certain younger boys for special tuition in Greek prose, in which he was a recognized scholar. Less than three mistakes earned a bar of chocolate; more than three a beating. But Trench was no ordinary flogger. He would offer his culprit an alternative: four strokes with the cane, which hurt; or six with the strap, with trousers down, which didn't. Sensible boys always chose the strap, despite the humiliation, and Trench, quite unable to control his glee, led the way to an upstairs room, which he locked, before hauling down the miscreant's trousers, lying him face down on a couch and lashing out with a belt. He achieved the rare distinction of being hated and despised by every boy who came in contact with him, and was therefore an obvious choice to be the youngest ever headmaster of Bradfield, and then of Eton.

At Eton he made the mistake of whipping the heirs of earls as though they were run-of-the-mill manufacturers' sons at Shrewsbury or Bradfield. One sensitive young viscount limped home and bared his tattered bum to his outraged father. Trench was sacked. He was appointed headmaster of Fettes.

New Statesman, July 1979

The saddest place on earth

Herman Melville, who wrote *Moby Dick*, once called Lima, Peru, 'the saddest place on earth'. I hope he is right and there is nowhere sadder.

My first impression was that Lima is a gigantic dustbin in which has been tipped all the rubbish from North America and industrial Europe. Almost all the cars, lorries and buses, for instance, are old, faulty and lethal.

If you saw a 1960 Volkswagen in Germany you would hail it as a collectors' item. In Lima, there are thousands of them. In the industrial democracies, tests and restrictions would drive these cars off the road. In Lima, though a test is formally demanded by law, there is no one to carry it out. So the slaughter on the roads continues.

That is only a rather silly example of what happens all over. There are none of the regulations which long years of social democracy have imposed on capitalism. Almost all the state machine is taken up by the army and the police, and there is nothing left over to enforce hygiene, sanitation, traffic and the like. There is no state health service and only a handful of publicly owned houses, which are let by lottery.

If Lima is a dustbin, Peru as a whole is a larder which is systematically raided by the same people who chuck their garbage back into the capital. In the week I was there, there was a drastic shortage of sugar. Queues formed from the early hours of the morning, and dreadful fights developed in them by midday.

The Peruvians are especially addicted to sugar, perhaps because they produce an enormous amount of it. But their government recently 'took advantage of a generous offer' to sell sugar at regulated prices to the United States.

So enthusiastically did they respond, in fact, that they committed the entire Peruvian sugar stock to be sold, and thus deprived about 90 per cent of the population of a food which they produce and enjoy.

There seems so little hope. A right-wing, elected government recently replaced a military junta which could not control inflation, but inflation is now running at 9 per cent a month, which means that prices more than double every year. The poverty is as horrible as it is unnecessary. Most of the thousands of children under the age of five who die every month could be kept alive with a tiny increase in spending on their health and diet.

I kept being overcome by an overwhelming desire to see the whole people rise up and smash to pieces everything which represents all this senselessness and horror.

Certainly, after a few days in Lima, it is much easier to understand the support for people like Che Guevara, and for the armed guerrillas in the countryside that are causing more problems for the Peruvian government and army than anyone officially admits. The industrial working class seems so *hidden* or isolated that it appears hopeless to rely on them.

And yet, and *yet.* Wishing something is not fulfilling it. A second, more sober look at Lima showed how unevenly the deprivation is spread and how dispersed the struggle is against it.

When Marx pointed to the working class as the agency of social change, it was not because they were in the majority, which they weren't, nor because they suffer worse than peasants, which they don't, nor even because they are more conspicuous than anyone else – but because they work collectively and cooperatively and therefore have the collective and cooperative strength to break the power of the capitalist machine.

In a strange way, a glimpse of a place like Lima makes it seem all the more vital to forge a power which can take on the oppression and defeat it.

The Peruvian government and its backers in the military and the state department seem almost to rejoice at the chaos on the Peruvian left – guerrilla wars and high votes for far left candidates on the one hand: almost complete abandonment of socialist organization in the trade unions and the industrial working class on the other.

If the direction changed, I imagine some smiles would quickly be wiped off some well-sugared faces.

Socialist Worker, May 1983

May Days and heydays

I went with a light heart to Newcastle on May Day on what I assumed would be a great workers' rally.

Twelve years ago I was in Newcastle on or around May Day for a hundredth anniversary meeting of the Trades Council. Jimmy Reid was the main speaker, but he didn't turn up. The meeting was chaired by an AUEW official, who told me blithely as he looked round the hall that there were, he thought, 'about 350 shop stewards here'. It was 1973, the year between the two great miners' strikes. Everyone was confident and proud of their movement in one of its strongest areas. The meeting was terrific.

I was in Newcastle last year too, for perhaps the best meeting of my life. It was a glorious June day and the Northumberland miners were holding a strike rally. Some 5,000 miners and their families marched into the park with their banners. They were full of confidence and pride. It was marvellous.

Last week's meeting had been carefully organized over many weeks. Derek Hatton, deputy leader of beleaguered Liverpool City Council, was the main speaker – but he didn't turn up.

When I got to the station there was no one to meet me, and I had forgotten the name of the hall. I wandered round the streets by the station searching for posters. There weren't any. I took a taxi to the university, to the poly, to every place in Newcastle I could remember ever speaking at. I rang the local paper. No one anywhere had heard of any Trades Council May Day meeting.

I went back to the station where, at last, someone *had* come to meet me. When I got to the hall I was shocked to find (at most) 120–130 people there.

The composition of the meeting was completely different to that of 1973. There were a handful of miners' wives there – friends I think of Ann Lilburn, one of the speakers – but pretty well nobody from the great rally the previous June.

The mood of the meeting was sad, low, rudderless. If it hadn't been for the Socialist Workers Party which supplied half the audience (at least) and five out of seven questions, it would have been the most gigantic flop.

Sitting there on the platform, I felt myself nibbled at by all kinds of heresies. Was it not true that the working-class movement *was* in decline?

Was it not true that the shop stewards of 1973 represented yards and factories which had since closed, with nothing to replace them? How could anything be built in a place like this, where getting on for 20 per cent of the workforce is unemployed, without the slightest hope of the kind of jobs which workers could expect in the 1960s and 1970s?

Then I got another shock. It came from a contribution from the floor. May Day, we were reminded, was a celebration of *international* working-class solidarity, and perhaps we ought to be talking not so much about the defeat of the miners in Britain, but about the great strike and lock-out of miners in South Africa. I realized I had spoken on May Day for three quarters of an hour without a single reference to any workers anywhere else in the world!

No wonder I had been so depressed. The insularity which infects us all when we feel low concentrates our minds on what we see around us – on the British working-class movement, whose traditional organizations and methods *have* been turned over and depleted in the last twenty years.

At the same time, however, in other countries huge working classes are being created almost every year. Countries and even continents where there was no working class fifty years ago are now teeming with a huge proletariat, much of it unorganized, but all of it exploited beyond belief, and showing strong signs of organizing and fighting back.

On the way back from Newcastle I picked up the *International Herald Tribune*, and read of two vast strikes in South Korea; of the lock-out in the South African goldfields; of the stirring of workers' unrest in the shanty towns around construction sites in Saudi Arabia.

Across the world, the working class is vastly bigger and more recognizable than it was in what seems to us to have been the 'heyday' of 1973.

If we lose sight of that, if we think for one moment of the working class as white, male shop stewards representing shipyard workers in Newcastle, then we are certain victims of gloom, introspection and, worse of all, inertia.

Socialist Worker, May 1985

Come here, Botham*

The first chapter heading of this book asks: 'Is Botham in?' The answer is yes, he is – just. He was selected for England in the last test against New Zealand, but only grudgingly. Mike Gatting, England's captain, explained that the real problem was Botham's bowling. Botham took a wicket with his first ball, another the next over, another soon after that. Then he scored an astonishing 59 not out in thirty-two balls. Before long, he was having a row with Somerset County Cricket Club Committee, which sacked his two friends Richards and Garner. The row seemed to inspire him. He ended the season with the most sustained display of boundary-hitting in the history of the game. Cricket lovers everywhere rejoiced – not just, I think, at the glory of the stroke play but because every Botham six and every Botham wicket cocked a mighty snook at the gentlemen of the MCC and the Test and County Cricket Board.

Most people who hate cricket complain about its dreariness. Nothing ever happens, they protest, and takes an inordinately long time about it. Fanatics such as myself – and there is nothing you can do about it once you have caught the cricket bug, it eats away at your better judgement for the rest of your life – reply that the dreariest parts of the game are often the most intriguing.

The hypnosis which the game works on us comes from the extraordinary balance between batting and bowling, a balance which almost always reasserts itself, just as one side is established in the ascendant. What appears to others as dreary is often just the balance holding steady, with batsmen and bowler unable to shift it in either direction. This claim, trotted out so often as an excuse for taking time off to watch cricket even when the weather is cold and nothing appears to be happening, will not really do, however. All of us who use it know that in the last resort the balance only fascinates because it can be broken; and when the balance *is* broken, fascination turns into delight.

Great specialist batsmen such as Geoffrey Boycott or Sunil Gavaskar afford endless hours of pleasure to fanatics. The same goes

---

*Review of *High, Wide and Handsome. Ian Botham: The Story of a Very Special Year* by Frank Keating.

for great specialist bowlers such as Ray Lindwall or Lance Gibbs. Any one of these, and many, many others like them, can break the balance. They do so by steady control, correctness, discipline, line, length, rhythm. They are specialists up against other specialists, and even a BBC commentator can follow what is going on.

But there are times when the balance is broken to pieces, when all the rules and disciplines are put to flight. These are the times which open cricket up to people who are not fanatics. They are brought about, almost always, by the great all-rounders – cricketers who are top-class batsmen and bowlers at the same time, who refuse to say which role they prefer, and who can on any day be as good at one as at the other. Such players invariably upset specialists, commentators and authorities. The reason for this is that they are, literally, carefree when they bat and when they bowl. When a specialist batsman fails – a little nick at the ball outside the offstump – his very livelihood is in jeopardy. The same fate threatens a specialist bowler when he fails to get that little nick, and ends up with nought for 60 in twenty overs. But the all-rounder bats and bowls knowing that if he fails, he can redeem his failure in the other role. So it is that, for the fanatics as well, the great all-rounders are the greatest gifts to an already gift-laden game.

The name of the greatest all-rounder of all time is not in any doubt. It is Gary Sobers. I speak as an authority, ever since at the age of nineteen I sat for two days on a desperately uncomfortable tin roof overlooking Sabina Park, Kingston, Jamaica, and watched him knock off the highest ever score in a test match (365) as if he was playing French cricket in a back garden. He wasn't remotely worried if he failed to get the runs, because he would then take the new ball, and try another record. If that failed, he could turn on his slow Chinaman, which he bowled better than anyone else in the world.

After Sobers, who? Some Australians who grew up when I did argue with some force for Keith Miller. As Frank Keating's book proves, however, Miller can quickly be rejected for second place. It goes, unquestionably, to Ian Botham. Indeed in one crucial respect, Botham beats even the great Sobers himself. Only twenty-two times in over a thousand test matches has a player taken five wickets in an innings and scored a hundred in the same match. Frank Keating tells us: 'Thirteen players have done it once; two – Sobers and Mushtaq Mohammad – have done it twice. *Ian Botham has done it five times.*'

Even more than Gary Sobers, Ian Botham exudes that carefree quality which marks the really great all-rounders. Sobers still has the record for the number of sixes in one over (fortunately televised). But Botham is a hitter of sixes to beat even Sobers hollow. One of the facts which inspired Frank Keating to write this book is that Botham's eighty sixes in the 1985 season was a County Cricket record. In one astonishing innings in July 1985 he hit the skilled Warwickshire attack for thirteen sixes out of a total of 138 not out – that is more than half his huge score in sixes alone! These sixes are not wild slogs. If they were, there could not be so many of them. Ian Botham hits in a glorious straight arc, with tremendous strength and accuracy. He obeys all the rules of the specialist but beats the specialist because he *dares*. He risks the absurd shot on the wide ball. No wonder, as Keating chronicles, that anyone who is the slightest bit interested in cricket shows some interest when Botham is in; and that the health and prosperity of the game in England depend heavily on his contribution.

Yet here is the mystery. This year, and last year, in his prime, at the peak of his success, Botham has been harassed by the gentlemen who run British cricket. Just before Christmas 1984, after what was plainly a set-up, Botham's house was raided by police. They went straight to a bag in a drawer in his bedroom, at the bottom of which they found 1.8 grammes of cannabis. He was convicted of possession, and fined. The hoo-ha in the press and from the authorities could hardly have been greater if Botham had tortured his best friend to death. Soon after-wards, the *Mail* newspaper started to persecute him with 'reminiscences' of a young woman who said he had smoked drugs on tour in Australia.

Botham unwisely sued for libel. The *Mail*, in its defence, organized 'investigators' to scavenge in his dustbins, and to dredge up any unfavourable gossip. As part of a deal to get the *Mail* off his back, Botham agreed to an article under his name in which he admitted he had smoked cannabis in his youth. Almost anyone who was a kid in the late sixties or early seventies could say the same, but the reaction from the authorities was astonishing. They banned Botham for most of the 1986 season, and deprived the dwindling and long-suffering cricketing public of their greatest entertainment. The barnacled boffins of the game weighed in. Fred Trueman, the Alf Garnett of cricket, said: 'Botham couldn't even bowl a long-hop.' Denis Compton said: 'He is a yobbo, who was never as good as he thinks.' Peter May and his selectors refused even to pick Botham for England after the ban had expired.

Was all this really because the game had been 'brought into disrepute' through Botham's article on cannabis? Cannabis is illegal, but it is not dangerous, as far as anyone in the world can discover. Nor is it addictive. There is some evidence (though even that is doubtful) that it leads to harder drugs, but what drug doesn't? Botham's confession that he had smoked the stuff in his youth was full of (rather uncharacteristic) remorse, and was plainly the result of a shabby legal deal. Can this absurd and extravagant punishment on all cricket lovers, backed up by all that absurd and extravagant language (Botham will live far longer in the record books than will Trueman or Compton, magnificent cricketers though both were), really have been because of cannabis?

I suspect there is much more to it than that. Micky Boulter, shop steward at the British Oxygen Company in Hackney in the days when there was a British manufacturing industry, knew as much about football as anyone I have ever met. He once described the typical English football boss as 'a blue-tie manager'. I never stopped to ask where the expression came from, so obvious was its meaning. Cricket, even more than football, is plagued by blue-tie managers – narrow-minded, small-hearted, utterly reactionary. Theirs is the attitude of the MCC member at Lords who called out 'Botham, come here!' as the great man was passing through the Long Room (the member got a suitably brusque reply, as Frank Keating is happy to report). The blue-tie managers like their players to be good-mannered and properly dressed, and above all to know their place. They prefer mediocrity on the field to insubordination off it. The attitude extends to their appreciation of cricket. They favour what Keating, in another phrase whose origin is uncertain but whose meaning is plain, describes as 'business strokes'. When Botham was bowled in a test match suddenly trying a 'reverse sweep', Peter May held a press conference. 'I have thumbed through the MCC coaching manual and found that no such stroke exists,' he told reporters. 'No such stroke exists', and yet, as Keating shows in a splendid rejoinder, most of the really great batsmen (not Peter May) have used it at one time or another. If players wear extravagant clothes which are not in the MCC manual, cutting their hair in a way which is not laid down in the MCC manual, and playing strokes which are not in the MCC manual, then what next? Might not the

MCC manual itself be challenged? Might not the hierarchical, snobbish undemocratic control of British cricket be threatened at its very
base? Like Sir Lester Deadlock in Charles Dickens's *Bleak House*, who
suspected a budding Wat Tyler in every guest who did not know with
what cutlery to eat fish, the controllers of cricket jump with horror at
every originality or improvisation lest it undermine their own long,
lamentable rule.

Frank Keating has done a great service not just to Ian Botham but to
all English cricket with this marvellous book. His object is simple: to
come to Botham's aid in his hour of need, and to put the record
straight about him. He has followed Botham's astonishing 1985 season
through every major match, describing and assessing each achievement. No one is better qualified to do that. For my money, Keating is
the country's top sports writer by a long distance (and there are many
other good ones). He writes pretty well about any sport, but cricket is
ingrained in him from his birth and upbringing not many miles from
the places where W.G. Grace performed his miracles. But the book is
not just a tribute from Frank Keating. From almost every county
ground, professional cricketers and umpires, old-timers and young-
timers, Australians, New Zealanders, Indians, Pakistanis, West Indians
are quoted in unstinting praise not only for Ian Botham's cricketing
ability but for the open-hearted and generous way he plays the game.
Almost all of them emphasize his friendship with his sporting opponents – something the blue-tie managers find deeply suspicious, if not
treacherous.

I am sorry to read in this book that Ian Botham is an 'independent
Tory' and (worse) that he admires Mrs Thatcher. But I am not inclined
to mix politics with sport. Indeed, the worst damage done to cricket
since the war has been that mixing of politics with sport which
knocked South Africa out of international cricket. The supporters of
apartheid mixed politics with sport so shamefully that they banned
people from playing cricket with one another because of the colour of
their skin. This outrage, which brought the entire sport into disrepute,
was greeted with unconcern by the same MCC gentlemen who have
apoplexy when cricketers say they smoked pot when they were kids.
Racialism is a million times more damaging to cricket than cannabis.
Where does Ian Botham stand on that?

He was offered, literally, a million pounds if he and his friend Viv
Richards went to South Africa as part of the public relations circus for

that country's racialist politics. He refused point blank. 'It was a hell of a lot of money,' he told Frank Keating.

> I said: 'What happens if Viv and I want to travel together? Or drive together? Or stay in the same hotel?' One of the guys said: 'Oh, no problem there at all. We'll make Viv an honorary white man.' That was it. *Honorary white man!* So if I go to Barbados and want to play cricket in Antigua, am I made an honorary black man? It's balls, the whole thing's total bollocks.

Ian Botham refused to join his England team-mates in their inglorious excursions to South Africa. When some Yorkshire representatives of the master race booed Viv Richards, Ian Botham was the first publicly to denounce them. And when a typical blue-tie manager from that county's cricket club (which still refuses to play a black man) came on the radio with typical blue-tie derision, Botham at once denounced him personally.

Ian Botham is a bitter enemy of racialism in sport, and so makes a poor Tory. If he continues, as he will, to lambast apartheid, he won't be asked too often to take tea with the Thatchers. When he suddenly decided, at the end of his astonishing 1985 season, to march from John O'Groats to Land's End to raise money for leukaemia research, there was, as Frank Keating persuasively proves, not an ounce of self-publicism in it. He knew his stunt could raise money, so he performed it – at great physical cost. Everyone quoted in the book comments on the infectious warmth of the man as he made his way south. But then he threw a punch at an interfering traffic cop. Much worse, he attacked the big companies for the paltry contribution they made to his appeal. He had discovered an old truth: 'the less people have; the more they give.' He gave voice to it angrily. And the blue-chip brigade, like the blue-tie brigade, grumbled over their lunches.

I have a serious quarrel with Frank Keating. He does terrible damage to adjectives. Adjectives are precious things, to be used always sparingly, with affection. They are (to make the point in nouns) the cream in the coffee, the salt in the stew. Too much, too randomly applied, ruins everything. Far too often, Frank Keating introduces his characters with two (or even three) slack adjectives. On one page we meet a 'strong and handsome' Simon O'Donnell, a 'snarling, aggressive, straight-backed' Geoff Lawson, a 'swift, hostile Craig McDermott', a 'wicked old Jeff Thomson', a 'gritty, youthful Doug Walters' and a 'simpering, sad Greg Matthews'. Phew! as Frank Keating would say. This sort of thing is bound to get ridiculous, and it does. On page 129 the unfortunate Greg Ritchie is described as 'pleasantly precocious, puppy-plump and pugnacious-looking'.

Frank doesn't write like this for the *Guardian* – does he have a good and faithful sub there who cuts out adjectives? There are some other examples of overwriting here. But not many. This is, despite these excesses, a delightful, challenging book, one of the best on cricket I have read for many a long year. It is enriched with Keating's prodigious memory for great cricketing occasions on almost every county ground. It is also beautifully produced (though, inexplicably, without an index). Best of all, it will make life even more exciting next time Botham's in.

London Review of Books, October 1986

Journalist in pursuit of story

The man on the phone was most insistent – and most impressive. He worked, he said, for British Telecom's accountants and had some documents about a huge share-dealing swindle which he wanted to pass on to me. He was off the next day to Blackpool, and had to see me that evening. No, it could not wait. Look, he went on urgently, he was frightened, and he wouldn't try again.

All right, all right, I replied. I would come right away and meet him as he suggested – outside a West End cinema. He could recognize me by the inevitable rolled-up *Daily Mirror* and the grey Beatles haircut.

Meeting such 'contacts' in the street can be extremely awkward and embarrassing. At one stage an elderly man drove his car right up to me, stopped abruptly, and flung open the door. I leaned inside and asked: 'Mr Edwards?' (the name the man had given me). 'No,' he said crossly. 'And I'm meeting my wife.' And here she was crossing the pavement, bewildered enough before I started my explanation, and totally confused when I had finished.

Eventually he arrived, quite unlike what I'd imagined, very young, very trendily dressed. He seemed genuinely scared and led me on a wild dance through the backstreets, eventually slumping down on a bench. He then announced that he was not Edwards at all, that he knew nothing at all about British Telecom and certainly hadn't got any documents. As I rose in some fury to go, he pressed me to sit down again, telling me he had *another* story, far more remarkable than anything about British Telecom; but he'd noticed I'd been writing about British Telecom and had used the bait to entice me out of the office.

He then embarked on a riveting saga about the supply of cocaine to a very important person.

The story was marvellous in its simplicity and in its sensationalism. He, the informant, was a receptionist who paid a large sum out of the company's petty cash every Friday for an envelope delivered by a despatch rider and collected the same day by the very important person. He could prove all this to me if I visited him the following day (he was not off to Blackpool) and witnessed the whole scene.

He wanted me to know that he was not interested at all in money. He did not want to be put up in a posh hotel (as he imagined most newspaper sources are). He only wanted to wreak vengeance on the very important person who was a hypocrite.

I became more and more absorbed. I started to plot with him how best we could catch the culprit with secret tape-recordings and 'snatch' pictures. I would have to discuss this, I said, with my editor, since it was all a bit big for me. He flattered me crudely, and successfully, by telling me he had singled me out from the whole field of journalism.

He said he knew I would want some proof to show my editor, and he had it. He had receipts for the envelopes, six of them in all, plus even a receipt from the local police station for a 'Christmas gift' which had been donated by the very important person.

I reached out my hand greedily but he said the documents were at home.

He promised to go and get them at once. He would not allow me to come with him, but he promised to meet me in an hour and a half's time in a pizza bar (which I named).

He said he ought to travel by taxi, and he lived in Acton. So I quickly pulled out my wallet and handed over all I had in it: £15, a reasonable estimate of the taxi fare from central London to Acton and back (in fact, I thought I was doing rather well out of the deal).

After an hour in the pizza bar I went home. He had not arrived. What could have happened? Had he been waylaid, had second thoughts, gone to the wrong pizza bar? The following morning I went early to the office and in mounting frenzy, rang every single branch of the vast organization headed by the Very Important Person in the story. I spoke to every single receptionist, and described my informant. Each one said they had never heard of anyone like that, and that it was 'most unlikely' that he existed.

It was only after about two hours of a precious morning that I started to realize the truth. I had been conned. Easily, ridiculously conned – and all for £15.

Dolefully, I recalled the last time this happened. In 1984, a man rang the *Mirror* office in Manchester claiming to have been signalman on a ship in the Falklands. He said he had in his possession the tapes from a signal from a flagship of the task force which spelt out the order for the sinking of the *General Belgrano*. The order made it clear that the cruiser was to be sunk in spite of instructions from the United States to the contrary.

The message was passed to me as the resident *Belgrano* expert. Once again, my enthusiasm knew no bounds. Somehow I persuaded the *Daily Mirror* to pay the fare for the man and his three mates to come to London from Liverpool. I met the man in a park and he told me breathlessly he had been holding this information for more than two years, but now he had nothing to lose since he was dying of cancer.

Disregarding his obvious state of good health and his tremendous appetite for beer (which I bought) I pressed him for the tapes. For a day and a night he kept ringing me saying the tapes were on the way. Finally, he was delivered up to the back door of the *Mirror* so drunk that he had to be taken to hospital. I never saw him again, and I never saw any tapes for the excellent reason that there weren't any.

There are those in the business who say that con artists are getting much cleverer nowadays, and that, as chequebook journalism becomes the norm rather than the exception, more and more top class swindlers are seeking to fleece 'up front' money from gullible journalists.

For my part, I seem to be plagued more than most with conmen, partly because my helpful colleagues at the *Mirror* are always keen to pass them on. I have discovered two basic rules: (1) the man who says he has a great story before he tells you his great story does not have a great story – indeed he does not have a story at all; (2) the person who says immediately that he doesn't want money for his information wants money for the information.

Nothing hurts quite so much as being conned.

On each of the two occasions above, as I gradually came to terms with the reality, I started to see the gaping holes in the informant's story. How *could* I have believed it? Every single aspect of it was shot through with nonsense.

I had behaved on both occasions (and on others I am too embarrassed to relate) like a baby with a new toy.

And yet, as the fury and the outrage dies, the regret dies quickly too. There's only one thing worse than believing people who are telling lies, and that is not believing people who are telling the truth. Scepticism may be the reporter's lifeline but cynicism is death. Better by far to be conned by the odd 'Mr Edwards', however monstrous his tale, than to run the chance of turning away some true story simply because it sounds fantastic. The more fantastic the story sounds, the more likely it is to be true.

So wherever you are, 'Mr Edwards', no hard feelings. And if I ever spot you on a bus or in the street, I want my £15 back.

UK Press Gazette, October 1987

The freedom to ridicule

When there is an attack raised in the press against Max Madden or Bernie Grant or Brian Sedgemore I am inclined to rush to their defence.

All three Labour MPs (Max in Bradford, Bernie in north London and Brian in east London) have bravely represented the persecuted racial minorities in their areas.

If the MPs are attacked, ostensibly for coming to the aid of Asian people in their constituencies and throughout the country, do they not deserve the support of all socialists? And is their recent House of Commons motion calling for the amendment of the blasphemy laws in the wake of Islamic fundamentalist outrage against Salman Rushdie's book *The Satanic Verses* not another example of their anti-racist convictions?

Brian and Max have both published strong defences of their motion. They have resisted criticism that they support the blasphemy laws by pointing out that their motion calls *either* for the amendment of the blasphemy laws to include Islam *or* for the repeal of the laws altogether. What further proof, they ask, could anyone need of their fairness of approach and basic hostility to blasphemy laws?

Unfortunately, the argument just does not work; indeed, it is ridiculous. Suppose for instance there was a law imposing capital punishment for certain types of murder – the 1956 Homicide Act is a good example. Would it be a sensible argument to demand *either* that the law applies to all forms of murder *or* be repealed?

Obviously not, for one alternative will mean that an ugly and repressive law is left on the statute book and even extended. The 'fair' alternative (that is, applying the death penalty for all murders) would end up being even more unfair than the existing law. Exactly the same argument applies to the MPs' attitude to the blasphemy laws.

The blasphemy laws are a hangover from the ecclesiastical courts, whose only interest was to preserve the established religion, usually against other rival religions. They were taken over by criminal courts in the nineteenth century and used in the struggle of the Establishment against the wave of dissent which was thrown up by the French Revolution.

They became the centre of a huge controversy in the 1880s when Charles Bradlaugh first won the right (so useful to people like Brian Sedgemore, Max Madden and Bernie Grant today) for people without strong Christian beliefs to sit in parliament. In 1881, a dissenter with the excellent (if slightly misspelt) name of G.W. Foote published *The Freethinker*, the journal of the Secular Society.

For this journal and other publications Foote was systematically prosecuted. He was convicted in February 1883 and sent to prison for a year. Two months later he came up again in court on another charge, and was taken from prison to his trial. He made a magnificent three hour speech on behalf of free thought.

In his speech Foote noted (as our three MPs have done) that religions which were not embraced by the established church had no protection from the blasphemy laws. He concluded, however, that this was further proof of the absurdity and oppressiveness of the laws themselves.

He asked the question: 'Is a church, any church, to be protected against ridicule, sarcasm or argument, or any other forms of attack?' And he replied:

> If a church cannot hold its own against such argument, let it go down.... To prosecute us in the interests of a church is to prostitute whatever is sacred in the name of religion and to degrade what should be a great spiritual power into a mere police agent, a haunter of criminal courts and an instructor of Old Bailey special pleaders.

The jury couldn't agree, and G.W. Foote wasn't tried again (though he served the rest of the year in prison).

After that the blasphemy laws were used sparingly, and then not at all until Mary Whitehouse tried to revive them in the 1970s.

We owe to people like Foote and Bradlaugh the freedom to say what we like about religion without fear of ancient, ecclesiastical and reactionary prosecution.

It is a great shame on Max Madden, Brian Sedgemore and Bernie Grant (and a sad comment on the cloying seductiveness of electoral politics) that they should have considered for a single moment, let alone in a House of Commons Order Paper, the resuscitation of these hideous laws.

In their eagerness to protect racial minorities in their constituencies they have not noticed that dark superstitions can work their suffocating powers on supporters of Islam just as much as on Christians.

All religions will at different times and for different reasons seek to raise themselves above the secular power, above reason and above free thought, and provoke laws to deny us the freedom to argue and to ridicule without which freedom no socialist can proceed.

Socialist Worker, February 1989

14. Inspirations

A socialist bookshelf

You have to look hard for some good news these bleak summer days, but I am cheered by two bits of it last week.

The first was that the takings at the bookstalls at *Marxism 83*, a week-long series of meetings, debates and discussions between Marxists, reached an all-time (and in the circumstances quite extraordinary) high of £9,000. More people came to *Marxism* this year than in any other, but the proportion of books sold to people who registered was higher, I gather, than ever before.

These fantastic sales among people who have not got very much money is further proof, if proof were needed, that socialists as a breed read more than anyone else. The ideas which keep people socialists against all the pressures of society push them more and more towards books.

But stop! Is there not some hideous deviation here? Is all this book-buying just a sign of property consciousness?

I remember during a day school for *Socialist Worker* readers in Manchester some ten years ago fleeing during a break to a secondhand bookshop with one of the school's organizers.

As I emerged with a couple of prize possessions, he remonstrated with me. Was this not just covetousness for possessions, a sort of obsession with belongings which had a distinctly bourgeois ring to it?

I supposed he was right, and hid the books shamefacedly. But on reflection, I realize he was not right at all. First, there is the old argument about private possessions and public property.

As John Strachey argued in his little book *Why You Should be a Socialist* nearly fifty years ago, the whole point about the public owner-ship and planning of the means of production is that it releases capital for producing things that people need *and want*. He argued for more public ownership and more equality not to abolish private possessions but to make them more widely available.

Then there is a special argument about books. However marvellous the progress in other forms of media such as tapes and videos, for people who think and who value ideas there is no replacement for books.

This is because books do not impose a pace on their reader. They can be studied at the reader's own level of concentration and consciousness. And then they can be re-read.

Of course public libraries are wonderful institutions, and under any system even remotely socialist would be expanded far beyond anything we have at present.

But there is a peculiar advantage in owning books, since they can be marked, stored away in shelves and in the mind, and returned to again and again when a new idea or argument comes along.

In an old questionnaire among Communists in Fife, the third or fourth question was: 'Are there any books in the house?' Plenty of workers, usually the best Communists, answered 'Yes'.

And that brings me to the second piece of good news. Last January I was driven from Harwich to Felixstowe by Dave Saunders, a seaman on a North Sea car ferry.

We were talking then about the collision of two ferries, which had killed six workers in dreadful circumstances.

As we came back to Harwich, Dave suddenly changed the subject and started talking about Shelley. As we went into his house, I fell eagerly on a big bookcase, full of old books of every description: Dickens, Shakespeare and Shelley.

Last week I was up that way again, for a meeting in Ipswich, led off with great vigour by Dave Saunders.

He was speaking for the workers on the ferries who had gone on strike against a crude attempt of the owners to sabotage their nationally agreed wage rise.

I was delighted to see that those workers won their fight (as far as I can see game, set and match). And I certainly believe that Dave Saunders's bookcase had something to do with it.

Tribunes and the people*

'Shakespeare was a Tory without any doubt.' Thus Nigel Lawson, in what must rank as one of the Great Asininities of the 1980s, in an interview in the *Guardian* in September 1983. Asked to explain himself Mr Lawson slid into characteristic incoherence:

'I think that in *Coriolanus* the Tory virtues, the Roman virtues as mediated through Shakespeare are ... it's written from a Tory point of view.'

In milder and more coherent prose, William Hazlitt, perhaps the greatest Shakespearean critic of all time, tended to the Lawson view: 'Shakespeare himself seems to have had a leaning to the arbitrary side of the question, perhaps from some feeling of contempt for his own origin, and to have spared no occasion of bating the rabble.'

In their different ways Lawson and Hazlitt are both wrong. But from the productions of *Coriolanus* I have seen over the last thirty years, it is easy to see how anyone could come to that conclusion.

The productions, without exception, have featured Coriolanus as a hero, the citizens as dupes and the tribunes as self-serving hypocrites.

This was true of the Coriolanus played by Laurence Olivier (1959), Alan Howard (1977), Ian McKellen (1986) and now Charles Dance. The present Royal Shakespeare production by Terry Hands seems to me even worse than his former effort in 1977, and that was unpolitical enough.

The *Coriolanus* Shakespeare wrote is something completely different to the stiff, unbalanced and unconvincing play which is constantly produced in our theatres.

Any socialist who goes to see *Coriolanus* must get seated early and listen, for the first few exchanges of the first scene of the first act lay the foundation stone for the entire play. The stage direction is apt: 'Enter a company of mutinous citizens, with staves, clubs and other weapons.'

In Terry Hands's production the citizens are all dressed up in the same silly black uniforms. They are easily convertible into a mob. But in Shakespeare's text each citizen has a character, and a separate argument.

---

*Review of *Coriolanus*, Royal Shakespeare Company production, January 1990

The first citizen takes the lead at once and proclaims: 'We are all resolv'd rather to die than to famish.' With this agreed, he goes to the second proposition: 'Caius Martius is chief enemy of the people.' There then follows a summary of the attitude of the Roman ruling class of the time which is not all that different from that of the British ruling class today.

> If they would yield us but the superfluity while it were wholesome, we might guess they relieved us humanely but they think we are too dear; the leanness that afflicts us, the object of our misery, is as an inventory to particularize their abundance, our sufferance is a gain to them. Let us revenge this with our pikes ere we become rakes, for the gods know, I speak this in hunger for bread not in thirst for revenge.

Immediately, the second citizen argues with the general view, pointing out Martius's services to the country, and demanding, 'Nay, speak not maliciously.' The argument goes on for a bit until the patrician Menenius arrives to stop the rebellion.

Menenius certainly was a Tory, not so much a Thatcher or a Lawson as a Whitelaw or a Macmillan, offering nice words and boring little homilies to the plebs he detests.

His chief opponent in the argument which immediately follows is the second citizen, the one who previously had doubts about so rash a course. When Menenius claims the senate cares for the people, the second citizen explodes in fury

> Care for us? True indeed, they ne'er cared for us yet suffer us to famish and their store-houses crammed with grain, make edicts for usury to support usurers, repeat daily any wholesome act established against the rich and provide more piercing statutes daily to chain up and restrain the poor.

Menenius tries to argue against this with a pleasing enough little metaphor about the limbs in mutiny against the belly which provides the nourishment for the limbs, but he is not very persuasive. And now, very early on in this first act, Caius Martius strides onto the stage apparently justifying everything the citizens say about him with his first sentence:

> What's the matter you dissentious rogues
> That rubbing the poor itch of your opinion
> Make yourself scabs.

He then delivers himself of the first of his many diatribes against the common people, calling them in quick succession, curs, geese and hares. He is beside himself with rage because he has just come from the Senate where they have made some concessions to the popular upsurge, granted slight reductions in corn prices and even agreed to the appointment of people's tribunes. Shouts Caius: 'The rabble should have first unroof'd the city ere some prevailed with me. It will in time win upon power, and throw forth greater themes for insurrection's arguing.'

He is against all concessions and would even take on all the demonstrators with his sword, had not a messenger suddenly announced the declaration of war with a neighbouring tribe, the Volsces. Martius immediately rushes off to war to become a great general and cover himself with blood and glory. One reason he loves war so much is that it provides plenty of opportunities to rid Rome and the patricians of 'our musty superfluity', by which he means the poor and the unemployed.

Back comes Martius from the conquered city of the Volsces. Corioles, to be acclaimed Coriolanus, and to seek the all-powerful post of consul. To do that, he must go through certain ceremonies to show his love for the people. He must appear in humble clothes in the marketplace, speak to the people and, if they ask, show them his wounds. He despises this ritual.

The fascination in his character lies not so much in his personal pride, which is prodigious, but in his inability to accept the advice of the Whitelaws and the Macmillans around him; to be nice to the people in order more effectively to rob them. He can't stand being nice to them. He hates their working clothes, their stinking breath, their vulgar accents. Above all he hates the tribunes, who come from his class but have agreed to represent another one.

The tribunes know perfectly well what Coriolanus is. He is (the word is apposite since it has Roman roots) a fascist. If he becomes consul, they reflect, 'our office may, during his power, go sleep'.

They therefore argue with the people to reject Coriolanus as consul. In the modern British theatre these scenes are always produced with a heavy bias towards Coriolanus. The tribunes are shown to incite the people against their will and better judgement. Once again, the text is different. The conversation between the tribunes and the citizens immediately after the 'humble pie' scene in the marketplace goes like this:

Sicinius (tribune): How now my masters have you chose this man?
First Citizen: He has our voices, Sir.
Brutus (tribune): We pray the Gods he may deserve your loves.
Second Citizen: Amen, Sir. To my poor unworthy notice, he mocked us when he begged our voices.
Third Citizen: Certainly, he flouted us outright.

Once more there is an argument. The First Citizen, who was the agitator in the first scene, now takes up the cause of moderation.

First Citizen: No, tis his kind of speech, he did not mock us.
Second Citizen: Not one amongst us, save yourself, but says he used us scornfully. He should have showed us his marks of merit, wounds received for's country.
Sicinius (tribune): Why so he did. I'm sure.
Citizens: No, no; no man saw them.

The citizens are disgusted by Coriolanus before even a tribune speaks a bad word of him. It is only then that the tribunes bring to bear the political arguments which, in the light of Coriolanus's contempt-uous behaviour and his record, are extremely serious ones.

The best arguments come from Brutus. In Hands's production these arguments are screamed and spat at the crowd as though the very decibel count would force them into the minds of the mob. In the text, though, they are powerful arguments about the advancing dictatorship.

When he had no power
But he was a petty servant to the state.
He was your enemy, ever spake against
Your liberties and the charters that you bear
I' the body of the weal

and again a bit later on:

Did you perceive
He did solicit you in free contempt
When he did need your loves: and do you think
That his contempt shall not be bruising to you
When he hath power to crush?

This is the argument used to incite people to action against tyranny. In the Paris Commune, for instance, the militants argued for the bloody hand to avoid the severed hand, for the terror of the many against the incomparably more horrible terror of the few.

The people respond, reject Martius for consul and, as he makes more and more angry noises against them, threaten to kill him. This threat is withdrawn by advice of the tribunes.

Eventually, as the play heaves back and forth from class to class, the tribunes decide on a compromise – banishment – which, like so many compromises since, proves disastrous to them and the people.

The people are *not* the collection of fickle idiots and their tribunes are not the screeching hypocrites who appear in Hands's latest production, and all the other prestigious productions of recent times. The people have a case, and they argue it sensibly between them. The tribunes have a very strong argument, and they put it straight to the people they represent.

When a senator asks if they intend 'to unbuild the city and to lay all flat' they answer with a great shout: 'the people are the city.'

This is not to pretend, Dave Spart-like, that *Coriolanus* is a revolutionary play against the fascist menace. That would be as ridiculous an interpretation as is the fashionable Lawson view. The people can be fickle: they do switch from side to side. They are as likely to murder a king as to worship him. Equally, their representatives are more likely to guard their own backsides than to fight for others of a different class.

Coriolanus is a complex character who gets our sympathy for his hatred of hypocrisy as much as he earns our contempt for his contempt of the common people.

This is probably the best political play ever written, precisely because it shifts and moves between arguments and counter-arguments not of dummies and stereotypes but of real human beings.

Shakespeare knew well enough from his own life experiences (the biggest Midlands riots against the enclosures took place not far from where he was born) that the people had a case. He was also nervous, as almost everyone is, of what may happen if the class born to rule and used to rule is suddenly toppled from power.

It is utterly ruinous of the play to take one side against the other, to glorify the excesses of Coriolanus or to make imbeciles of the tribunes, as this most recent production has done.

Bertolt Brecht loved *Coriolanus* more than any other play. He spent hours with it, rehearsing it, adapting it and even rewriting it to make sure the people had a proper say. In the end he admitted he could not improve on the original. What a tragedy it is that to please the likes of

Nigel Lawson so many modern producers of *Coriolanus* do not learn the same lesson.

Socialist Worker Review, January 1990

Almighty Godwin*

Don't be deceived by the title or subtitle. This is not the biography of a family and it is not about the Godwins and the Shelleys. Perhaps the publishers persuaded William St Clair against his better judgement to downgrade his hero in the title and to include the Shelleys, who are more famous. This rich, glorious book is, however, a biography of William Godwin – no more, no less. St Clair himself is described on the dust-jacket as a 'senior Treasury official', a horrifying disclosure which emerges elsewhere in the book only in parenthesis (the French monarchy was forced to appeal to the Third Estate, St Clair tells us, because it failed to 'control the public sector borrowing requirement' and the philosopher Malthus discovered in the early nineteenth century what HM Treasury has discovered in the late twentieth – that the 'great economic answer to social misery is to make it worse'). How St Clair gets on with his Malthusian colleagues at HM Treasury day by day is a perpetual wonder to the reader of this book, where, like his subject, he emerges as a genuine Whig, a creature not so much of the French Revolution as of the Enlightenment.

William Godwin was brought up in England's bleakest countryside, the Cambridgeshire Fens, and in one of its bleakest religious traditions. By the time the people of Paris stormed the Bastille in 1789, he had thrown off all the superstitions and cruelties of his upbringing and his faith, and was writing the great work which was to make him, during the 1790s, at once the most famous and the most notorious of all

---

*Review of *The Godwins and the Shelleys: The Biography of a Family* by William St Clair.

the writers of that tempestuous decade. *Political Justice* took its theme from the Marquis de Condorcet, Baron d'Holbach, Volney, Diderot and the other great Enlighteners of pre-Revolutionary France. Human beings, it asserts, are above all perfectible. They need look nowhere else for improvement but to themselves. Women are equal to men. Religion is superstition, marriage an 'odious monopoly', riches and poverty unnecessary evils. People can and should live in harmony, happiness and relative equality, and the only obstacle which stands in their way is their own inability to think for themselves and to apply calm and reason to the chaos around them.

Political Justice is a rigorous, exciting and often ferocious attack on the established order in Britain in 1793, much of which is still with us two hundred years later. It was reinforced the following year by the more readable *Caleb Williams*, Godwin's first novel. The tyranny of society in general is symbolized by the aristocratic monomaniac Lord Falkland, the good sense and misery of its common people by the aristocrat's servant, the narrator, who spends much of the book in prison.

> 'Thank God,' exclaims the Englishman, 'we have no Bastille! Thank God, with us no man can be punished without a crime!' Unthinking wretch! Is that a country of liberty, where thousands languish in dungeons and fetters? Go to, ignorant fool, and visit the scenes of our prisons! Witness their unwholesomeness, their filth, the tyranny of their governors, the misery of their inmates! After that show me the man shameless enough to triumph and say, England has no Bastille!

Political Justice was published in the same month that England declared war on Revolutionary France, and *Caleb Williams* burst on a reading public that was being systematically terrorized by blood-curdling descriptions of what the Jacobins were doing in Paris. Publishing anything critical of the British government or favourable to the French was already a dangerous business. *Political Justice* was not prosecuted – it sold at one pound sixteen shillings a copy and was therefore thought unlikely to get into the hands of the sort of people who were reading Thomas Paine's *Rights of Man*. *Caleb Williams* was not prosecuted, on the grounds that it was a novel and decent people did not take novels seriously. But Godwin's friend and fellow freethinker Thomas Holcraft, along with other members of the London Corresponding Society, were prosecuted for treason (opposing the government) – and were found not guilty after Godwin himself, at great risk,

published a pamphlet attacking the prosecution as corrupt and politically motivated. Holcraft and his colleagues were luckier than their
brilliant and courageous comrade Joseph Gerrald, who argued the case
for freedom of republican speech in an Edinburgh court and was
despatched to Botany Bay, where he died within a year.

As the post-Revolutionary repression rose to a crescendo many of
the 1793 revolutionaries fled the field. Godwin himself identified 1797
as the year of the great turn. Perhaps the most decisive events were the
failure of the French Army to land in Ireland in December 1796 (success would certainly have cut the British tyranny short) and the subsequent collapse of the naval mutiny at the Nore. From 1797 onwards, at
any rate, Godwin found himself deserted by former allies and benefactors, James Mackintosh, Thomas Wedgwood, Samuel Parr. In his
magnificent open letter to Parr in 1801 he mused on the phenomenon of
political apostasy, and restated his faith in the 'progressive nature of
man', and in the fundamental notions of the much revised *Political
Justice.*

Even by 1801, however, Godwin was embarked on what St Clair
properly calls a 'long slow retreat'. It was to go on, with incessant
'retractations', for the rest of his life. As early as 1795 he shamefully
attacked the opposition to the government's Two Acts, which banned
political meetings and 'seditious' publications. Yet by the time he
wrote 'The Reply to Parr', he was a symbol of everything the King, his
courtiers and their government found disgusting about Jacobins. This
was partly because of his views on politics but mostly because of his
attitude to women's rights, marriage and sex. In his early writings,
perhaps under the monastic influence of his upbringing, Godwin
suggested that in the great scheme of things relations between men
and women were a 'trivial matter'. Mary Wollstonecraft soon put paid
to that notion. When he met her first at dinner in 1792, Godwin was
irritated by her bubbling assertiveness. But he met her again, and his
tempestuous relationship with her in 1796 and 1797, their brief life
together as husband and wife, and Mary's quite unnecessary death
during the birth of her daughter Mary profoundly affected his writing.
The exposition of women's rights in *Political Justice* was rather dry.
After Mary's death he set to work to write a tribute to her, and it was
these *Memoirs* which earned him the full fury of the anti-Jacobin
hysteria. Then as now, it was much easier for reactionaries to attack
the personal behaviour of their opponents than to argue with their

politics. The Jacobins, it was said, were all loose-living libertines. Mary Wollstonecraft had conceived her daughters out of wedlock. No doubt that had something to do with her most appropriate death. It was a short step from exposing these 'loose morals' to denouncing the philosophy which inspired them – indeed the very word 'philosophy' became, in those dreadful days, a word of abuse. It was better not to think at all, since any thought could lead to having children out of wedlock.

Godwin was first pilloried, then forgotten. By 1810, though he was still writing third-rate plays, novels and even Bible stories, few people who admired *Political Justice* knew that its author was still alive. He had married again, started a children's bookshop, and was absorbed, almost to the end of his life, in finding money to keep out of the debtors' prisons.

One such admirer was the young Shelley. He had read the first edition of *Political Justice* and much preferred it to all the others. Shelley was a revolutionary. He revelled in the 'spirit of 1793'. As soon as he heard (in 1812 from the apostate poet Southey) that Godwin was alive, he was impatient to meet him and to correspond with him. The two men immediately plunged into argument. Shelley wanted to form a political association, a party of like-minded revolutionaries. Godwin angrily cautioned him against any such scheme. Each person should arrive at his opinions *individually*, he insisted. Political associations only inflamed the passions and dimmed the light of reason. Shelley replied, equally angrily, that in the twenty years since *Political Justice* had been written not much had been achieved by all the individually thinking men and women who agreed with it. Now, surely, was the time for action to implement the ideas. Godwin nagged on and on, and finally dissuaded Shelley from his purpose.

St Clair describes this as a 'debate between the younger Godwin and the older Godwin'. Shelley took his stand on the first edition of *Political Justice*, and in his youth, when writing for a Whig Party paper, Godwin himself had strenuously defended the rights of men and women with similar opinions to associate with one another. Here was the old philosopher warning his protégé against the enthusiasms of his own youth. But there was a further, deeper difference between the two men which St Clair has also detected. Godwin was an egalitarian in thought, but 'in action only a Whig'. He was frightened by and suspicious of all forms of collective action. At every political meeting he had ever attended he had seen 'how the enthusiasm was lighted up, how the flame caught from man to man, how fast the dictates of sober reason were obliterated by gusts of passion'. These were precisely the flames of revolution which excited Shelley.

St Clair is firmly on Godwin's side in the argument. Of Shelley, he does not really approve at all, though he can't help but admire his poetry. The characterization of Shelley here is the crude early nineteenth-century stereotype. Shelley was a 'spoilt young man', a 'fanatic'. He took up causes and dropped them at will. He 'never liked history'. He was 'never in doubt'. At one stage St Clair guesses (this strange episode has never been satisfactorily explained) that Shelley adopted a child from a Naples street in order to replace his own dead baby daughter – and then placed the adopted baby in a convent where he never visited her. Shelley, it is suggested, was heartless and selfish with those close to him and, after he married Godwin's daughter, especially so with his poor old father-in-law. In an extraordinary appendix, St Clair suggests that Shelley did not write the notes, or essays, which illuminate *Queen Mab*. The pirated editions of the poem in the early 1820s print at the head of each note the picture of a small hand. This illustration St Clair suggests, indicates that someone else wrote the notes. He even names the author as Erasmus Perkins, a Shelley admirer, who helped to circulate *Queen Mab* among the pirates.

The stereotype nowhere fits the reality. Shelley's political ideas remained consistent throughout his life. He was not spoilt – he was cut off from his family's fortune as soon as he was expelled from Oxford. 'A Philosophical View of Reform', the pamphlet he wrote in 1820 (it wasn't published for a hundred years) starts with a brilliant short history of the world and its culture which could hardly have come from a history-hater. He was not a fanatic – he was always listening and learning from what others had to say. He constantly doubted and tested even his most fervent convictions (a single reading of the 'Ode to the West Wind' is enough to prove that). He was a generous man, especially to Godwin, to whom he gave thousands of pounds for nothing, and whose praises he never stopped singing. 'You will see,' he wrote in his poem to Maria Gisborne, Godwin's former admirer,

> That which was Godwin – greater none than he
> Though fallen – and fallen on evil times – to stand
> Among the spirits of our age and land,

Before the dread tribunal of To-Come
The foremost ...

As for the notes to *Queen Mab*, William St Clair's theory can quickly be refuted. One of the notes (accompanied, like the others, by the tell-tale 'hand') is a slightly edited version of 'The Necessity of Atheism', which Shelley wrote at university. Its authorship is not in any doubt at all, unless William St Clair would have the ubiquitous Erasmus Perkins at Shelley's elbow at Oxford in 1811. This refutation is, in any case, hardly necessary since the style of the notes is so obviously Shelley's – there are so many phrases which can be found in so many of his other pamphlets ('A Letter to Lord Ellenborough', for instance) – that no one who admires Shelley's prose as much as his poetry could doubt for a moment that he wrote the *Queen Mab* notes.

If St Clair is irascible and sometimes patronizing towards the Shelleys, he is nothing of the kind towards Godwin. The Great Philosopher would have been delighted to know that his life would be written by such a devoted biographer who records his subject, his times and his books with the enthusiasm of a writer who does not have to make his living or his reputation from any of them. Before I read this book I had Godwin down as a dry old opportunist. I agreed with the American visitor who spoke of his 'great head' full of 'cold brains'. This marvellous book has banished that picture for ever. Godwin, for all his 'long slow retreat', did not sell the pass. He defended Robespierre in 1794 and Napoleon in 1815. He preferred the gains of the French Revolution to the feudalism it replaced. His ideas were too firmly held to be rejected because the times changed or the money ran out. He enjoyed conversation and argument every bit as much as books. He was loved by all his children, Mary most of all. It was right and proper that he should have lived even for such a short time with Mary Wollstonecraft. His *Political Justice* and her *Vindication of the Rights of Woman* 'stand together on the shelf', in St Clair's memorable metaphor, 'like a colossal Pharaoh and his consort; enduring monuments of the spirit of the age'.

London Review of Books, September 1989

Coleridge's early visions*

I confess I started this book in an uneasy temper. Richard Holmes's first major work, his 1974 biography of Shelley, had a more profound effect on me than anything I have ever read except Shelley himself, to whom, anyway, I was led by Richard Holmes. Though it merged my revolutionary opinions with Shelley's majestic poetry, Holmes's *Shelley: The Pursuit* was not a dogmatic book. Christopher Booker, whose political opinions have grown steadily more reactionary, also enjoyed it. It was a biography of such devoted and loving care that it was difficult to see how Richard Holmes, who published this book when he was 29 years old, could possibly move forward from it.

Though I knew pretty well nothing about Coleridge, except what Hazlitt (and Shelley) had written about him, it seemed indisputable that, on any reckoning, a move from Shelley to Coleridge was a step back. All through the 1980s I have imagined Richard Holmes working away on Coleridge, and worried about how he was coping. The very decade itself loomed ominously around him. Shelley was just right for the early 1970s. Would Coleridge seem just as right for the 1980s?

In the slightly pretentious last lines of his Preface, Richard Holmes writes 'He (Coleridge) is the visionary hero of my book, a hero for a self-questioning age.'

Self-questioning age be blowed. This has been a downright reactionary and backward age, as indeed were the late 1790s and early 1800s which form the backcloth to this first volume. In the sudden switch from prevailing revolution to prevailing reaction, former revolutionaries behave in different ways. Some stand firm by the ideas, as did Shelley, and to a lesser extent Shelley's father-in-law, William Godwin. Others, like Coleridge's undergraduate friend Bob Southey, do a complete about-turn, and make no attempt to deny it. Others twist and turn from one position to another, on the one hand unable to write off the invigorating idealism of their youth, on the other unable to shout out loud for a change which seems either impossible or preposterous or both. Such people are inclined to shift their ideas, their writings and their conversation according to the mood of the company. They are

---

*Review of *Coleridge: Early Visions* by Richard Holmes.

always seeing both sides of the argument so clearly that they do not know which side they are on. Their indecision turns invariably into self-pity and then to self-contempt. Nowadays the slogan which justifies all this is 'new realism'. This phrase appears at least twice in this biography in contexts which suggest that Richard Holmes himself is advocating Coleridge's 'new realism' to his readers in the 1980s, every bit as enthusiastically as he advocated Shelley's revolutionism in the 1970s.

Coleridge's conversion to new realism was rapid. At Cambridge and soon afterwards he was, by the later definition he gave the word, a Jacobin, or at least an extreme Democrat (then a term of abuse to the upper classes). His ill-fated journal, the *Watchman*, and, above all, his fiery speeches to vast crowds from the pulpits of the growing industrial cities, especially Bristol and Birmingham, were indistinguishable in content (if superior in style and delivery) from anything put out by the more infamous radicals of the day. When he settled in Somerset and enticed William and Dorothy Wordsworth to take a house at Alfoxden, the Home Office sent a spy to keep in touch with the activities of the two subversives. The spy left when he discovered that the most subversive thing the poets ever did was go for endless walks in the Quantock Hills.

There was some truth in Coleridge's own assertion in 1809: 'my little world described the path of revolution in an orbit of its own'. He was far more interested in setting up a perfect colony in which he and his friends could live and dazzle each other with their geniuses than he was in the effect the French Revolution might have on anyone else. It was he who invented the term 'Pantisocracy' to describe his plan to go with Robert Southey and any other intelligent man or woman of letters who would join him to found the perfect colony in America. Everyone would contribute to the necessary work, and, in the vast amount of spare time left over, would educate and entertain one another. The plan foundered on innumerable problems. Southey caused an awful fuss by asking what status servants would have in the new communes. Southey could not tolerate Coleridge's instinctive notion that the servants should have equal status with their masters. No one for a single moment imagined a perfect society where servants did not exist.

Once Pantisocracy was dropped, it became necessary to sound the revolutionary retreat right here in England. This Coleridge did most eloquently, and rapidly persuaded Wordsworth to do the same. 'The

Language of the Rights of Man' Richard Holmes explains, 'had been modified into what may be called the Rights of Nature.' Coleridge himself wrote in a letter to his brother (in words which almost exactly recall Wordsworth's famous poem Tintern Abbey): 'I love fields and woods and mountains with an almost visionary fondness – and because I have found benevolence and quietness growing within me as that fondness increased, therefore I should wish to be the means of implanting it in others.'

The same letter explained to his brother how Coleridge intended to live on the new handsome annuity conferred on him without condition by Tom Wedgwood. The argument was that the new thought which would now replace the rather vulgar ideas of the French Revolution would be based not on human beings but on fields and woods and mountains. The visionary enthusiasm of the early 1790s in which men like Coleridge looked to changes which would affect human beings was replaced by the 'visionary fondness' they felt for the inanimate countryside. All this is nothing but introspective nonsense. It is all very well to enjoy the countryside and the wonders of nature; fine indeed for poets to describe such things. But to reject ideas which are based on human thought and action in exchange for sybaritic contemplation of nature is nothing but to beat a retreat. Arguing against William Godwin and those like him who contended that there was a permanent drive towards human progress, Coleridge asked incisively: 'Is the march of the human race progressive, or in Cycles?' In cycles, certainly, but what causes those cycles is surely to be found not in fields and woods and mountains but in the minds and actions of human beings.

Richard Holmes and many other Coleridge-lovers would well reply that politics is not everything. They might insist that where Great Poets are concerned politics is next to nothing. That could hardly be said of Coleridge, however, and not just because this first volume covers in great detail one of the most tempestuous decades in British political history. Coleridge's reputation as a poet may be based on glorious ballads like the 'Ancient Mariner' or 'Kubla Khan,' which describe nature all the time and politics not at all. But Coleridge flung himself into Radical politics in the early 1790s with all the enthusiasm with which he denounced them in the late 1790s. He was not just a poet, indeed as far as most people who had heard of him at that time were concerned he was not even mainly a poet, but a journalist with a terse writing style, a thirst for campaigning and investigation, and a powerful platform in the *Morning Post.* Moreover, as this volume makes quite clear (and Richard Holmes is far too good a biographer not to notice it) Coleridge's political backsliding is closely connected to a lot of other backsliding. Boris Kagarlitsky recently wrote a book about the twentieth-century Russian intelligentsia which he describes in his title *The Thinking Reed.* Coleridge was perhaps more than any of his contemporaries a Thinking Reed: brilliant, witty, infectiously enthusiastic but a reed shaken by whatever wind happened to blow in his direction.

In his preface, Richard Holmes sets the standards by which this biography must be judged. 'If he (Coleridge) does not leap out of these pages – brilliant, animated, endlessly provoking – and invade your imagination (as he has done mine), then I have failed to do him justice.' All these aspects of Coleridge certainly do leap out of this book. Richard Holmes may have lost some of his radicalism, but he has lost none of his biographer's skill.

> Coleridge arrived at Lamb's with three ponderous German dictionaries; a set of 17th century political dialogues; a huge box of letters, poems and sermons; a pair of razors and a soap box; and a voluminous five-penny floral dressing gown decorated with hieroglyphics, in which he used to sit translating Wallenstein looking suspiciously like a conjuror according to Lamb.

These images go on and on. Coleridge is never dull. But there is another side to Richard Holmes's hero, which protrudes so bluntly from the biography that the very status of hero is cast in doubt. Coleridge was forever prevaricating, forever a victim to 'the fatal genius of being all things to all men'. If he met up with a crowd of Republicans he would make jokes about the King; but in Germany where his fellow English students were all for King, Pitt and Country, he led the singing of Rule Britannia. No jingoistic balderdash was too crude for this most refined of all the poets; no one more certain to be pitied (or despised) than himself. His worst habit was constantly to apologize for his excesses, or his lack of excesses. He exploited to the full the old trick of the British upper classes; charm through self-denigration. Kitty Wedgwood, the wife of Coleridge's benefactor, wrote: 'An excessive goodness and sensibility is put too forward, which gives an appearance, at least of conceit, and excites suspicion that he is acting.' Shelley had it right, as usual.

You will see Coleridge, he who sits obscure
In the exceeding lustre and the pure
Intense irradiation of a mind
Which, with its own internal lightning blind,
Flags wearily through duskness and despair,
A cloud-encircled meteor of the air,
A hooded eagle among blinking owls.

This is only volume one (it shouldn't be: one huge volume would have been much better than two, with a gap – and another £16.95 I suppose – in between) and there is, I suspect, worse to come. Holmes's Shelley excited and inspired me; his Coleridge merely interests (and faintly disgusts) me. I suppose that is the price that must be paid in a 'self-questioning age'.

Literary Review, October 1989

Discovering Shelley

I share with Shelley a rotten education at University College, Oxford.

On many journeys to the college's football changing rooms, I passed, with only a moment's hesitation, a huge gilded cage, under a dome. Inside, on a marble slab borne up by angels and sea lions, as though from the deep, was, and still is, the statue of a beautiful young man, emphatically naked. A typewritten note stuck rather shame-facedly on the wall told me that this was Percy Bysshe Shelley, who had been an 'alumnus' of University College, Oxford, from 1810 to 1811. I remember asking the dean of the college why Shelley had spent so little time at the university. 'Oh,' muttered the dean, embarrassed, 'he was drowned.' And so, of course, he was – eleven years after he had been expelled from University College for writing the first atheist pamphlet ever published in English.

The naked Shelley was the subject of much sport each summer I was at Oxford. As a climax to what is known as Eights Week, the future leaders of the nation would mourn yet another disaster for the University College First Eight by squeezing between the bars of Shelley's cage, and wreaking havoc on his statue. 'We've got Shelley's balls!' was the plummy cry of triumph which would echo through the quadrangles at three or four in the morning.

The authorities shrugged their shoulders and sought out a mason, who replaced the missing parts.

The castration of Shelley at British places of learning has not been confined to rowing oafs. Ladies and gentlemen of letters have been at it far longer, and with far greater effect. I still have a slim navy blue volume, entitled *Shelley*, which I was forced to buy at school. Its editor is one A.M.D. Hughes. In his 'selected works', there is no *Queen Mab*, no *Revolt of Islam*, no *Mask of Anarchy*, no *Peter Bell*, no *Swellfoot the Tyrant* – no *ideas* of any description. In the Penguin edition of Shelley, published in my last year at school (1956), the editor, a celebrated lady of letters called Isobel Quigly, writes: 'No poet better repays cutting; no great poet was ever less worth reading in his entirety.' She sets to her scissors with a will, extracting with devoted thoroughness every trace of political or social thought from Shelley's work.

In the beautiful Nonesuch edition of *Shelley: Selected Poetry, Prose and Letters*, published in 1951, the editor, a well-read gentleman called A.S.B. Glover, rejoices as he leaves out two of Shelley's greatest longer poems, both political from start to finish. '*Peter Bell* and *Oedipus* [*Swellfoot the Tyrant*]' writes Mr Glover, 'are mainly of interest as proof that a great lyric poet may fail lamentably outside his own proper field.'

Similarly, Kathleen Raine in her selection of Shelley in the Penguin 'Poet to Poet' series, writes: 'Without regret, I have omitted *Laon and Cythna* (later revised and renamed *The Revolt of Islam*), and a great deal of occasional political verse by Shelley the student activist in which the inspirers had no hand.'

These are just a few examples from my own literary upbringing and education. They are repeated over and over again in perhaps a hundred castrated editions of Shelley over the last 150 years.

The castration is horrible. The treatment of Shelley's 'Philosophical View of Reform', for instance, is almost incredible. It was written at the height of Shelley's literary powers. It ranks in style and in content with the most famous radical pamphlets of our history – with Tom Paine's *Rights of Man*, with Mary Wollstonecraft's *Vindication of the Rights of Women*, with the pamphlets of Bentham or Robert Owen or Marx and

Engels. It was available and known to all the people who had access to Shelley's notebooks after his death. Yet it stayed there, not even transcribed, for *one hundred years* after it was written. And even then – in 1920 – it was published only as a collector's item for members of the Shelley Society.

Shelley's most explicit work on sex and love, *A Discourse on the Manners of the Ancient Greeks, Relative to the Subject of Love*, was held back even longer. It first appeared in an edition edited by Roger Ingpen in 1931, 113 years after it was written, and even then it was privately printed.

By this process of censorship and omission, Shelley has been sheltered from young people at school and university even more carefully than have most other radical or revolutionary writers. He is regarded as 'too complicated' for study by 'O' level classes. And, to judge from the questions asked about him at 'A' level, he is very complicated indeed! The questions are almost exclusively about Shelley's 'linguistic' or 'lyrical' qualities. In 1967, for instance, students for the 'A' level English literature paper set by the Joint Matriculation Board (Liverpool, Sheffield, Leeds, Manchester and Birmingham Universities) were asked to study *Prometheus Unbound*. The question put to them after all their study was: 'What are the outstanding poetic qualities of the songs and lyrics in *Prometheus Unbound*?'

In all the English literature papers set by the three main examination boards – the Joint Matriculation Board, Oxford, and Cambridge – from 1961 to 1977, there is only one question, from Oxford in 1974 – 'How does Shelley handle the theme of liberty?' – which concedes that Shelley had any political ideas at all.

The most time-honoured rule for teaching anything at our schools and universities is that people should stick to what Mr A.S.B. Glover calls 'their proper field'. Science is science, law is law, literature is literature and politics is politics. Each must be isolated. The separation is enforced with special fervour for poetry and politics. For poetry can inspire people. And it is extremely important for the 'fabric of society' that inspirations should be kept away from politics, and especially from anything which smells of subversion. So poetry is judged 'as poetry', by standards set down by 'experts' on poetry. Politics, students are reminded sharply, has nothing to do with it.

It is all humbug. George Orwell, who could sniff out humbug quicker than most, wrote shortly before he died:

The more I see the more I doubt whether people ever really make aesthetic judgements at all. Everything is judged on political grounds which are then given an aesthetic disguise. When, for instance, Eliot can't see anything good in Shelley or anything bad in Kipling, the real underlying reason must be that one is a radical and the other a conservative, of sorts. Yet evidently one does have aesthetic reactions, especially as a lot of art and even literature is politically neutral, and also certain unmistakable standards do exist, e.g. Homer is better than Edgar Wallace. Perhaps the way we should put it is: the more one is aware of political bias the more one can be independent of it, & the more one claims to be impartial the more one is biassed.

To remove from writers their political ideas is even more insulting than to judge them solely on their politics. What people think usually, if not always, determines what they write. When writers think about their fellow human beings and the political relationships between them, those thoughts become essential to their writing, and to the understanding and enjoyment of it.

In Shelley's case, censorship of his ideas is more than insulting. It is totally destructive. For Shelley thought about politics intensely, all his life. His revolutionary ideas were the main inspiration for the great bulk of his poems and essays.

For people who agree even with some of those ideas, the discovery of the real Shelley is an astonishing experience. 'At last', wrote the philosopher Bertrand Russell, 'at the age of seventeen I came across Shelley, whom no one had ever told me about. He remained for many years the man I loved most among the great men of the past.'

At last! At the age of seventeen! It took me twice as long, but it was no less exciting. I read the unadulterated Shelley with a mixture of fury and excitement: fury at what had been hidden by my education; excitement at what was opening out in front of me. The feeble fop on that marble slab vanished altogether. In his place appeared a restless agitator, who spent his short life challenging every received opinion and every arbitrary authority. Behind the other-worldly lyrics I had learned at school, I found poems which had inspired generations of workers to political action. I came face to face with Shelley's gigantic intellect, and was re-educated. He became for me like a great tree of knowledge and I like a squirrel, scampering down each undiscovered branch.

The 'Romantic poets' (Byron, Keats, Wordsworth, Southey) became not Romantic at all but every one of them creatures of the social convulsions which shook Europe in the wake of the French Revolution. Shelley introduced me, perhaps most crucially and most disturbingly, to feminism, to its literature and its struggles. He led me back to Condorcet, Diderot and Mary Wollstonecraft, and on to the nineteenth-century feminists, to the suffragettes and to the Women's Liberation movement, which is still fighting for the ideas expressed so eloquently by Cythna in *The Revolt of Islam*. All these things were hidden both from my patrician education and from the curiously masculine Marxism to which I graduated.

From *Red Shelley*, 1981

A stone's throw from Windsor Castle

All through his short life Shelley loved bizarre happenings and unpredictable human behaviour, so he would have enjoyed himself a lot at Windsor Girls School on 22 June. About a hundred and fifty people came together to celebrate his work. Was this an academic gathering, a place where scholars could show off their latest pedantry to their peers? Not at all. It was organized by Val Price, who works in computers, and Brian Edgar, a secondary-school teacher, on behalf of the Windsor and Maidenhead Labour Party. The idea came to Val Price about a year ago. Shelley, she knew, had lived at Marlow. Should not the Labour Party organize a function there to celebrate his contribution to British radical ideas over nearly two centuries? A committee was promptly set up. They couldn't find a suitable room in Marlow, so they settled for Windsor Girls School, and fixed on 22 June as the anniversary of Shelley's drowning at the age of twenty-nine.

Tickets were sold; auditions held for poetry readings; invitations sent out. The result was a grand gathering. Edward de Souza read some of Shelley's political poems with tremendous force. The winner of the audition to read 'Men of England' was a young black woman. Lesley Saunders, a Greenham Common campaigner and local Labour

Party member, read some of *her* poems, including a rumbustious reply to John Betjeman which she called 'In Praise of Slough' – 'those bombs aren't such a huge joke any more.'

The main session over, we were offered Judith Chernaik on Shelley's feminism or Elma Dangerfield on Byron and Shelley or Marilyn Butler on the background to the politics of the Romantic poets. I had heard Judith a few times before, and reckoned Elma Dangerfield probably a bit right-wing for me, so I plumped for Marilyn Butler. After about two minutes I found myself longing to be an undergraduate at St Hugh's College, Oxford, reading English literature and specializing in the Romantic poets. Butler was terrific.

Five out of six of the Romantic poets, she said, were overtly and obviously radical, if not revolutionary, at least for long periods of their youth. Yet the attitude to these poets in modern places of learning is less political than ever. The field is dominated by American critics who place the poets, not in the setting of revolutionary France (where their ideas sprang from), but in counter-revolutionary Germany of the same period. This period is fashionable in modern America because it has 'strong vibes for the right wing'. Critics there (and here) saw in the Romantic poets a 'recovery of the religious tradition' overlaid with a lot of mystical claptrap. 'What is out of fashion,' said Marilyn Butler, 'is what the poets were saying.'

She called this 'pure intellectual escapism', and proceeded to prove it with an analysis of the treatment of India and the Orient by the Romantic poets. In the 1780s, she said, Warren Hastings had hoped to rule India through Indians, without imposing a British civil service or a British army. For this purpose, he needed to sow a gentle, rather radical view of the Hindu people and their customs and art in the minds of cultured Englishmen. So he arranged for two brilliant hacks to come out and translate Hindu folklore. The result sold well among the gentry and the rising bourgeoisie in Britain. Hindu gods and especially goddesses were portrayed as peaceful, prosperous types who meant well. Wives had a lot of husbands and the stories about them were overlaid with an exciting aura of sexual liberation. The more restrictive tales of Christian folklore (like Eve and the apple) were stood on their head.

Then came Napoleon and his expansive imperialism in the East, which threatened the most profitable of all British plunder abroad – in India. It now became necessary for the British to protect their 'trade' with a much more ruthless show of force against the Indians, and especially against those treacherous princes who were hobnobbing with Napoleon. At once, the whole of British literature about the Far East changed. Poor old Bob Southey (he who in his youth had written the revolutionary epic *Wat Tyler*) was whistled up to deliver the goods. *The Curse of Kehama* (1810) showed the Hindu princes (especially those who flirted with Napoleon – the worst of them actually looked like Napoleon) as vile, degenerate tyrants representing an intolerable culture which only good old Christianity could civilize. The stage was set for the brutal 'civilizing' imperialism necessary to keep the other 'civilizing' super-power out of India.

Marilyn Butler then mentioned a name I had not heard for a long time: Constantin François Volney, author of *The Ruins: A Survey of the Revolutions of Empires*. This great book (written during the French Revolution, and kept in print by British radical publishers from the time it was first translated in 1795 until the early years of this century) exposed among many other things the intellectuals who are bought by society and subject their skills and their learning to the power and profit of the people who run the world. It was the duty of intellectuals, Volney argued, to resist such prostitution, to think for themselves, against the stream, before they could put their abilities to proper use. Volney was a powerful influence on the British Romantic poets, on Byron and especially on Shelley. When Byron came to write *Childe Harold*, he was hard enough on the great Oriental tyrants, their cruelties and their despotisms, but he was just as hard on the Christian alternative. You cannot supplant one tyranny with another, was his theme (forerunner, perhaps, to the modern slogan: Neither Washington, nor Moscow).

Marilyn Butler finished her talk by restating the duty of people who teach Romantic poetry to examine what the poets are saying and the toadying pusillanimity (she would not use such language) of academics and teachers who dare to present Byron or Shelley or Keats as purveyors of 'literature' which might just as well commend itself to Reagan or Thatcher. Most of this was new to me. The combination of scholarship and commitment was intoxicating. I felt a bit like some watcher of the skies when a new planet swims into his ken, or even like the stout imperialist bastard Cortez on his peak at Darien. And all this happened, not a stone's throw from Windsor Castle, at a function organized by the Labour Party in a constituency where the Tory majority is something more than 23,000. As the man said, if winter comes, can spring be far behind?

A liberated woman in an unliberated time*

From the moment Byron met Shelley in 1816, the two men argued. At the root of the argument was Shelley's belief in human perfectibility: the notion that humankind could and should be improved far beyond most people's wildest dreams. When the two men met again in Venice in 1818, and rehearsed the arguments, Shelley wrote a poem about it, 'Julian and Maddalo'. Julian puts the Shelley argument:

> 'We might be otherwise; we might be all
> We dream of, happy high, majestical.
> Where is the beauty, love and truth we seek
> But in our minds? And, if we were not weak,
> Should we be less in deed than in desire?'
> 'Ay, *if* we were not weak – and we aspire,
> How vainly! to be strong,' said Maddalo.
> 'You talk Utopia.'

The argument raged on, and pretty sharp it was too. But it was not resolved.

A close observer of this argument when it first broke out in 1816 was Mary Wollstonecraft Godwin, then eighteen, who had eloped with Shelley two years earlier. While the two geniuses argued away in the Swiss mists, the teenager wrote a story about a man created by another. The story became more popular by far than any of the most popular works written by either Byron or Shelley, and (unlike anything either

---

*Review of *The Journals of Mary Shelley 1814–1844. Part I 1814–1822*, edited by Paula R. Feldman and Diana Scott-Kilvert.

of the poets ever wrote) entered deep into the imagination of many millions of people all over the world.

Was it just a horror story, this *Frankenstein*? Or was it an allegory which flowed directly from the argument which raged about its author as she wrote it?

Reactionaries, who for some reason have always made common cause with Mary Shelley (she married Shelley after his first wife committed suicide later that year, 1816) have been quick to interpret Dr Frankenstein as Shelley himself, playing with revolutionary ideas which were bound to turn against him. They miss the whole point of the story. The monster himself is not naturally violent, or even anti-social. All his instincts are kindly, humble, cooperative. He is also exceptionally clever, and has fantastic physical prowess. It is only because he *seems* ugly and monstrous that people shun him. He needs his creator to explain his origins to the human race. But Dr Frankenstein has deserted him. This *desertion* is what finally drives the monster to violence and destruction.

Everything written or spoken by Mary Shelley in her journals or anywhere else before she wrote *Frankenstein* suggests she was firmly on Shelley's side in the argument with Byron. She too was for the perfectibility of the human race; for the highest possible revolutionary aspirations. What worried her was the level of commitment of wealthy or well-born revolutionaries who played with revolutionary ideas, only to abandon them as soon as they were successful. A revolution abandoned by the brilliant men and women who helped to set it in motion, she believed, was doomed.

With all this, Shelley agreed. Indeed, he was the first to be struck with the significance and the excellence of Mary's novel. He fought against her modesty, and persuaded her to revise it and prepare it for publication. In the first volume of these journals, which they kept together, there is plenty of evidence on both sides of the grand egalitarian love affair in which they were engaged. 'She feels as if our love would alone suffice to resist the invasions of calamity,' wrote Shelley. Mary testified to this again and again. 'Sunday 30th October, 1814. Talk with Shelley all day.' '6th November, 1814. This is a day devoted to love and idleness.'

In January 1815 she wrote to Shelley's friend, Jefferson Hogg: 'I who love him so tenderly and entirely, whose life hangs on the beam of his eye and whose whole soul is entirely wrapped up in him....'

This was not conventional romantic love, which both scorned. It was a meeting of ideas, a blending of intellectual and physical attraction. In the summer of 1817, Shelley paid tribute to it in his dedication to Mary of 'The Revolt of Islam':

Thou friend, whose presence on a wintry heart
Fell like bright spring upon a herbless plain,
How beautiful and calm and free thou wert
In thy young wisdom, when the mortal chain
Of Custom thou didst burst and rend in twain,
And walk as free as light the clouds among ...

After the First Journal, which is full of this passion and mutual intellectual respect, Shelley drops out. Mary continues in a more subdued and repetitive tone to chronicle her way through the ordeals which tormented the love affair for the next five years. In 1818, their daughter Clara died, aged two, in Venice. Their beloved Willmouse, aged five, died the following year. The sad little Shelley cavalcade shifted restlessly across Italy, and Mary had somehow to cope with the complicated domestic arrangements, and above all with the non-paying guests.

Claire Clairmont, her stepsister, who had managed to accompany Shelley and Mary even on their elopement, was always there or thereabouts, to Mary's increasing irritation. Claire has since been rescued as a woman in her own right by Richard Holmes's magnificent biography of Shelley and by Marion Stocking's edition of her journals. But Mary couldn't stand her. Her indignation with Claire's constant claims on Shelley's affections and concerns keeps breaking out in the Journals: 'June 8, 1820: A better day than most and good reason for it.... C away at Pungano.'

If she wasn't being irritated by Claire there was certain to be another querulous begging letter from her father, William Godwin.

The grand love affair of 1814 to 1817 was badly bruised by all this, of course, and Shelley played his part in the bruising. The dream of women's liberation as an idea, when read in youth in the pages of Mary's mother, Mary Wollstonecraft, was tarnished in real life, with real babies to look after and real households to manage. On 18 June 1822, six weeks before he died, Shelley wrote to a friend:

It is the curse of Tantalus that a person possessing such excellent powers

and so pure a mind as hers [Mary's] should not excite the sympathy
indispensable to their application to domestic life.

This was a far cry from the uncritical adulation of the early years.
'Domestic life' had not even been anticipated in that rapturous dedication of 'The Revolt of Islam'.

The wonder, however, is not so much that the love affair lost its
glitter after years of drudgery and grief – what love affair does not? The
wonder is that this extraordinary woman rose above all these difficulties. She kept up her prodigious self-education, matching even
Shelley book for book. She taught herself Greek. She started more
novels. Her wit and temper flash out from time to time from behind the
wall of reserve she built round herself in her journal. She described the
German writer Christopher Wieland as

> one of those men who alter their opinions when they are forty and then,
> thinking that it will be the same with everyone, think themselves the only
> proper monitors of youth.

When the bore Tom Medwin came to stay, interminably, she
described him as being 'as silent as a firescreen but not half so useful'.
The explorer Trelawney remarked on what must have been her most
striking characteristic:

> She had the power of expressing her thoughts in varied and appropriate
> words, derived from familiarity with the works of our most vigorous
> writers.... This command of language struck me the more as being
> contrasted with the scanty vocabulary used by ladies in society.

She strove, as her mother had done, to behave as a liberated woman in
an unliberated world – and perhaps as a result of that was able to
struggle back to the surface again after each tremendous blow. She
could not, however, survive the greatest blow of all: Shelley's absurdly
early (and absurd) death by drowning when he was twenty-nine, and
she just twenty-four. Mary's spark, which had lit Shelley up from the
moment he first met her, was doused forever. Though I have tried
hard, I confess I haven't been able to finish any of the novels she wrote
after his death. None of them, for certain, is a patch on *Frankenstein*. All
of them are plagued by precisely that 'Custom' whose chains, for
Shelley, she had burst and rent in twain in her youth. She came to
rejoice in the normality and mediocrity of her only surviving child and
to cherish her reputation in London society. She recalled the radi-

calism of her youth only in her determination not by a single syllable to betray what Shelley thought and wrote.

These journals, whose first part covers the period to Shelley's death, are often dull. They are sometimes no more than a list of books without even an adjective to suggest what she thought of them. But they are brilliantly illuminated by the editors' notes and quotations. The whole production is worthy of the finest traditions of the OUP, which has not always been kind or fair to Shelley and his circle.

If I have a criticism, it is that the scholarship does not have about it enough of the enthusiasm which scholars tend to suspect, but which so often enriches their scholarship. *The Journals of Claire Clairmont* have, for me, the edge. Marion Stocking, their editor, never wavers for a moment in her scholarship, but neither is there a shred of doubt of her admiration for the commitment to her subject. Mary Shelley deserves at least as much from her editors.

The Spectator, August 1987

An astonishing woman: Olive Schreiner

In the late summer of 1900, the radical journalist Henry Nevinson, who was covering the Boer War for the *Daily Chronicle*, came to Cape Town and met some important people there. 'But I encountered' he later wrote

> another figure of far greater interest to me even than the pianist or the Attorney General.
>
> It was at a meeting of women – the first women's meeting ever held in Cape Town I believe. The burning of farms and villages way out on the veldt, away from the railways, had just been ordered by Lord Roberts, and it must be remembered that by Dutch law half the farm is the wife's private property.... No wonder that indignation ran high.
>
> Mrs Sauer presided at the meeting, and though a few English women

were present the audience were mainly Dutch. The third speaker rose amid the breathless silence of expectation. I described her at the time as 'a short heavy brown-eyed woman, but when she began to speak she was transfigured'. Indeed, though she stood perfectly still, she was transfigured into flame. Indignation can make the dumb to speak and the stones be eloquent. But this woman was not dumb and was no stone. I have heard much indignant eloquence, but never such a molten torrent of white hot rage.

It was overwhelming. When it suddenly ceased, the large audience, about 1,500 men and women, could hardly gasp. If Olive Schreiner, for of course it was she, had called on them to storm the Government House, they would have thrown themselves upon the bayonets.

Where had she come from, this astonishing woman? She had been born the ninth child out of twelve to Protestant missionaries in the Karoo, the desert country in the North of the Cape Province. Her father was German – a Lutheran; her mother the daughter of a Yorkshire nonconformist minister. Five of the children died in infancy, and Olive's three Christian names were derived from those of her three dead brothers. Her father broke the strict rules which prevented missionaries from trading, and dabbled unsuccessfully in various business ventures. He was rejected both by respectable missionaries and by respectable businessmen. Olive grew up in fearful poverty, made worse by her parents' aspirations and by her mother's belief in the purifying virtues of corporal punishment.

On every side, there was nothing but religious and racial bigotry. Although Rebecca Schreiner, Olive's mother, passed on some of her formal learning, the only book which was respected in the household was the Bible.

Before she was seventeen, however, thanks in the main to the privately financed public libraries of South Africa, Olive Schreiner was an atheist and a feminist and had already started work on an atheist, feminist masterpiece which was to make her famous. A wandering missionary had introduced her to Herbert Spencer's *First Principles*. Then she read Gibbon's *Decline and Fall of the Roman Empire*; and Shelley – all of him. ('I used to read Shelley's poems,' says her heroine in her novel, *Undine*, 'It was wicked, but I used to wish I could have seen him.') She read ceaselessly and voraciously through any literature which questioned or undermined the received notions of her upbringing. When she was nineteen she went to work as a governess in the Cradock district of the Karoo. When she left for England seven years later at the age of twenty-six, she took with her the manuscript of three novels, all of which had been written in and about South African frontier country.

She took the manuscript of *The Story of an African Farm* to Chapman and Hall, who agreed, after some hesitation, to publish it in a small edition under a masculine pseudonym. In its first year of publication, 1883, there were two editions. In the next forty years, there were twelve more. By the time Olive was overwhelming the women of Cape Town at the meeting described by Henry Nevinson, her famous novel had overwhelmed the literate public of three continents, and had sold a fantastic hundred thousand copies. *The Story of an African Farm* made her famous in the highest circles. When a biography was published in 1948, twenty-eight years after her death, the foreword was written by Field Marshal Smuts, who had recently been Prime Minister of South Africa. Concluded Smuts: 'I love her, as I love Emily Brontë.... Such women cast a radiance on this sombre scene in which we carry on the human struggle.'

The Story of an African Farm was popular in other circles, too. Mary Brown, a friend of Olive Schreiner, recalled:

> I asked a Lancashire working woman what she thought of *Story of an African Farm* and a strange expression came over her face as she said: 'I read parts of it over and over.' 'What parts?' I asked, and her reply was: 'About yon poor lass' (Lyndall) and with a far-off look in her eyes added: 'I think there is hundreds of women that feels like that and can't speak it, but *she* could speak what we feel.'

I suspect that that reaction would have given more pleasure to Olive Schreiner than all the accolades of South African field marshals or of London literati.

The attraction of *The Story of an African Farm* was not so much in the plot, though that flows freely enough, as in the combination of exuberance and sensitivity in the writing; and in Olive's uncanny ability to weave the fantasies of childhood into the aspirations and yearnings of loveless adults. The novel is about a woman's battle to preserve her own identity in the unlikely surroundings of Olive's childhood, and the tragedy which, perhaps inevitably, accompanies her success. When the publisher suggested that the book would sell better on railway bookstalls if only the heroine married the hero at some stage or other, he was struck dumb by a mighty blast of Schreiner indignation. That would have emasculated the whole book, destroyed its entire point, didn't he understand? He conceded at once.

Of the other two novels whose draft the young Olive Schreiner took to England in 1881 *Undine* was never touched again. She showed the draft to her friend Havelock Ellis, but begged him to burn it. Her husband Samuel Cronwright had never heard of it when he found bits of it in her papers after her death. Fortunately, Havelock Ellis had kept the rest, and *Undine* was published posthumously, though in only two rather small editions.

The other novel, *From Man to Man*, was, quite literally, her life's work. From the moment she started work on it in the diamond fields of Kimberley at the age of eighteen to her death forty-seven years later, her letters are full of her frustrations and hopes over what she always regarded as her greatest book. It was revised in almost every part, picked over and again and again threatened with the furnace. She wrote of it as others might write of their lovers, treacherous but irresistible. 'I love my new book so,' she wrote to Havelock Ellis in 1887, 'a hundred times better than I ever loved *An African Farm*'. And again, two years later: 'Not Lyndall, not even Waldo [of *The Story of an African Farm*] have been so absolutely real to me as she [Rebekah] and Bertie.'

But she couldn't get it right. 'I guess it's more likely to make an end of me than I am ever to make an end of it,' she wrote to Ellis, prophetically. For she never lived to see it in print. It wasn't published until 1926 – six years after she died. Her husband wrote a long, fussy introduction explaining that the book was unfinished, and adding a pathetic two-page postscript about the possible endings which Olive had suggested to him.

These serve only to disappoint and confuse the reader. The ending, I suspect, was exactly as Olive Schreiner intended it. She did not want either of her two 'beloved' women to die. On the other hand her deep suspicion of the real world, especially the real world of men, and her intense faith in a perfect state of egalitarian monogamy would not permit a happy, adulterous ending. I am quite content that she *did* finish her book, even if she could never quite admit it.

What parts of this book were first conceived in her prolific youth, and what parts were added later? We know she wrote the Prelude, The Child's Day, one of the most thrilling pieces of writing in all our literature, one winter in Italy in 1888. Her description of how she wrote it is full of the restless inspiration which kept her forever on the move all through her life.

> I was sitting at my dear old desk writing an article on the bushmen, and giving a description of the skulls; when suddenly, in an instant, the whole of the little Prelude *flashed* on me. You know, those folded-up views of places one buys; you take hold of one end and all the pictures unfold one after the other as quick as light? That was how it *flashed* on me. I started up and paced about the room. I felt absolutely astonished. I hadn't thought of my novel for months, I hadn't looked at it for years. I'd never dreamed of writing a Prelude to it – I just sat down and wrote it out. And do you know what I found out – after I'd written it? – that it's a picture in small, an allegory of the life of the woman in the book!! It's one of the strangest things I know of. My mind must have been working on it *unconsciously*, although I knew nothing of it – otherwise how did it come?

The background and characters in the story are not very different from their predecessors in *Undine* and *African Farm*. In all that revising and rewriting, no doubt, Olive gradually grafted on the thoughts and experiences of her later life, especially those she shared with leading socialists and radicals in Britain: Eleanor Marx, Edward Carpenter, Henry Salt and many others. She had been a fighter, a writer, a pamphleteer for women's suffrage, women's liberation and independent socialist representation in parliament, both in Britain and in South Africa. Her youthful idealism, accrued by reading books and thinking, had grown into enriched, seasoned, perhaps confused ideas. It was her impulse to transmit these ideas which inspired all that interminable rewriting of *From Man to Man*.

The result is that the plot appears to falter, and even to get lost in huge chunks of Rebekah's thinking and secret letter-writing. Many admirers of *Story of an African Farm* were irritated by what they felt was over-indulgence in propaganda at the expense of the novel. Certainly, the impatient reader can easily get fed up. *So please be patient with these passages.* They are vital to the book, which is a frail thing without them. They are not just didactic propaganda. They are the thoughts of Olive Schreiner, sensitively and powerfully expressed as an argument between a woman and herself, which is just how Olive Schreiner came to them, and how she held on to them and refurbished them as she met others who shared them.

Everything she believed is there. First, the universe is not a thing of 'shreds and patched and unconnected parts'. On the contrary, it is

'one, a whole, and it lives in all its parts'. She rewrites in prose poetry
the famous lines of Shelley's *Prometheus Unbound*:

> Man, one harmonious soul of many a soul,
> whose nature is its own divine control
> where all things flow to all as rivers to the sea ...

The whole philosophy and culture of the society in which she lived was
founded on the notion that only a few, a tiny class, could enjoy the
benefits of education and ease. But it was founded on a terrible weakness: '*Where the mass remain behind, the few are ultimately drawn back.*'

> Is it not a paradox covering a mighty truth that not one slave toils under the
> lash of an Indian plantation but the freedom of every other man on earth is
> limited by it? That not one laugh of lust rings but each man's sexual life is
> less free for it? That the full all-rounded human life is impossible to any
> individual while one man lives who does not share it. Bring up your rears!
> Bring up your rears!

This leads the suburban mother to explain to her children why the
popular notions of racialism were so horrible.

Though the terror of British imperialism had blinded Olive to the
racialism of the Boers with whom she sided in the war, she never lost
sight of the menace of racialism, nor of the way in which it would
engulf her country in a tidal wave of tyranny if it were not resisted. The
only world she would tolerate, however distant it seemed from
anywhere at the time she wrote, was a world of equal, independent and
interdependent human beings, none in the least bit reliant on another's
weakness or poverty. I suppose I have read hundreds of expressions of
common interest; of the old socialist notion that an injury to one is an
injury to all – but none so compelling or exciting as Rebekah's in *From
Man to Man*.

And so Rebekah warms to her main theme: the subjection and
humiliation of women. Olive wrote in another letter about *From Man to
Man*:

> To me there is nothing else in the world that touches me the same way. You
> will see, if you read my novel, that all other matters seem to me small
> compared to matters of sex, and prostitution is its most agonising point.
> Prostitution, especially the prostitution of men of themselves to their most
> brutal level, can't really be touched till man not only says but feels that
> woman is his equal, his brother human to whom he must give as much as he
> takes.

The novel is about prostitution of married women, of seduced women and of men who care little or nothing for either.

Its faults are very obvious, and have been rehearsed often enough by the experts. In their biography, *Olive Schreiner* (André Deutsch, 1980), Ruth First and Ann Scott show how little *From Man to Man* takes into account the independent sexuality of women. It is also a bit of a cheek to take the title for the book from a quotation which calls for charity ('From man to man nothing matters but charity') and yet to show no charity at all to the wretched males in the book, nor even to the gossiping women, Veronica and Mrs Drummond. Yvonne Kapp in her biography of Eleanor Marx has shown how much damage Olive Schreiner's urge to overwhelm her friends did to Eleanor. And in her novel about Eleanor, *The Daughter*, Judith Chernaik's Olive is a rather selfish and demanding companion. Rebecca West once described Olive Schreiner as 'a geographical fact', and the dominating, sometimes even bullying side of Olive's nature is a strong feature of this book. Even worse is her tendency to be tempted by the First Deadly Sin of any agitator – sanctimoniousness. But all of this taken together cannot for a single moment resist the magnetic power of Olive Schreiner's writing, nor the infectiousness of her ideas.

'I have always built upon the fact', she wrote as she toiled with the book in one of her dreaded and finally lethal attacks of asthma 'that *From Man to Man* will help other people, for it will help to make men more tender to women, because they will understand them better; it will make some women more tender to others; it will comfort some women by showing them that others have felt as they do.'

Although her bitterness about the careless sexual appetite of men is perhaps more explicit in this book than in any of her other writing, Olive Schreiner was not anti-male. She wanted men to be equal, not inferior to women. After the publication of *Woman and Labour*, her unequivocal appeal for women to work independently of men, she wrote to her sister, Ettie:

> One thing that I have been glad of about my book is that so many men have written to me about it. You know what a bitter opponent of any emancipation for women old Merriman has always been. My book hadn't been six days in Cape Town when I got a long letter from him saying how much he had enjoyed reading the book – how beautiful it was. The only thing was that man was such a brute that my ideas could not be realized.

Although women might understand *From Man to Man* better and sympathize with it more instinctively, it is compulsory reading for men. As Olive's 1948 biographer Vera Buchanan-Gould put it in a chastening passage:

> What moved Olive to write so passionately was her belief that men are unaware of what they are doing when they seduce or betray a woman. To them their act is merely a momentary aberration from the normal standard of behaviour and is very quickly forgotten. But for the woman, seeking for affection and finding only lust, that moment may have physical, emotional and psychological repercussions which cannot as easily be dismissed.

I was affected far more by *From Man to Man* than I was by *The Story of an African Farm, Woman and Labour* or any other Olive Schreiner work, much though I love all of it. I finished my 1927 edition (third impression) and reflected sadly that it would only reach the few in my generation who scour through secondhand bookshops; or who are lucky enough to find it in a library.

In a review I wrote of the biography of Olive Schreiner by Ruth First and Ann Scott I included a few quotes from this novel to whet people's appetites and followed with what I thought was a brave but futile appeal: '*From Man to Man* went into at least three editions after Olive's death, then vanished into an obscurity from which I beg some lively publisher (why not Virago?) to rescue it.'

As though to prove that dreams as well as nightmares can come true, here it is.

Introduction to *From Man to Man* by Olive Schreiner,
published by Virago in 1982

Shaken by John Reed

John Reed's *Ten Days That Shook The World* shook *me* to pieces. I went to Glasgow in 1961, when I was twenty-three, to start a career and seek, as soon as possible, an editor's chair and a seat in parliament. John Reed triumphantly rescued me from both.

There have been hundreds of good books about the Russian Revolution but no one captures the thrill of its democratic spirit quite like John Reed. Karl Marx taught him that revolution was necessary not just to dispossess an exploiting class but also for the exploited class to rid itself of the 'muck of ages'. In 1917, he could see it happening. The muck of ages was disappearing all over the place, and in its place all the aspirations and hopes which lie so low, so long, among so many were suddenly blossoming.

> All Russia was learning to read, and reading – politics, economics, history – because the people wanted to know.... Russia absorbed reading matter like hot sand drinks water, insatiable. And it was not fables, falsified history, diluted religion and the cheap fiction that corrupts – but social and economic theories, philosophy, the works of Tolstoy, Gogol and Gorky. Then there was the Talk beside which Carlyle's 'flood of French speech' was a mere trickle. Lectures, debates, speeches in theatres, circuses, school-houses, clubs, Soviet meeting rooms, Union headquarters, barracks.... For months in Petrograd and all over Russia, every street corner was a public tribune. In railway trains, street-cars, always the spurting up of impromptu debate....

A Central Committee member of the Bolshevik Party spelled out for John Reed the basic principle of the Revolution: 'The initiative of the new society will come from below.' And in a mighty speech at the Smolny Institute Trotsky warned that the Russian Revolution would either spread to Europe or it would die. It did not spread; so it died, and the dictatorship which succeeded it bent its mind and muscle to a single purpose: to wipe out the revolution and the revolutionaries.

John Reed led me on to read insatiably about the Russian Revolution, and then to look at everything else from a different angle – 'from below'. It seemed suddenly obvious that there was nothing for it but to be a revolutionary, 'Not in Utopia – subterranean fields', as Wordsworth warned before his fire went out, 'But in the very world ... or not at all.'

Real change cannot come from general secretaries any more than from benevolent kings or patronizing parliaments. It will only come when masses stir themselves as they did in the Petrograd John Reed described.

For nearly thirty years I envied John Reed his luck at being with his notebook in Russia 'in full tide of insurrection'. Never in my lifetime, I mourned, would it happen to me, especially not in the 1980s. Now, after the last six months, who knows?

Independent on Sunday, March 1990

Orwell and the proles

Everyone else seems to be doing it, so I did it too. I re-read *1984* by Geroge Orwell, and I marked this passage:

> The future belonged to the proles. And could he be sure that when the time came the world they constructed would not be just as alien as the world of the Party? Yes, because at the least it would be a world of sanity. Where there is equality, there can be sanity.
>
> Sooner or later it would happen, strength would turn into consciousness. The proles were immortal, you could not doubt it when you looked at that valiant figure in the yard.
>
> In the end their awakening would come. And until that happened, though it might be a thousand years, they would stay alive against all the odds, like birds passing on from body to body the vitality which the Party did not share and could not kill.
>
> All round the world, in London and New York, in Africa and Brazil, and in the mysterious, forbidden lands beyond the frontiers, in the streets of Paris and Berlin, in the villages of the endless Russian plain, in the bazaars of China and Japan – everywhere stood the same solid, unconquerable figure, made monstrous by work and childbearing, toiling from birth to death and still singing.
>
> Out of those mighty loins a race of conscious beings must one day come. You were the dead; theirs was the future. But you could share in that future if you kept alive the mind as they kept alive the body and passed on the secret doctrine that two and two make four.

Poor George Orwell (and *1984* in particular) have been ground down almost to nothing in the awful mill of the Cold War. In the West, he has had to put up with the most revolting flattery from those who say that *1984* is *all* about Russia: that it is Russian horror alone which he had brilliantly exposed.

From the East (and from official Communists everywhere) Orwell has had even worse service. He has been denounced as pessimistic, nihilistic and even anti-working class. He has been ridiculed as a Hampstead intellectual who sold out to the CIA.

The Western flatterers forget that *all three* warring super-continents in *1984* have developed the same system, not through conquest, but through the choice of their rulers.

Orwell's prediction was that *all* the power blocs would grow increasingly similar in style and character – a prediction which every minute is being brilliantly fulfilled.

The Eastern critics forget passages like the one above (and many others) when Orwell's perennial optimism and good humour break out from behind his gloomy descriptions of what he saw as an extremely gloomy society.

Both sets of critics forget, above all, the working class, which as this passage shows, Orwell did not forget, even at the end. Of course he did not know or care much about working-class organization, about the relationship between party or class.

Of course, he *was* a loner, with all sorts of weird and often quite horrible ideas about nationalism and people's instinctive 'love of country'. Of course he was a male chauvinist of the most patronizing and often vulgar variety.

But for all that you've really got to hand it to him. He was among the very first to see through Stalin's Russia for the bureaucratic tyranny which it was: and to detect how such a tyranny necessarily took the path of counter-revolution when a revolution broke out anywhere, as in Spain in 1936 and 1937.

While much 'better trained' and 'conscious' socialists were looking to Stalin's Russia for salvation, Orwell was denouncing it and exposing it, not as a Cold War diatribe, but as part of a life's devotion to the common people. He exposed Russia precisely because he saw things from the point of view of the proles.

He and his books will survive attacks from Moscow and praise from Washington, because his basic message is stronger than either of them: A plague on both your houses. The future belongs to the proles.

Socialist Worker, January 1984

Karl Marx and Rosa Luxemburg

Just as socialism is being 'written off' by all important people today, so in his lifetime (1818 to 1883) and ever since, Karl Marx has been 'written off' by each successive generation of politicians and intellectuals. At his funeral in Highgate, North London, the graveside oration was made by his collaborator and friend, Frederick Engels. In a short, simple speech Engels summed up Marx's enormous contribution to civilization. Just as Darwin discovered that mankind had developed from animals – the law of evolution – so Marx discovered

> the simple fact, hitherto concealed by an overgrowth of ideology, that mankind must first of all eat and drink, have shelter and clothing, before it can pursue politics, science, religion and art; and that therefore the production of the immediate material means of life and consequently the degree of economic development ... form the foundation upon which the forms of government, the legal conceptions, the art and even the religious ideas of the people concerned have been evolved ... instead of vice versa as had hitherto been the case.

Marx argued that all human history was dominated by a tussle for the wealth between classes, one of which took the wealth, and used it to exploit the others. As science and technology developed, so one exploiting class was replaced by another that used the resources of society more efficiently. The necessity for exploitation, he observed, had ended with capitalism. If the working class, the masses who coop-erate to produce the wealth, could seize the means of production from the capitalist class, they could put an end to exploitation forever and run society on the lines of the famous slogan: 'From each according to his abilities, to each according to his needs.'

Famous people throughout history have scoffed at Marx as a remote academic, who wrote for intellectuals and not for the masses. This entirely misses the main inspiration of Marx's life. Here is Engels again, by the graveside:

> Marx was before all else a revolutionary. His real mission in life was to contribute in one way or another to the overthrow of capitalist society and of the forms of government which it had brought into being.... Fighting was his element.

When Marx's daughter Eleanor asked him for his favourite character in history, Marx replied immediately: 'Spartacus'. The fighting spirit of the slave revolutionary against the Roman Empire inspired Marx's enthusiasm for the class struggle in his own time. It was, as he put it, all very well for people to understand the rotten world they lived in. The point, however, was to change it.

How could it be changed? It certainly was no good just thinking about a new society, or trying to attract others to it by example. Exploiters who amassed their power and wealth by robbing workers were not sentimental or namby-pamby about it. They would hold on to their wealth and power, if they had to, by force. They would never surrender that power and wealth, however intellectually or morally unjustifiable it was. It was up to the exploited class – the working class – to seize the means of production in a revolution. No one could do it for them. Socialism could not be introduced by utopians, dictators, benevolent or otherwise, or by reforming intellectuals and politicians. The first precondition for socialism was that the wealth of society had to be taken over by the workers.

Marx faced up squarely to an argument which is common enough 150 years later. How, he was asked, can you expect the workers to change society? Are they not the most damaged victims of class rule? Are they not religious, racist, nationalist, dirty and violent?

Marx reacted angrily to this abuse. He had spent a lot of his time with the workers of Paris when he was exiled there in the late 1840s. He knew that there were among the workers people of outstanding courage and self-sacrifice, and that workers' attitudes could quickly change when they took part in collective struggle such as a strike.

But he was not, as so many middle-class socialists can be, a worker-worshipper. He realized that an exploiting society corrupts everyone in it: the exploited as well as the exploiters. Not to put too fine a point on it, capitalist society covered everything in shit. And that was the best argument of all for a workers' revolution; he wrote:

> This revolution is necessary not only because the ruling class cannot be overthrown in any other way, but also because the class overturning it can only in a revolution succeed in ridding itself of all the muck of ages and become fitted to found society anew.

While reforms are carried out in the name of workers by someone from on high, the muck of ages sticks to them. The hierarchies created by exploitation encourage even the most degraded and exploited worker to seek someone else whom he can insult and bully as he himself is insulted and bullied. In such circumstances, workers will take pride in things of which there is nothing to be proud: the colour of their skin, their sex, nationality, birthplace or God. These are selected for them by custom, inheritance or superstition, and have nothing to do with their abilities or characters. They are the muck of ages. How are they to be shaken off? Is someone else to do it for the workers? Or should they do it themselves, by organizing their producing power, their own strikes, demonstrations and protests?

When people asked Marx for blueprints of a socialist society, he steadfastly refused to supply them. He would not, he said, 'provide them with recipes for their cookbooks'. The question 'what is socialism?' is, he argued, inextricably entwined with another: 'how can socialism be achieved?' No socialist utopia was worth the paper it was written on if its authors expected the workers to be passive while the utopia was achieved. The seed of the new society could only be sown in the struggle against the old one. The only way labour could be emancipated from capital was by the active struggle from below – and a struggle from below could not and would not be set in motion from above.

In 1864 Marx wrote the articles for the first International Working Men's Association. The first clause started: 'Considering that the emancipation of the working classes must be conquered by the working classes themselves.' That clause was written on the cards of every member of the International. It was the very lynchpin of Marx's socialism.

Seven years after the International was formed, the people of Paris, led by the working class in the city, rose, threw off the muck of ages, and set up their own administration: the Paris Commune. It only lasted a couple of months, when it was drowned in the most ferocious ruling-class slaughter. Marx responded at once with one of the most powerful political pamphlets in all history, which he read out loud to a meeting of the International's executive. The Commune's outstanding achievement, he said, was the self-emancipation of the working class:

> They have taken the actual management of the revolution into their own hands and found at the same time, in the case of success, the means to hold

it in the hands of the people itself; displacing the state machinery of the ruling class by a governmental machinery of their own. This is their ineffable crime!

What kind of a society did they set up? 'The Commune,' Marx reported,

was formed of the municipal councillors, chosen by universal suffrage in the various wards of the town, responsible and revocable at short terms. The Commune was to be a working, not a parliamentary body, executive and legislative at the same time. Instead of continuing to be the agent of the central government, the police was at once stripped of its political attributes and turned into the responsible and revocable agent of the Commune. So were the officials of all other branches of the administration. From the members of the Commune downwards, the public service had to be done at workmen's wages. The vested interests and the representation allowances of the high dignitaries of state disappeared along with the high dignitaries themselves.

The Commune worked. That was no surprise to Marx, for he saw in the Commune 'the produce of the struggle of the producing against the appropriating class'. It was the living expression of the self-emancipation of the working class.

The other aspect of the Commune which appealed to Marx was its democracy. He liked the fact that it was elected, and the way it was elected. The Commune was infinitely more democratic than any parliamentary democracy the world has known. The executive, as well as the political assembly, the judiciary, the police, education, science, industry and finance – all these became, in the two most consistent words in the pamphlet, 'responsible' and 'revocable'. Marx had seen how workers chose their own representatives in their workplaces. They chose the people they most trusted for positions which held no privilege and no extra wages. Those elected were subject to constant questioning and, if they did not carry out their mandates, to recall. That was a natural way for people to choose their representatives. It brought the representatives close to their electors. It was a democracy which the common people could trust.

The caricature of Marx painted by his enemies over the past 130 years is that he was a tyrant with no interest in democracy. Edmund Wilson, in his famous introduction to his book *To the Finland Station*, which is about the growth of socialist ideas from the French to the Russian Revolution, wrote that Marx 'was incapable of imagining democracy'. Well, Marx wasn't terribly interested in imagining anything. But what attracted him to politics in the first place was a loathing for tyranny and a yearning for democracy. In his youth he was known by everyone as 'an extreme democrat'.

Marx himself wrote how his passionate longing for democracy brought him to socialism. No democracy was worth its name if industry, finance, law and the armed services stayed in the hands of a completely unelected and irresponsible minority. The democratic element in such a democracy was certain to be corrupted and eventually squeezed out. For a democracy to deserve the name, labour had to emancipate itself and, as part of the process, democratize all the areas of society which were constipated by class rule. 'Democracy,' wrote Engels in 1845, 'nowadays is communism ... democracy has become the principle of the masses ... the proletarian parties are entirely right in inscribing the word "democracy" on their banners.'

The point about socialism is that it would replace a hierarchical, bureaucratic and undemocratic society – capitalism – with a genuine democracy in which the working people controlled their own representatives, and the representatives acted accordingly.

These elements – the self-emancipation of the working class through their own struggle and the democratic society which follows such emancipation – are the heart of socialism. Without them, socialism is dead. All the other features of a socialist society – the planned economy, for instance – depend on a self-emancipated working class and a real democracy. A socialist economy cannot be planned for workers unless the workers are involved in that plan. It took a plan to build the pyramids, but the slaves who built them are not reported to have rejoiced that this new planning brought anything but a life and death under the whip. Like everything else about socialism, the plan depends on who are the planners and how they got there. Socialism depends upon control from below, and control from below can never be brought about from above.

Marx died in 1883, when socialism was still a subject for minorities. He did not live to see the huge growth of the German Social Democratic Party, which claimed it was based on his principles.

As long as the ruling class in Germany withheld the vote and suppressed the growing labour movement, it seemed obvious to most people that socialism could come only through a revolution. But as more and more workers were given the right to vote, and as the trade unions grew into enormous and influential organizations, most socialists started to sing a different tune. In 1898, Eduard Bernstein wrote a pamphlet, which was instantly denounced by other Social Democratic leaders – though they secretly agreed with it. Bernstein argued that the vote and the unions changed the socialist perspective. With the vote and the unions, the working class could be emancipated without a revolution: by getting socialists elected to parliament and there passing laws to change the system. This could be done without antagonizing the government or the state, and without calling on people to risk anything, or indeed to do anything or to think anything. All they would have to do was vote.

Bernstein's book provoked a furious response from another leading member of the German Social Democratic Party: Rosa Luxemburg. Her central point was that Bernstein's argument was not just an argument about means and ends – but about socialism itself:

> People who pronounce themselves in favour of the method of legislative reform in place of and in contradistinction to the conquest of political power and social revolution, do not really choose a more tranquil, calmer and slower road to the same goal, but a different goal. Instead of taking a stand for the establishment of a new society, they take a stand for the surface modification of the old society. Our programme becomes not the realization of socialism, but the reform of capitalism.

Capitalism, she argued, was not made by laws, and would not be undone by laws. It was an economic system, which had to be replaced by another economic system.

The worst part of Bernstein's proposals was that they left the masses passive: unable to throw off the muck of ages, and so unable to change society. This passivity would, she predicted, make it difficult for the Bernstein reformers to carry out even their most marginal reforms. But the main point about them was that by changing the means of getting socialism, they changed the meaning of socialism itself.

Rosa Luxemburg's attack on Bernstein – it was titled *Social Reform or Revolution* – was published in 1900. She returned to the attack six years later in another even more remarkable pamphlet called *The Mass Strike*. Its inspiration was the Russian Revolution of 1905. She watched with increasing excitement as hundreds of years of tyranny in Russia were brought to a halt, not by gradual reforms or by the resurfacing of the old society by wise men at the top, but by the most cataclysmic upheaval from below. She contrasted the slow, steady, ordered march of the German trade unions, through their conferences, sporting associations, libraries, offices and marble halls, with the uprising of Russian workers, many of whom were not even members of trade unions.

> While the guardians of the German trade unions for the most part fear that the organizations will fall in pieces in a revolutionary whirlwind like rare porcelain, the Russian Revolution shows us the exactly opposite picture: from the whirlwind and the storm, out of the fire and glow of the mass strike and the street fighting, rise again, like Venus from the foam, fresh, young, powerful, buoyant trade unions.

Better by far a group of raw workers in struggle than a committee of long-organized trade unionists solemnly selecting candidates for a parliamentary party. The pamphlet throbs with the living spirit of the self-emancipation of workers in struggle: the same spirit which had excited Marx at the time of the Commune. Against the passive piece-meal progress of Bernstein she counterposed the 'living political school', the 'pulsating flesh and blood', the 'foaming wave' of the workers in struggle, breaking down the wall of capitalism and in the process purging themselves of the muck of ages.

This argument between Eduard Bernstein and Rosa Luxemburg has been going on in different tones all through this century. The enormous majority of socialists and even Marxists have taken Bernstein's side. The reformists offered real reforms, many of which affected the real lives of working people. They offered a clear instrument by which the reforms could be carried out: by electing Labour or social-democratic governments and passing new laws in parliaments; and they demanded from the masses very little – only the vote. How much more 'sensible' and 'practical' it seemed to get socialism through peaceful parliaments than by revolutions which were vague in theory and dangerous in practice!

A perfect example of the Bernstein method in action was a motion in the British House of Commons which was debated on 20 March and 16 July 1923:

> That, in view of the failure of the capitalist system to adequately utilize and organize natural resources and productive power, or to provide the

necessary standard of life for vast numbers of the population, and believing that the cause of this failure lies in the private ownership and control of the means of production and distribution, this House declares that legislative effort should be directed to the gradual supersession of the capitalist system by an industrial and social order based on public ownership and democratic control of the instruments of production and distribution.

The debate was ended by the leader of the Labour Party, Ramsay MacDonald, with the words: 'I am in favour of socialism.' He lost the vote in the House of Commons that day: 121 MPs voted for socialism; 368 for capitalism.

But a few months later Ramsay MacDonald got his chance. He led the Labour Party to its first election victory, and became prime minister. His government lasted less than a year. It did nothing.

MacDonald's Labour Party was returned to office again in 1929, pledged to rid Britain forever of the 'scourge of unemployment'. A million people were out of work. Two years of Labour policies later, there were three million out of work, and MacDonald joined the Tories in a national government.

Labour and social-democratic governments have been elected throughout Europe all this century. Their model has been Bernstein's – to enact socialist measures through parliament. When every one of these governments left office, capitalism was stronger and socialism weaker. As Rosa Luxemburg had predicted, the enthusiasm for gradual means has gradually erased the ends. No Labour or social-democratic party now puts forward motions in parliament to get socialism by 'gradual supersession', or by any other means for that matter. Instead, they have come to admit that they do not want socialism at all. They prefer, as Rosa Luxemburg predicted, a 'reformed capitalism' – a 'different goal'.

When socialism lost its soul – the self-emancipation of the working class, and a democratic society organized from below – it ceased to be socialism, and became something completely different.

From *The Case for Socialism,* 1990

Index